Small Scale Industries
State and Liberalisation

Small Scale Industries State and Liberalisation

Dr. Sweta Mishra

RADHA PUBLICATIONS
New Delhi-110002

First Edition 2005
ISBN 81-7487-365-1

Radha Publications
4378/4B, Ansari Road, Daryaganj
New Delhi-110002
Ph. 23254306, 23261839

Printed in India

Nitin Garg for Radha Publications, Laser Typesetting by Deep Printers, and printed at R.K. Offset Press, Naveen Shahdara, Delhi-32

Dedicated to my husband

Dr. Anil Dutta Mishra

who played the most vital role during this work.

Preface

In a developing economy like ours, where capital is scarce and there is regular and sizeable expansion of the labour force, emphasis on small sector is inevitable. The place accorded to small scale industries sector in the process of economic development and particularly in the process of industrialisation by policy-makers has been quite significant.

The programme of small industry development in India is more than 35 years old, and is perhaps the most established of any developing country. Development of modern small industries, infact, has been one of the most significant and characteristic features of planned industrial development in India.

Small industry sector in India has grown into prominence over the years through its multi-faceted contribution and role. As part of the industrial strategy, it occupies a significant position serving specific purpose. Small scale industries have been steadily enlarging its area of operation by entering new product lines not produced earlier in the small scale sector, in locations where small industry was not that well known, and by promoting entrepreneurs with varied backgrounds. This sector has considerably diversified its production and is manufacturing a wide variety of products including the sophisticated items which are either export-oriented or are import-substitution products. The sector has sizeable share in India's index of production, employment generation, increase of national income and foreign exchange earning.

These far reaching developments and the scale and scope of operation of small scale industries have brought to the fore the importance of administrative and institutional assistance provided to small scale industry sector.

Realising that the panacea of our economic problem lies in the promotion and development of small scale and cottage industries, efforts have been made in the past and are still being made to protect and promote this sector, through Governmental intervention. Accordingly, the Government have set up organisations at the Central and State levels. The Central as well State Governments have put in place an impressive institutional support structure to cater to the needs of small scale industries. There are a number of institutions and agencies engaged in the areas of credit lending, technology support services, infrastructural services and a host of marketing and support related services.

Amongst various other promotional bodies, Small Scale Industrial Development Corporations were set up at the Centre and the State levels, to identify the problems of small scale sector and provide all assistance for their promotion. Moreover the new economic policy and changes in industrial policy of the Government of India has provided added strength for the promotion of SSIs and we hope that these opportunities will be exploited by National Capital Territory of Delhi more effectively.

In view of the above mentioned facts, an attempt has been made in this work to analyse the role of State in promotion of Small Scale Industries and the functioning of DSIDC. Besides, an attempt has also been made to provide some meaningful suggestions so that DSIDC can become effective institution for the promotion of Small Scale Industries. The basic research for this work was done during my doctoral pursuit. The present work is a revised and updated version of that.

In the course of completion of this work, I received immense help and encouragement from various sources. I shall be failing in my duty, if I do not acknowledge my gratitude to them.

First of all my grateful thanks are due to the officials, particularly to Shri Raju Sharma, IAS, Director, Office of the Development Commissioner, Small Scale Industries (during the period of my research) Ministry of Industry, Government of India, Shri P.N. Mishra, Joint Director (Admn.), Department of

Industry, Government of NCT of Delhi, Shri U.K. Vohra, Private Secretary, Minister of Industry, Government of NCT of Delhi, Shri P.M. Bakshi, Public Relation Officer, DSIDC and Shri O.P. Dhingra, Company Secretary, DSIDC, for their kind co-operation. Discussions with them on the problem concerned proved to be very useful. Any amount of thanks will be too little to record my appreciation for them.

My thanks also goes to the respondents both small scale entrepreneurs and DSIDC officials for sparing their valuable time and responding to the printed questionnaire as also frank discussion on the problem. But for their help and co-operation my attempt would have proved a dream unfulfilled.

I would like to express my sincere gratitude to my supervisor, Dr. R.B. Jain, Professor of Political Science, University of Delhi, Delhi, who not only consented to be my supervisor but also gave his guidance and critical comments which enabled me to complete the study in record time. Despite his pressing engagements, he was always ready to guide me in shaping the data and information in present form. Words fail me to express my feelings for him who apart from being my teacher, is a fatherly figure.

I am extremely grateful to my teachers Professor M.P. Singh, Professor M. Mohanty, Professor S.K. Chaube, Professor Subrata Mukherjee, Professor Mahendra Kumar, Professor Neera Chandhoke and Professor Bidyut Chakravarty, for all the help, they extended to me from time to time in the course of the study.

I am highly indebted to my father, Prof. S.N. Mishra, who has been a guiding spirit throughout my life and especially in my academic pursuits till now.

Thanks are also due to my mother, Smt. Nirmala Mishra, brother Manish and sisters Sumita, Sangita, Supriti and Shruti, who helped me in so many ways by providing a congenial atmosphere at home which made it possible for me to concentrate on my work.

No words can express the constant flow of energy that the very touch of my lovely daughter, 'Sanstuti' provided me even during the most tiresome moments.

I really do not understand, how to thank my in-laws who, graciously enough, spared me from every responsibility to complete this work.

During the final stages of the book, I received immense cooperation, help and encouragement from my Principal, Dr. Surjeet Kaur Jolly. Her qualities of both head and heart so immensely inspired me in taxing hours that I find words inadeguate to express my deep gratitude and sincere thanks to her.

I am also very thankful to Dr. Amita Singh, Reader, Centre for Law and Governance, Jawahar Lal Nehru University, Dr. Sushma Yadav, Reader, Delhi College of Arts and Commerce and Dr. Ram Avtar Sharma, Principal, Maharaja Agrasen College, who acted as friend, philosopher and guide, encouraged me and gave valuable suggestions throughout the study. Any amount of thanks will be too little to record my appreciation for them.

Thanks are also due to my friends, Chaitali, Maneesha, Nuti, Renu, Ritu, Rajendra, Rajesh, Sanjay, Sanjeev and Surendra, for their help and suggestions throughout the period of my research. Among the seniors, I gratefully acknowledge the constant moral support and occassional discussions with Alka Dhameja, Durgesh Nandini and Uma Medury.

I am very grateful to the staff members of the Library of Indian Institute of Public Administration, New Delhi, the Ratan Tata Library, Library of Institute of Economic Growth, the Central Reference Library, Arts Faculty, University of Delhi, Delhi and Library of Development Commissioner, Small Scale Industry, Nirman Bhavan, New Delhi. I would particularly like to thank Mrs. Sunita Gulati, Deputy Librarian, Indian Institute of Public Administration, New Delhi, who was always ready to help and in the process also taught me to operate the library computer.

My thanks are also due to Shri J.N. Chawla and Shri Shekhar Chaturvedi, for their patience and keen interest in bringing out several drafts and giving the final shape to the study.

I would also like to thank Shri Nitin Garg, Radha Publications, New Delhi, for bringing out the book in a nice form and that too within record time.

Last but not the least, I would like to extend my thanks to all of them, whose names do not appear here, but their help is in my memory.

SWETA MISHRA

LIST OF TABLES

No.	Name of Table	Page No.
1.1	Norms for Definitions of SSI	7
1.2	Definition of SMEs in Asia and other Countries	13
2.1	Growth of Public Enterprises	48
3.1	Overall Performance of SSI Sector after Liberalisation	92
3.2	Plan Expenditure and Outlay on Small Scale Industries Programme in Five Year Plans	96
3.3	Evolution of Investment Limit for SSIs	100
3.4	Progressive Reservation of Items for Exclusive Manufacture in the Small Scale Sector	101
3.5	Anticipated Level of Production and Exports During 1979-80	104
3.6	Targets of Output, Employment and Exports for Different Village and Small Industries	105
3.7	Share of Small Scale Industries in Total Exports	108
3.8	Progress of SSI Sector Under Different Plan Periods	109
3.9	Targets During Eighth Plan Period in Small Scale Sector	111

3.10	Growth Rates of Small Scale Sector (Unregistered Sector of the National Accounts and the SSI Sector from the Annual Survey of Industries)	112
3.11	Cumulative No. of SIDO Units Registered on Permanent Basis with States/UTs	112
4.1	Specialized Training Institutes	122
4.2	Break-up of Extension Services	128
4.3	Budgetary Provision for SSI Promotion	129
4.4	Consultancy Services Provided by the SISI During 1992-93	134
4.5	Scheme-wise Assistance of SIDBI	145
4.6	Performance of District Industries Centre	154
5.1	Population and Number of Workers Engaged in Industries in Delhi State: 1921-1951	160
5.2	Growth of Industries in Delhi	161
5.3	Product-wise Profile of Industrial Units in Delhi	163
5.4	(A) Industrial Areas Developed by DDA	167
5.4	(B) Industrial Areas Developed by Co-operative Societies	167
5.4	(C) Industrial Areas Developed by Directorate of Industries	168
5.4	(D) Industrial Areas Developed by DSIDC	168
5.5	Possible Industrial Pollution Control Measures from Different Sources	175
6.1	Highlights of the Working of the DSIDC	189
7.1	Whether the Unit was Registered as SSI Unit?	215
7.2	Awareness About the Policy of the Government towards SSIs	216
7.3	Knowledge About Institutions Organisations Promoting SSIs	217
7.4	Knowledge About the various Activities of the DSIDC	217

7.5	Whether received any Financial Assistance in the form of Loan/Subsidy from Financial Institutions/Banks at the time of setting up the unit?	218
7.6	From where do you get Raw Materials for the Project?	219
7.7	Did you find difficulty in procuring Raw Material?	220
7.8	Does Government help in importing Raw Materials?	220
7.9	Does DSIDC give any help in procuring Raw Materials?	220
7.10	Where do you market your product?	222
7.11	Do you find difficulty in Marketing your Projects?	222
7.12	Does DSIDC provide any Marketing Assistance?	222
7.13	Do you face any problem while Exporting?	223
7.14	Does DSIDC provide any help in Exporting your products?	223
7.15	Did you purchase your machinery on Hire-Purchase?	224
7.16	Knowledge about DSIDC's Technical Consultancy Organisation?	225
7.17	Did you receive any help from DSIDC's Technical Consultancy Organisation?	226
7.18	Have you ever participated in any Exhibition/Trade Fair ?	226
7.19	Are you satisfied with the functioning of the DSIDC?	227
7.20	Are you satisfied with the organisational structure of the DSIDC?	229
7.21	Does DSIDC provide any assistance in making the SSIs Environment Friendly?	231
7.22	Do you think that the DSIDC has an obligation to make new Environment Friendly technology available to the SSIs?	231

8.1	Awareness About the Policy of the Government towards SSIs	236
8.2	Knowledge About Institutions/Organisations Promoting SSIs	237
8.3	Knowledge About the various activities of the DSIDC	238
8.4	Does Government help in importing the Raw Material?	238
8.5	Does DSIDC give any help in procuring the Raw Materials?	238
8.6	Does DSIDC provide any Marketing Assistance?	239
8.7	Does DSIDC provide any Exporting Facility?	239
8.8	Knowledge About DSIDC's Technical Consultancy Organisation	240
8.9	Are you satisfied with the functioning of the Technical Consultancy Organisation?	240
8.10	Have you ever participated in any Exhibition/Trade Fair ?	241
8.11	Are you satisfied with the functioning of the DSIDC?	242
8.12	Are you satisfied with the organisational structure of the DSIDC?	242
8.13	Does the DSIDC provide any assistance in making the SSIs Environment Friendly?	245
8.14	Do you think that the DSIDC has an obligation to make the new Environment Friendly Technology available to the SSIs?	246

LIST OF CHARTS

No.	Name of Charts	Page No.
3.1	Plan Expenditure and Outlay on Small Scale Industries Programme in Five Year Plans	97
4.1	Support Agencies and Specialised Services for SSIs	125
5.1	Population and Number of Workers Engaged in Industries in Delhi State : 1921-1951	160
5.2	Growth of Industries in Delhi	162
6.1	Turn Over of **DSIDC** during the last 10 years	190
7.1	Number of Entrepreneurs Interviewed	214
7.2	Purchase of Raw Material	219
7.3	Place for Marketing of Product	222
7.4	Knowledge About **DSIDC's** Technical Consultancy Organisation	225

LIST OF ABBREVIATIONS

APSSIDC	Andhra Pradesh Small Scale Industrial Development Corporation
ARI	Agro and Rural Industries
ASI	Annual Survey of Industries
BOD	Board of Directors
CFTC	Central Footwear Training Centre
CIHT	Central Institute of Hand Tools
CITD	Central Institute of Tool Design
CMD	Chief Managing Director
CSIR	Council of Scientific and Industrial Research
COB	Carrying On Business
DDA	Delhi Development Authority
DEPAs	District Enterprise Promotion Agencies
DFC	Delhi Financial Corporation
DGS&D	Directorate General of Supplies and Disposals
DIC	District Industries Centre
DKVIB	Delhi Khadi and Village Industries Board
DSIR	Department of Scientific and Industrial Research
DSIDC	Delhi State Industrial Development Corporation
DVB	Delhi Vidyut Board
EDIs	Entrepreneurship Development Institutes
EDP	Entrepreneur Development Programme
FASII	Federation of Association of Small Industries of India

FERA	Foreign Exchange Regulation Act
FICCI	Federation of Indian Chambers of Commerce and Industry
FTSs	Field Testing Stations
HARDICON	Haryana Delhi Industrial Consultants Limited
ICICI	Industrial Credit and Investment Corporation of India
IDBI	Industrial Development Bank of India
IDR	Industries Development and Regulation Act
IDEMI	Institute for Design of Electrical Measuring Instruments
IFC	Industrial Finance Corporation
IFCI	Industrial Finance Corporation of India
IITF	India International Trade Fair
IIC	India Investment Centre
ILO	International Labour Organisation
IPR	Industrial Policy Resolution
IRCI	Industrial Reconstruction Corporation of India
ISI	Indian Standards Institution
ISO	International Standard Organisation
ITC	Integrated Training Centre
ITPO	Indian Trade Promotion Organisation
ITI	Industrial Training Institute
KVI	Khadi and Village Industries
KVIC	Khadi and Village Industries Commission
LIC	Life Insurance Corporation
LSI	Large Scale Industry
MCD	Municipal Corporation of Delhi
MLAs	Member of Legislative Assemblies
MNCs	Multi National Corporations
MPD	Master Plan for Delhi
MRTP	Monopolies Restrictive Trade Practices
NABARD	National Bank of Agriculture and Rural Development
NAYE	National Alliance of Young Entrepreneurs
NCR	National Capital Region
NCT	National Capital Territory

NEF	National Equity Fund
NGOs	Non-Governmental Organisations
NIESBUD	National Institute for Entrepreneurship and Small Business Development
NISIET	National Institute of Small Industry Extention and Training
NPC	National Productivity Council
NSIC	National Small Industries Corporations
PDTCs	Prototype Development and Training Centres
PMRY	Prime Minister's Rozgar Yojana
PPDC	Product cum Process Development Centres
R&D	Research and Development
RBI	Reserve Bank of India
RTCs	Regional Testing Centres
SEBI	Securities Exchange Board of India
SEEUY	Self Employment for Educated Unemployed Youth
SFC	State Financial Corporation
SICOM	Small Industrial Corporation of Maharashtra
SIDBI	Small Industries Development of India
SIDC	State Industrial Development Corporation
SIDCO	Small Industries Development Corporations
SIDO	Small Industry Development Organisation
SIETI	Small Industry Extension Training Institute
SIP	Statement of Industrial Policy
SISI	Small Industry Service Institute
SME	Small and Medium Enterprises
SSE	Small Scale Enterprises
SSIs	Small Scale Industries
SSIB	Small Scale Industries Board
SSICs	State Small Industries Corporations
SSIDC	State Small Industries Development Corporation
SSIDCO	Small Scale Industrial Development Corporation
SSS	Small Scale Sector
SWS	Single Window Scheme

TCO	Technical Consultancy Organisation
TDC	Technology Development Cell
TDMF	Technology Development and Modernisation Fund
UNDP	United Nations Development Programme
UNESCO	United Nations Educational Scientific and Cultural Organisation
UNIDO	United Nations Industrial Development Organisation
USSR	Union of Soviet Socialist Republic
UTs	Union Territories
UTI	Unit Trust of India
VSI	Village and Small Industries.

Contents

Preface		*vii*
List of Tables		*xi*
List of Charts		*xv*
List of Abbreviations		*xvii*
1.	Introduction	1
2.	Role of the State in Industrial Development: The Indian Context	34
3.	Industrial Policy of the Government of India: Retrospect and Prospect	66
4.	Institutions Promoting Small Scale Industries	121
5.	Industrial Profile of Delhi	159
6.	DSIDC-Genesis, Objectives, Administrative Structure and Functions	186
7.	Perception of the Entrepreneurs Regarding the Functioning of **DSIDC**	213
8.	Perception of the Officials of **DSIDC** with regard to its Role in Promotion of Small Scale Industries	235
9.	Conclusion	249
	Bibliography	*274*
	Appendices	*295*

1

Introduction

During the British regime the policy of our foreign rulers was that of 'laissez faire'. This was in the interest of British industries which had already spread their industrial tentacles throughout the country and were in a position to compete with any industry of any foreign country. The policy of the British Government was not to encourage industries in India and whatever industries had already come up to leave them in their infancy at the disposal of the circumstances. Thus industry in India, during the British rule, was like a child without proper nursing. As such industries were suffering in India for want of State encouragement and help. In course of time almost all our industries became sick in absence of raw material, required tools and proper care and suffered heavy losses, while the industries owned by Britishers were becoming more and more prosperous. This state of affairs continued till the Provincial Autonomy was granted to India under the Government of India Act, 1935, which was enforced in April, 1937.

The popular Provincial Ministries were not competent to deal with large-scale industries, as it was a Central subject, but they tried their best to give impetus, protection and encouragement for the development of small industries and village and cottage industries, by making available a number of facilities. Thus, the year 1937 was the beginning of State intervention in respect of Small Scale Industries (SSIs) in India.

After independence, the Government of India, was committed to the promotion and encouragement of village and SSIs, though later on the accent was shifted to large scale and tiny industries, specially the key industries and defence industries. However, side by side, efforts were also made to give State help to small sector for the benefit of small and poor entrepreneurs.

The primary responsibility for executive action in regard to the development of SSIs and implementational plan to assistance is that of State Government, as under the Indian Constitution, the Small Scale Sector (SSS) is a State subject. The strategy relating to development of industries in general and SSIs in particular in the States and Union Territories is looked after by the Directorate of Industries in each State and Union Territory.

Another agency that has been set up at the State level in most States is the State Small Industries Development Corporation (SSIDC). The SSIDC undertake a number of commercial activities. The most important among these are distribution of scarce indigenous and imported raw materials, construction and management of industrial estates, supply of machinery on hire-purchase basis, procurement of orders from Government departments to be sub-contracted to small industries, assistance in export marketing and, in certain circumstances, provision of financial, technical and managerial assistance to small enterprises.

The State also helps in the marketing of SSI products. In accordance with the Government policy, SSIDC gives preference to those SSI products, with ISI markings in implementing their marketing strategy for the SSI units and to tap markets locally and abroad.

Another area where the State comes to the help of SSI is the rehabilitation of sick units. A separate cell is set up by SSIDC to identify sick units and formulate programmes for their revival.

The lack of access of the SSS to the organised capital market and the consequent operation of these units with a thin capital base reflect the need of the scheme for participation in the capital structure of small-scale units through State agency. Besides strengthening the capital base of the units, this scheme fortifies their position to raise long and short term borrowings. The grant of interest free loan through refund of sales tax has also become a popular mechanism for extending financial assistance to industrial units by the State.

The State Governments are required to provide loans to the industrial co-operatives.

In case where power is supplied by private agencies, the State examines whether the tariff could be so adjusted as to make supplies to small industries at concessional rates. If it is found that the supply of power at concessional rates entails a loss to the electricity supply undertakings, such loss is met by the Central and the State Government in equal proportions. Where power is supplied by the Electricity Board, the State Government allows a rebate to SSIs.

Importance of Small Scale Industries

For a developing country like India, the real progress lies both in its industrial and agricultural development. While industrialisation on the whole plays a significant role in the development of a country, for countries like ours, development of SSIs has its special significance as they have a long tradition. They have played a vital role in the overall economic development of our country where millions of people are unemployed or under-employed, where most of the entrepreneurs are capable of making only small investment and where there is chronic shortage of resources to procure sophisticated machinery and modern technology. They have also played a strategic and significant role in promoting rapid industrial growth by providing greater employment opportunities, bringing about reduction in regional imbalances and removal of economic backwardness of the rural and underdeveloped segments of the country.

The industrial structure of the country has been divided into three parts–Large-scale industries; Medium-scale industries; and Small-scale industries. The categorisation is done on the basis of actual financial investment in a particular unit. Of the three kinds, SSIs have the most important role in economic advancement of India.

In a developing economy like ours, where capital is scarce

and there is regular and sizeable expansion of the labour force, emphasis on SSS is inevitable. The place accorded to SSIs sector in the process of economic development and particularly in the process of industrialisation by policy makers has been quite significant.

The programme of small industry development in India is more than 35 years old, and is perhaps the most established of any developing country. Development of modern small industries, in fact, has been one of the most significant and characteristic features of planned industrial development in India.

Over the years, the various Industrial Policy Resolutions and statements have accorded a strategic position to SSIs. The Industrial Policy Resolution(IPR), 1948 specially stated that "cottage and SSIs have a very important role in the national economy. These industries are particularly suited for better utilisation of local resources and for the achievement of local self sufficiency, in respect of certain type of essential consumer goods like food, cloth and agricultural implements".[1] The IPR, 1956 visualised integrated growth of both the large and SSSs and recognised the social and economic contribution of the SSS. It also proposed a programme of establishing Industrial Estates. The IPR, 1977 emphasised a policy of reservation of items exclusively for SSIs. The Industrial Policy statement of 1980 gave a predominant place to SSSs and widened the scope of such industries to include those having an investment from 1 million rupees to 2 million rupees. The IPR, 1990 raised the investment ceiling in plant and machinery for SSIs to Rs. 60 lakhs. It reserved 836 items for exclusive manufacture in the SSS. A new scheme of central investment subsidy exclusively for the SSS in rural and backward areas capable of generating higher level of employment at lower capital cost has been implemented. To ensure adequate and timely flow of credit for SSIs, a new apex bank known as Small Industries Development Bank of India (SIDBI) has already been established.

Small industry sector in India has grown into prominence over the years through its multi-faceted contribution and role. As part of the industrial strategy, it occupies a significant position serving specific purposes. SSIs have been steadily enlarging its areas of operation by entering new product lines not produced earlier in the SSS, in locations where small industry was not that well known, and by promoting entrepreneurs with varied backgrounds. This sector has considerably diversified its production and is manufacturing a wide variety of products including the sophisticated items which are either export-oriented or are import-substitution products. The sector has sizeable share in India's index of production, employment generation, increase of national income and foreign exchange earning.

These far reaching developments and the scale and scope of operation of SSIs have brought to the fore the importance of administrative and institutional assistance provided to SSI sector.

Despite comprehensive programme of assistance provided by the Government and a number of facilities available to SSS by industrial estates, it is hampered by several problems. A large number of small-scale industrial units are still in the paralysed condition suffering from several handicaps like finance, raw material, marketing etc.

Concept of Small Scale Industries: A Historical Background

The term "small scale industry" has many synonyms, such as, "small enterprise", "small undertaking", "small unit", "small scale sector", "small industrial enterprise", "small industry" etc. In fact, these terms are used by different authors to convey the same meaning.

The concept of SSIs, as it has developed over the years, is one of the confusion and lacks clarity. Neither the Government, nor the planners could provide a clear and graphic definition. SSIs have been defined differently in various countries and their definitions have been changing from time to time. There is no single functional economic criterion by which small, medium and large industries can be distinguished. The definitions adopted in different countries have been evolved in the context of their specific circumstances. This is obviously due to the fact that the concept of SSI is not an absolute concept. It is a relative concept and has to be understood in the context of the stage of economic development attained and the political and social environments existing in a particular country. The concept fell a prey to diverse circumstances, to which the Indian economy was subjected. Obviously SSIs were not given so much importance during the British rule as is given today. Now we have a pragmatic approach to the concept in view of the prevailing economic conditions, gradual industrial development and the difficulties that arise in the implementation of planned programmes. Hence, the concept has undergone change from time to time. Before Independence, the present SSI was meant to denote the village and the urban cottage industry.[2] This group included a variety of industries ranging from bee-keeping and lac cultivation to hand-spinning and weaving, sandal wood and ivory carving, manufacturing of cutlery, locks, iron safes etc. In fact, the term "cottage and SSIs" was used in juxtaposition to the large scale industries established under the influence of Western ideas. They were, therefore, "indigenous" or "native" to the country and were often regarded as a part of our heritage.[3]

Government have, however, adopted formal definitions in order to identify the small-scale industrial units which could be eligible for fiscal incentives and financial and input assistance. The definition of SSIs has been modified several times in order to meet the need of time. The various definitions of SSIs are given below. Table 1.1 shows the periodic revisions in the definition of SSIs as made by the Government of India.

The Industrial Commission (1918) described SSIs as organised industries carried on in a workshop or factories having a simple operation with a provincial character.[4]

The Fiscal Commission (1949-50) defined a SSI as one which was operated with hired labour of usually 10 to 50 hands.[5]

According to the Committee on Finance for the Private Sector, SSIs are those which are not integrated with rural economy and in which the investment of capital and labour are relatively small, i.e., units with assets between Rs. 10,000 and Rs. 5 lakhs engaged largely in the production of articles that are ancillary to or competitive with the products of so called large scale industries.[6]

Professor K.T. Shah was the first Indian Economist, who realising the importance of SSIs in India, tried to give a workable

Table 1.1
Norms for Definitions of SSI

Year	*SSI*	*ANC*	*TINY*	*EOU*	*SSSE*	*SSSBE*	*Remarks*
1950	Gross investment in fixed assets: not exceeding Rs. 0.5 million	Did not exit	Did not exit	Did not exit	Did not exit	Did not exit	Employment less than 50 workers per day (with the use of power) or less than 100 workers per day (without the use of power)
1958	Gross investment in fixed assets: less than Re. 0.5 million.	-	-	-	-	-	Same as above, except that the criteria based on the employment 'per day' was henceforth replaced by a 'per shift' provision.
1959	Gross investment in fixed assets: value of machinery (original).	-	-	-	-	-	Same as above, except the criteria based on the employment 'per day' was henceforth replaced by a 'per shift' provision.
1960	Gross investment in fixed assets: value up to Re. 0.5 million.	Value of gross fixed assets up to Re. 1 million.	-	-	-	-	The employment condition was dropped from the definition.
Original	Value of Plant and Machinery Only						
1966	Up to Re 0.75 million	Up to Re. million.	-	-	-	-	-
1975	Up to Re. 1 million	Up to Rs. 1.5 million	-			-	-
1977	Up to	Up to	Up to	-	-	-	* Units located in rural

Contd. Table 1.1

Norms for Definitions of SSI

Year	SSI	ANC	TINY	EOU	SSSE	SSSBE	Remarks
	Re. 1 million.	Rs.1.5 million.	Re. 0.1 million.*				area/towns with a maximum population of 50,000 (as per the 1971 Census)
1980	Up to Rs. 2 million.	Up to Rs. 2.5 million.	Up to Re. 0.2 million.**	-	-	-	** Units located in rural areas/ towns with a maximum population of 50,000 (as per the 1971 Census). Census).
1985	Up to Rs.3.5 million.	Up to Rs. 4.5 million.	Up to Re. 0.2 million.***	-	Up to Re. 0.2 million.***	-	*** Units located in rural areas and towns with a maximum population of up to 0.5 million (as per the 1981 census).
1991	Up to Rs. 6 million.	Up to Rs. 7.5 million.	Up to Rs. 0.5 million@	Up to Rs. 7.5 million.@	(b)	Up to Re. 0.5 million.@	@ The location-specific condition was withdrawn. (b) The SSSEs classification was suspended in 1991 and replaced by the term 'SSSBEs.'

Contd. Table 1.1

Norms for Definitions of SSI

Year	*SSI*	*ANC*	*TINY*	*EOU*	*SSSE*	*SSSBE*	*Remarks*
1997	Up to Rs. 30 million.	Up to Rs. 30 million.	Up to Rs. 2.5 million.	Up to Rs. 30 million.	-	Up to Re. 0.5 million.	
1999	Up to Rs. 10 million.	Up to Rs. 10 million.	Up to Rs. 2.5 million.	Same as SSIs	-	Up to Re 0.5 million.	

Notes: SSI–Small Scale Industry, ANC–Ancillary Industry, TINY–Tiny Unit, EOU–Export Oriented Unit, SSSE–Small Scale Service Establishment, SSSBE - Small Scale Service & Business (industry related) Enterprise.

1. Women Entrepreneurs' Enterprise as defined, for the first time, in 1988 laid down that an enterprise owned and administered by a woman entrepreneur, with a minimum financial interest of 51 per cent of the share capital and giving at least 50 per cent employment to women would be treated as 'Women's Enterprise'. The investment ceilings were kept at par with the limits specified in 1985 for other units, i.e. upto Rs. 3.5 million for SSI units and upto Rs. 4.5 million for an ANC. This definition was revised in August, 1991 by dispensing with the employment criterion for women workers. Currently, the Women's Enterprise is defined as a small scale industrial unit/ industry-related service or business enterprise managed by one or more women entrepreneurs in which she/ they individually or jointly have a share of capital of not less than 5 per cent as proprietors/ partners/ shareholders/ directors of private limited companies/members of co-operative societies.
2. For an ancillary unit, there was a requirement to supply at least 50 per cent of its production/services to other undertakings, which in 1988 was modified to a limit of 30 per cent and then in 1991 again raised to 50 per cent.
3. Export oriented units are under an obligation to export at least 30 per cent of annual production by the end of the third year and onward from the year of commencement of production.
4. An SSI unit cannot be controlled or owned or be a subsidiary of any other industrial undertaking.

Source: Government of India, SIDBI Report on Small Scale Industries Sector 2000, Small Industries Development Bank of India, New Delhi, 2000, p. 28

definition of these industries. He said:

A small-scale or cottage industry may be defined to be an enterprise or series of operations carried on by a workman skilled in the craft on his own responsibility, the finished product of which he markets himself. He works in his own home with his own tools and materials and provides his own labour or at most the labour of such members of his family as are able to assist. These workers work mostly by hand labour and personal skill, with little or no aid from modern power driven machinery and in accordance with traditional technique. Such supplementary energy as is provided by animal power may add to the economy and efficiency of the industry. He works, finally, for a market in the immediate neighbourhood, that is to say, in response to known demand with reference to quality as well as quantity.[7]

Jawaharlal Nehru seemed to be more clear in his mind when he maintained separate entities of cottage and SSIs. He was of the view that small industry was the middle sector and it would overlap both the cottage and the large scale industries.

Till independence, SSIs remained composite in character. The environment of post-independence period made little change in their concept. The Industrial Policy Resolution of 1948 and the document of First Five Year Plan maintained the existing concept of SSIs. The only criterion to define small industries, was their non-registration under the Indian Factory Act 1948. Thus, the SSI includes all units which (a) use power and employ less than ten workers or (b) do not use power and employ upto 20 workers. Later on, during the performance of First Five Year Plan, the distinction of SSIs with village industries was made. As a result, the SSIs were defined as a group of those industries which were not forming the integral part of village economy. So by the year 1954 when International Planning Team came to India, the SSI had a separate entity as the Government had recognised the full meaning of the concept.

The Development Commission (1955) defined a SSI as one which had capital asset not exceeding Rs. 5 lakhs and employing less than 50 workers if power is used; or less than 100 workers, if no power is used.[8]

This definition worked for a few years and then it ran into

difficulties. The growing feeling was that it was neither productive nor in the economic interest of the country, to deny financial and technical aid, simply because a unit has been successful in expanding itself beyond the arbitrary ceiling set by the above definition.

A revised definition of SSIs was consequently adopted in 1966. According to this definition, an industrial unit with a capital investment of not more than Rs. 7.5 lakhs in plant and machinery is considered as a small scale unit.[9] In calculating the value of plant and machinery, the original price paid by the owner (whether new or second hand) is taken into account. For ancillary industries, the ceiling was fixed at Rs. 10 lakhs.[10] The sixth decade of the present century saw another change in the "usage of the term SSIs". It was referred only to mean modern equipment, techniques of production and management.[11]

Again in 1975, in view of the rise in prices, the Ministry of Industries and Civil Supplies revised the definition of SSIs so as to include all industrial establishments with a capital investment in plant and machinery (fixed capital) of not more than Rs. 10 lakhs, irrespective of the number of persons employed.[12]

The investment limit for SSIs was revised from Rs. 10 lakhs to Rs. 20 lakhs, for ancillary units from Rs. 15 lakhs to Rs. 25 lakhs in the Industrial Policy announced on July 23rd 1980.[13]

The revised definition of small-scale and ancillary industrial undertakings, as published in notification No.SO 202(E) dated 18-3-1985 is given as follows:

A small-scale industrial undertaking is an undertaking having investment in fixed assets in plant and machinery held on, ownership terms or by lease or by hire purchase not exceeding Rs. 35 lakhs. An ancillary industrial undertaking is one having investment in fixed assets, in plant and machinery whether held on ownership term or by lease or by hire purchase not exceeding Rs. 45 lakhs.

In 1990, once again the investment ceiling of small-scale units was revised upwards. This was announced by the Minister of the Industries, Shri Ajit Singh, in his policy statement in Parliament on May 31, 1990. The definition notified on 2-4-1991 is as follows:

A small-scale industrial undertaking is an undertaking in

which the investment in fixed assets in plant and machinery, whether held on ownership terms or on lease, or by hire-purchase, does not exceed Rs. 60 lakhs. An ancillary undertaking is one which is engaged or is proposed to be engaged in the manufacture or production of parts, components, sub-assemblies, tools, intermediates or rendering of services and undertaking supplies, renders or proposed to supply, render not more than 50 per cent of its production or services, as the case may be to one or more other industrial undertakings and whose investment in fixed assets in plant and machinery, whether held on ownership terms, or on lease, or on hire-purchase, does not exceed Rs. 75 lakhs.[14]

In 1997, the Union Government once again increased the classification limit for industrial units as SSI to Rs. 3 crore from the current Rs. 60 lakh, to give a boost to the SSS. According to the notification, for classification as a SSI, an industrial undertaking should have investment in fixed assets in plant and machinery not exceeding Rs. 3 crore, whether held on ownership terms or on lease or on hire-purchase basis. Regarding ancillary industrial undertaking, an industrial undertaking engaged or is proposed to be engaged in manufacturing or production of parts, components, sub-assemblies, tooling or intermediaries, or rendering of services, and undertaking supplies or renders not more than 650 per cent of its production or services to one or more industrial undertakings, and whose investment in fixed assets in plant and machinery does not exceed Rs. 3 crore.[15]

According to the current definition (effective 1999), a small scale industrial undertaking is that, in which investment in plant & machinery, whether held on ownership terms, or on lease, or by hire purchase, does not exceed Rs. 100 lakhs. Same limits are prescribed for ancillary undertakings.[16]

No small scale or ancillary industrial undertaking will be considered a SSI or ancillary undertaking if it is a subsidiary of, or owned or controlled by any other industrial undertaking.

In India there exists no separate definition of medium enterprises and as such no specific definition of small and medium enterprises. At the international level, the size of a unit in most of the countries is determined either by the number of workers

Table 1.2 : Definition of SMEs in Asia and other Countries

Country	*Category of Industry*	*Criteria/Country's official definition*
Australia	Manufacturing Services	Small enterprises ≤ 100 employees. Medium enterprises ≤ 20 employees.
Belgium	SME	Annual staff average of 50 employees. Annual turnover (VAT excluded) ECU 4.2 million. Balance-sheet total of ECU 2.1 million.
Canada	Manufacturing	Independent firms having <200 employees.
China	SME	Depends on product group usually <100 employees; investment ceiling 30 million Yuan (US$8 million).
Denmark	Manufacturing	<500 employees. Production units with more than 5 employees.
France	SME	10–499 employees
Germany	SME	<500 employees
Greece	Small Enterprises	<50 employees
	Medium Enterprises	50 - 500 employees
Indonesia	SME	<100 employees
Ireland	SME	<500 employees
Itlay	Small Enterprises	<200 employees
Japan	Manufacturing	<300 employees or asset capitalisation <hundred million Yen.
	Wholesale Trade	< 50 employees or capitalisation < 30 million Yen
	Retail Trade and Services	<50 employees or capitalisation < 10 million Yen
Korea	Manufacturing Services	<300 employees <20 employees
Malasiya	SMIs	<75 full time workers or with a shareholder fund of <RM 2.5 million (US$1 million).
	Sis	Manufacturing establishments employing between 5 and 50 employees or with a shareholders fund up to RM 500,000.
	Mis	Manufacturing establishments employing between 50 and 75 full time employees or with shareholders fund between RM 500,000 to RM 2.5 million.

Contd.

Country	*Category of Industry*	*Criteria/Country's official definition*
Mexico	Micro	< 15 employees and gross Income/Sales < US$ 175,000.
	Small	15-99 employees and gross Income/Sales <US$ 175,000.
	Medium	100-249 employees and gross Income/ Sales <US$ 3,500,000.
Netherlands	Small Enterprises	<10 employees
	Medium Enterprises	10-100 employees
Philippines	Small Enterprises	<200 employees, revenue <P 40 million.
Portugal	SME	<500 employees. <Esc 2400 million in sales (value for 1993) is not controlled more than 50% by any company (nor does it hold over 50% of any other company).
Singapore	Manufacturing	<S $ 12 million fixed assets
	Services	<100 employees
Spain	Small Enterprises	<200 employees
	Medium Enterprises	<500 employees
Sweden	SME	Autonomous firms with <200 employees
Switzerland	SME	No fixed definition
Taiwan	SMEs	In manufacturing, mining and construction-invested capital is <NT$40 million or the number of regular employees not to exceed 200.
	SSEs	In manufacturing and construction–sales turnover <NT$120 million or regular employees to be <20.
Thailand	Labour intensive sectors	<200 employees
	Capital intensive sectors	<100 employees
United Kingdom	SME	No fixed definition
United States	Very Small Enterprises	<20 employees
	Small enterprises	20-99 employees
	Medium enterprises	100-499 employees
Vietnam	SME	No fixed definition, generally <200 employees.

Sources: 1. Handbook on Foreign Direct Investment by Small and Medium-sized Enterprises –Lessons fromAsia, UNCTAD, Geneva, 1998.
2. Globalisation and Small and Medium Enterprises (SMEs) - Vol. I Synthesis Report, OECD.

employed and/or by a measure of assets (capitalisation sales, etc.) The general practice is to define the size of the unit (both in the manufacturing and services sectors) in terms of the number of employees followed by assets size. The prevailing definitions in some Asian and other countries are listed in Table 1.2.

II. Parameters of Research of the Present Study

Statement of the Problem

India, as a whole, has been rich in its arts and handicrafts since time immemorial and Delhi occupied a special place in this field. During Mughal period it saw the zenith but with the sweeping changes in history, the British Imperial Power which ruled India converted the scenario. The Britishers introduced factory goods manufactured in Britain, as a result, the traditional arts and crafts started languishing. The necessity to correct this imbalance, though realised in the pre-independence period, became much sharper with the attainment of freedom in 1947. The Government by adopting the process of planned economic development came forward with a number of programmes to ensure that industrial activity in large, medium and small sectors picks up quickly, not only to provide greater employment to large number of people but also to develop an element of self-sufficiency in our national economy.

Realising that the panacea of our economic problem lies in the promotion and development of small-scale and cottage industries, efforts have been made in the past and are still being made to protect and promote this sector, through Governmental intervention. SSS has large number of advantages ranging from level of technology to manpower conditions–both skilled and unskilled.

Amongst various other promotional bodies, Small-Scale Industrial Development Corporations (SSIDCO) were set up at the Centre and the State levels, to identify the problems of SSS and provide all assistance for their promotion. Moreover the new economic policy and changes in industrial policy of the Government of India has provided added strength for the promotion of SSIs and we hope that these opportunities will be exploited by National Capital Territory of Delhi more effectively.

Further in view of the vital importance given to SSIs sector, the researcher was tempted to examine the role, organisational structure as also functioning of one such organisation. However, for the present study, Delhi State Industrial Development Corporation (DSIDC) was chosen because it is first and foremost Corporation which is playing a vital role in promotion of small-scale industries sector. The SSIDCO exists in almost all States and Union Territories of the country which could have been studied. However, on following considerations, DSIDC was selected for the present study.

1. Geographical compactness of the sample.
2. DSIDC having had the privilege of receiving guidance, help and consultancy from several agencies located in the capital city.
3. DSIDC having benefitted by availability of support services, technical know-how, equipment and maintenance facilities and other inputs.
4. DSIDC being in a privileged position in matters of large inland and overseas market.
5. DSIDC having taken large number of activities and associated itself with the Entrepreneur Development Programme in the past.

The above mentioned facts weigh heavily in favour of selecting DSIDC in order to obtain realistic insights into its functioning. It is but natural that selection of such topic for study is bound to project certain facts and information which could be successfully utilised in policy formulation as far as development of SSIs is concerned.

Survey of the Literature

As the present inquiry is concerned with the SSIs, an attempt is made here to review the earlier studies on the subject in order to obtain greater insights into the subject and define the parameters of the present study. A number of studies on SSIs in India have been conducted by scholars and practitioners. In one of the earlier works, Staley, Eugene and Morse, Richard, (1955) in their study, Modern Small Industry for Developing Countries, discuss issues connected with the development of SSIs and technical assistance, guidance and promotion of modernisation on competitive basis of small industries, small industries in transition, resource use and development strategy. They also competently answer what small industries can do and cannot do, explicating the complimentarity of relationship of small and large industries employment bias and decentralisation. An useful contribution is an extensive review of small industries programmes in various countries.

Basu, S.K. (1957) in his study, Place and Problems of Small Industries, has made an attempt to examine the problems of SSIs and assess their place in the country's Second Five Year Plan. The scope of the study has been strictly confined to an appraisal of the financial problems of such industries. The author critically examines the part played by the State Financial Corporations with regard to the provision of finance to small industries and indicates the possible lines along which their working may be improved and they may provide industrial finance. Finally, the author makes an attempt to assess the place of such small-scale power - driven industries in the economy of the country in the light of the controversy which was set on foot after the Draft Plan was published.

Ramakrishna, K.T. (1961) in his study, *Finances for Small Scale Industries in India*, has highlighted the role of Government agencies and institutional finance. Non-institutional agencies such as money lenders and indigenous bankers are excluded. The study is confined to financial assistance by a State in the shape of direct credit under the State Aid to Industries Acts, non-financial assistance in the form of external aids and credit from the State Financial Corporations, State Bank of India, Commercial Banks, Scheduled and Non-scheduled; and Co-operative Banks. It also deals with finance for SSIs in highly industrialised nations; such as Japan, Germany, Switzerland, France, Great Britain and the United States.

Balakrishnan, G. (1961) in his study, *Finance Small Scale Industries in India 1950-52*, gives a detailed account of the finances of a sample of small-scale units in modern industry in India. The author discusses the economic and industrial developments during 1950-52 and also examines the financial experience of about 10 SSIs. Finally, the author examines the financial experience of large companies vis-a-vis the small companies.

The UNESCO Research Centre (1962), in its study, *Social Aspects of Small Industries in India: Studies in Howrah and Bombay*, observed that the industrial entrepreneurship sprang up gradually owing to a shift in the entrepreneurs from their traditional occupations to industry. This might have been due to their educational attainment which stimulated prospective entrepreneurs to come out with a resolve to succeed.

Iyengar, K.S. (1968) in his study, *The Philosophy of Small Scale Industrial Management*, aims to present the importance of the vital techniques that have to be implemented in SSIs. The book is divided into six parts. Each part deals with the major divisions of the management study. In the first part, 'Management in Principles', the author discusses the present day business trend and the principles of modern management. In the second part, 'Marketing', he defines the scientific methods of fixing price, besides product-planning and other important features relating to marketing. The third part, 'Production', presents the fundamental aspects of scientific methods of production necessary for small units. The fourth and the fifth parts, 'Personnel' and 'Control' are respectively designed to embrace the scientific principles vital for all manufacturing units. The last part, 'Management in Practice' deals with such business-ethics, that is the latest trend of management thought.

Singh, Kumar Ramchandra Prasad's (1969) study, *State and Industrialisation of Developing Countries with Special Reference to India*, is an analytical study of the role of State in the industrial development of developing countries. It deals with the rationale of rapid industrialisation and with the study of the costs of industrialisation. It also summarises some of the widely held views on obstacles to the industrial growth of an underdeveloped economy, discusses the role of State in removing these obstacles and in creation of proper atmosphere for making industrialisation a rapid process. Besides, it also deals with the manifold aspects of the problems of financing the industries of underdeveloped countries with special reference to India and tries to examine and analyse how State paternalism has helped the growth of industry in some important countries of the world.

Singh, Nau Nihal's (1970) *Scientific Management of Small-Scale Industries*, enumerates the problems of small-scale enterprises and suggests a comprehensive system of scientific management which could be profitably employed by the small industrialists. The author shows how–with the application of modern methods of management–the small-scale enterprises can cut down production cost, standardise, improve the quality of their products and achieve sustained growth in a competitive economy.

The study by Vepa, Ram K. (1971), *Small Industry in the Seventies*, deals in depth with many of the key areas vital to the future growth of small industries viz., policy and organisation, credit, modernization (including appropriate technology) training and consultancy, and finally, marketing (including export promotion). It also describes in some detail the experiences of Japan and India in this field and status of small industries in other countries of Asia, Middle East, Africa and Latin America. A model of a Development Programme weaving the various facets together is also outlined.

Ramakrishnan, P. (1975) in his study, *New Entrepreneurship in Small-Scale Industries in Delhi*, had studied 94 new small-scale units started after 1965 in 11 categories of modern industries in Delhi city. The units have been divided into three categories viz., those that succeeded in production, those who failed and those that dropped out after the initial production. The study revealed that social status, occupational background of the entrepreneurs and education were responsible for growth of entrepreneurship.

Bharti, R.K.'s (1978) *Industrial Estates in Developing Economies*, presents a comprehensive and critical survey of the programme of industrial estates in the developed and developing countries. The book is divided into three parts. The first part deals with the objectives, policies and progress of industrial estates programme in developing economies. The second part makes a full and detailed study of different aspects of industrial estates in the Indian context. The third part gives first-hand information about industrial estates in Madhya Pradesh. It also gives the findings and suggestions for making industrial estates more effective. The author concludes the study with some concrete and logical suggestions with a view to making industrial estates a potent and effective tool for industrializing the economy of the country.

Pareek, H.S. (1978) in his study, *Financing of Small-Scale Industries in a Developing Economy*, highlights in brief the socio-economic background of Rajasthan and focuses attention on the rationale and growth of small-scale industrial units in the State. The study also highlights the problems of SSIs with particular reference to finance and brings home to the readers an analysis of the capital structure of 181 small-scale units of different capital sizes belonging to various industrial groups. The study reviews the role of financial institutions and State agencies in extending credit to small-scale industrial units and pinpoints their attitude on indifference in catering to the needs of the tiny units.

Sanghvi, R.L.'s (1979) *Role of Industrial Estates in a Developing Economy*, is primarily based on the field survey of six industrial estates located in South Gujarat region. Broadly, it endeavours to analyse the role of industrial estates in the industrial development and to evaluate the achievements and shortcomings of the programme and policy of industrial estates in India in general and in Gujarat in particular. It also attempts to throw light on a number of issues in connection with the programme of industrial estates such as their size, location, efficiency, utilisation and their impact on industrial dispersal and area growth. It also examines the implications of slow moving and non-starter estates in the framework of social Cost-Benefit Analysis.

Mathur, S.P.'s (1979) *Economics of Small Scale Industries*, is a study on the Economics of SSIs, particularly of Agra District. The author has undertaken this study to have a deeper probe into the malaise and to appraise critically the ills which prevent the smooth growth of the SSS, which is vital for the economic emancipation of the country. It endeavours to bring out the aberrations in State Policy, and factors responsible for improper utilisation of raw materials, man-power, and capital resources. The author also deals with the promotional aspect of the industry.

Carr, Marilyn's study, *Developing Small-Scale Industries in India: An Integrated Approach,* provides a clear insight into the working of a unique and successful scheme which entrepreneurs with the necessary training, financial backing and the right product have launched into small industries with considerable success. The book discusses how an outside agency can act, as a catalyst in helping to bring Government schemes to fruition. Besides, the book also includes a number of case studies of enterprises which have been established through the work of the programme.

Deshpande, M.U. (1982) in his study, *Entrepreneurship of Small Scale Industries,* has observed that the backwardness of the Marathwada region is mainly due to a lack of prospective entrepreneurs in the region. According to him, the policies of the Government, the upper strata of society, social and political leadership, occupational background, family aspirations, and general infrastructure are important factors which contribute to the development of entrepreneurship. His study also indicates that the emergence of entrepreneurship is not merely a psychological or socio-psychological phenomenon but it is also conditioned by the political milieu and the administrative system and the commitment to economic development.

Vepa, R.K.'s (1983) *Small Industry Development Programme,* seeks to summarise the Indian experience in the growth of small industry and the policy considerations as well as the problems in it. It covers issues relating to policy, organisational structure, and international co-operation in addition to providing details about various programmes of small industrial development in the country and their linkages with other development programmes. The book also provides guidelines for appraisal of these programmes.

Pradhan, Gopinath's (1985) *Industrial Estates and State Development,* analyses the contribution made by the programme in terms of its potential for creating a new industrial climate for fostering actively the development of SSIs. Towards this end, with the help of empirical evidence, supported by statistical tests, the author points out the emergence of better product - mix, a superior form of organisation and a new class of technically qualified and educated entrepreneurs in the units functioning in the industrial estates.

Mohanty, Bedabati (1986) in her book, *Economics of Small-Scale Industries*, makes an analytical study of the different aspects of various SSIs in India. The book makes an indepth analysis of the production cost, investment, employment generation and future prospects of various SSIs then in operation in the district. The book throws light on the various problems of SSIs. Statistical tables along with detailed analysis have attempted to explain the existing problems of these industries.

Dawar, Ram's (1986) *Institutional Finance to Small Scale Industries*, attempts to examine the hire-purchase schemes of the National Small Industries Corporation Limited (NSIC) and the State Small Industries Corporations (SSICs), particularly the Andhra Pradesh Small Scale Industrial Development Corporation (APSSIDC). An appraisal of the operation of the hire-purchase schemes of these institutions has also been attempted. The evaluation of the performance of the units assisted by the Corporations, with the help of different accounting ratios, is one of the distinctive features of this study.

Mishra, S.N. and Sharma, Kushal (1986) in their study, *Organisational Requirements of Village and Small-Scale Industries*, have examined the action plan of the District Industries Centre (DIC) of Alwar District in Rajasthan and have tried to evaluate the functioning of different organisations engaged in the task of expansion of Village and SSIs. Finally, based on the perception of officials and entrepreneurs, they have tried to identify the problem areas. They have also attempted to seek suggestions from the sample respondents of both the sets i.e. the beneficiaries and the officials, in regard to organisational requirements and performance of existing organisations.

Mehta, Anil (1987) in his book, *Organisation and Working of Industrial Estates*, analyses organisation and working of industrial estates and evaluates the achievements and short-comings of the problem. Besides dealing with the conceptual framework of the programme, it also attempts to throw light on a number of issues such as working of industrial estates in India and abroad, infrastructural facilities, institutional assistance, marketing, finance and workers problems with reference to industrial estate.

Vinze, Medha Dubhashi's (1987) book, *Women Entrepreneurs in India*, provides a detailed industrial profile of Delhi as also the facilities made available to the entrepreneurs by the Government and different other agencies. Attempt has also been made to find out the basic ingredients of entrepreneurship and achievement motivation. The book tries to assess the role of women in socio-economic development of the country in a historical perspective and examines the factors which help or hinder the women in playing a positive role in socio-economic development of the country. Finally, it provides the empirical view of the problem in which attempt has been made to provide the perception of the sample respondents on different aspects of the problem.

Gupta, M.C. (1987) in his book, *Entrepreneurship in Small Scale Industries*, has studied entrepreneurial performance of 60 small entrepreneurs, taking 20 each from Kanpur, Allahabad and Gorakhpur, in Uttar Pradesh. In his study he deals in detail with the essential qualities and functions of entrepreneurs, policy framework and support systems to develop entrepreneurship in the small sector. He makes recommendations for framing policies in future and outlines the role of the Government in developing entrepreneurship in the small industry sector.

Saxena, K.K. (1987) in his book, *Regional Input-Output Model for Small Scale Industries*, has made an attempt to explain the importance of the SSIs in the industrial set-up of the Rajasthan's Economy through input-output analysis. The study measures the inter-sectoral dependence among the SSIs in Rajasthan and have found out the key sectors by calculating the different types of multipliers. Finally, the author makes the comparison of the small and large scale industries in the input-output framework.

Jaimini, R.K. (1988) in his study, *Management of Small-Scale* Industries, makes an attempt to analyse the complex profitability situation in which the Indian paper industry has sailed during the study viz., 1976-83. The author analyses the profitability of the paper industry of India on the basis of investment turnover. Profit margin of the selected units and the profit margin of this industry have been analysed and evaluated to interpret their impact on return on investment. The author also analyses the return on investment and profitability in relation to owners equity. Further the author examines and discusses the problems confronted by the paper industry from time to time. They have been spotlighted with a view to analyse the cause that have hampered the growth of this industry and reduced its overall profitability. Finally, certain suggestions for the improvement of profitability and for the overall development of the industry have been given.

Vepa, R.K. (1988) in his study, *Modern Small Industry in India Problems and Prospects*, first outlines the progress made over the last thirty years. He then identifies some key areas which, he argues, need greater attention on the part of policy-makers if the small industry sector is going to successfully meet the challenges posed by modern technology. These areas include technology support, credit flow, and market assistance. The author also identifies thrust areas which are likely to gain in importance as we enter the next decade and suggests a strategy for micro-planning at the field level.

Tyabji, Nasir's (1989) *The Small Industries Policy in India*, is divided into four parts. In the first part, the basis for understanding the developments in the field of small-scale production is set out by elaborating the process of evolution of an industrial capital. In the second part, the structure of several industries in which units of small size predominated is analysed. The conclusion is reached that at the beginning of the period preceding the formulation of the Second Five Year Plan, the system of commodity production subordinate to merchant, and sometimes to usurer capital, was the predominant structure in these industries. The third part, examines both the evolution of the small industries policy and its development. It consists of a study of the ways in which the development strategy to be followed by the country after independence was refined and elaborated in the course of the national struggle. The development of the concept of planning is described, and the positions on planning taken by various strata and classes articulated. In the fourth and final part of the book, the author has made an attempt to measure the results of the Small Industries Policy and the impact of general economic development, on the growth of the SSS.

Hamid, Syed Abdul's (1989) *Management Development of Small Scale Industries*, explores the possibility of setting up various types of Small Scale and Cottage Industries in the Jammu and Kashmir State with a view to provide a sound base for the future industrialisation in the State. The book deals with an overview of the economy of Jammu and Kashmir State and also examines the existing industrial structure of the State. Apart from this, it also highlights the urgency of setting up cottage and SSIs based on local skill and indigenous raw-material in the State. Finally, the author concludes that the State of Jammu and Kashmir possesses enough potentialities in respect of cottage and SSIs but it demands a greater deal of effort on the part of the Government and its various agencies.

Khanka, S.S. (1990) in his study, *Entrepreneurship in Small Scale Industries*, studied 50 small-scale entrepreneurs in a notified backward region of the Kumaun division of Uttar Pradesh regarding the emergence, performance and problems of entrepreneurship. A guiding assumption of this study is that true display of the entrepreneurial role and attributes can be well seen only in the case of small-scale entrepreneurs. This study brings under its purview entrepreneurial setting, entry into entrepreneurship, financing of entrepreneurship, entrepreneurial performance and their problems. Finally, the author lays stress on the policy implications to provide liberal incentives and concessions to the entrepreneurs to encourage, promote and strengthen the small units in backward areas.

Kaveri, V.S. (1990) in the study on *Development of Small Scale Industries–Some Issues*, has analysed the development of small scale industry in two sections. Section 1 relates to policies of the Government and institutional network to provide financial assistance. Section 2 attempts to examine the performance of small-scale industrial sector in terms of investment, production, employment and number of units.

Rao, V.S.P. and Nagaiya, D. (1991) in their study, *Small Industry Development in India*, probe deep into the process of small industry development in India during the last four decades. The book is divided into five sections. The first section deals with the concept, nature and the philosophical background of Small Industry in India. The second section traces the development process initially followed by the various measures taken by the Government to support small industry. In the third section, the reasons for high mortality rate are presented. The fourth section deals with interesting case studies focusing attention on the need to develop small units in backward areas. Recent trends in small industry development are presented in the final section.

Saigal, Omesh's, *et.al.*, (1994) *Problems and Prospects of Industrial Development in a Metropolitan City*, is substantially based on the scholarly deliberations of a seminar organised by the DSIDC. Some of the constructive suggestions put forward are that in future only environment friendly hitech industries which are less taxing on infrastructure be permitted in Delhi and for that technically qualified youth be trained and encouraged to take up entrepreneurship, existing industries be shifted from non-conforming areas to other parts of National Capital Region (NCR); SSIs be motivated to upgrade the technology to make the production more efficient and environment friendly; proper linkage between industry and institutions be established; the multiplicity of authorities administering industries be done away with and one leading institution like the DSIDC be declared as nodal agency for administering and monitoring industrial activity in Delhi.

Rao, Ch. Umamaheshwara's (1995) *Small Scale Industries,* probes deep into the problems faced by these industries and raises certain fundamental and theoretical implications of the public attitudes and policies towards them. The book is divided into two parts. In the first part, the author discusses the meaning, economic implications, classification and occupational structure of SSIs. In the second part, the policy aspects such as problems of organisation, labour mobility and public aids are discussed. The author also investigates the maladies besetting these industries, financial, technical and managerial and discusses the pros and cons of the steps taken by the Government to overcome these difficulties.

Kumar D., Narendra's (1995) *Entrepreneurship in Small Scale Sector*, gives a brief historical outline of Indian Entrepreneurship: Entrepreneurship Development in the SSS; and Entrepreneurship Development Programmes. It also provides a back-drop of the Industrial Economy of the Chittoor District and socio-economic setting of entrepreneurship–covering the social setting of Entrepreneurs and their economic status. Apart from this, it discusses the factors influencing entrepreneurship covering entrepreneurs' ambitions; compelling factors; facilitating factors; Government facilities and incentives; and help expected from the Government promotional agencies etc. Finally, it discusses the progress and problems of enterprises.

Rao, T. Venkateshwara (1995) in his book, *Development of Small Scale Industries*, deals with the DICs and their relevance in the promotion of SSS. The author discusses the organisational structure of the DICs, identifies its strengths and weaknesses and also the functional linkages of DICs with other industrial promotion and financing agencies. The author makes an attempt to study the relative performance of DICs in Andhra Pradesh *vis-a-vis* at the all India level. He evaluates the inter-regional and inter-district performance of DICs in Andhra Pradesh and also deals with the performance of DIC assisted SSI units. Finally, an attempt has been made to analyse the role of DICs in Self Employment for Educated Unemployed Youth (SEEUY) programme and the progress achieved thereof and to study the role of DICs in Artisan Development Programmes based on case studies of select artisan complexes.

Hundekar, S.G., *et.al.*, (1998) in their study, *Challenges Before Small Scale Industries*, have dealt with issues relating to SSIs. It highlights the need for financing SSS; its role in Indian economy; problems, prospects and performance of this sector; financial requirements of rural units; identification and rehabilitation of industrial units and impact of new economic policy on the growth process of SSS. Moreover, focus has been pinpointed to the specific industries like cotton, paper mills, etc.; operational efficiency of small and medium scale industries in Malaysia; women entrepreneurship in Manipur of North Eastern Region and Fund flow–Cash flow analysis of industries.

The above mentioned surveys or studies are not comprehensive or full either in approach or analysis of the problems of SSIs. All the above mentioned researches and studies are mainly related either with the financial aspects or with the role of industrial estates in removing regional imbalances. None of these studies deal with the role of the State in promotion of SSIs in India. In addition, there is no exclusive study on the role and functioning of the DSIDC and thus the survey is being undertaken.

Objectives of the Study

In the light of the introductory background, the statement of problem, selection of Delhi for the study purpose and overview of literature, the main objectives of the present study are:

1. to analyse the role of the State in industrial development of the country in general and SSIs in particular;
2. to discuss in detail the industrial policy of the Government towards the SSIs;
3. apart from the activities of the Small Industrial Development Corporation in promoting SSIs, to study in detail other supporting organisations in promotion of SSIs;
4. to examine the role of the DSIDC as a specialised agency of the State;
5. to depict the genesis, objectives and administrative structure of the DSIDC;
6. based on the organisational structure, to provide a broad classification of the functions of the DSIDC;
7. to test empirically the perception of the officials of the DSIDC in regard to its role in promotion of SSIs;
8. with the help of the field survey of a few enterprises to assess the perception of entrepreneurs in regard to the functioning of the DSIDC; and
9. finally, based on the available data and information, to suggest whether DSIDC requires a thorough restructuring for better performance and how to maintain co-ordination with other promoting agencies active in National Capital Territory of Delhi.

Hypotheses

To achieve the objectives of the present study, a few main hypotheses have been developed for final testing. They are as follows:

1. In the broader framework of the State activities, the development of SSIs is not only essential for the overall well-being of the society but also to sustain the basic requirements of the society;
2. SSIs serve as a conduit to the overall industrial development of the country;
3. Perfect inter-organisational co-ordination (between Small Industries Development Corporation, State Financial Corporations, Small-Scale Industries Development Corporation, etc.), may provide greater scope for the promotion of SSIs;
4. The helping and co-operative attitude of DSIDC may encourage the new entrepreneurs to enter into the small-scale industrial sector;
5. The accessibility of raw material, will provide greater scope for higher production; and
6. Finally, better marketing facilities of finished goods, will help accelerate the growth of SSIs.

Methodology

As regards the methodological aspect of the study, we have followed both the method of historical and survey research. To put it differently, it has been based both on the method of desk research and empirical investigation. The primary data has been collected with the help of the planned document, the policy papers and guidelines issued from time to time. Apart from the primary source, the books and journals available with the libraries on the problem have also been made full use of.

For empirical study we have sought the co-operation of the officials and employees of the DSIDC. A detailed formal and informal discussion supported by a structured and guided schedule, served on them, was the main source of primary data and information. Apart from the officials and employees of

DSIDC for detailed information in regard to the role performance of DSIDC, the entrepreneurs engaged in various enterprises in the different industrial estates were selected on the basis of random sampling for the detailed interview.

The data and information so collected have been tabulated, analysed and presented in the form of book.

A detailed schedule was prepared for the respondents in English and it was served on sample respondents. But in course of interview they were translated into Hindi. Before serving the schedules on sample respondents, they were pretested. While pretesting the schedules, it was noticed that some questions required to be revised. As such, nearly ten questions were removed and equal number of questions were added after pretesting. The questions in the schedule were basically of two types – fixed answer questions and opinionative questions.

In course of serving the schedules on respondents it was felt that desired information was not coming out due to formal environment of interviews. As such we also depended on informal discussion which proved quite useful.

As regards the sample size, we chose 120 entrepreneurs and 25 officials for interview purpose. The officials belonged to the DSIDC. The 120 entrepreneurs, selected as sample belonged to different trades like–steel rolling, toy making, furniture works, leather works, garments, shoe making etc. The 120 entrepreneurs belonged to three industrial areas of Delhi *viz.*, Okhla Industrial Area, Wazirpur Industrial Area and Anand Parbat Industrial Area. Out of the 120 entrepreneurs, 60 entrepreneurs belonged to Okhla Industrial Area, 40 to Wazirpur Industrial Area and 20 to Anand Parbat Industrial Area.

A lot of inconvenience was faced by the researcher during the course of the field work. Being a lady, the researcher faced lots of problem in visiting the industrial areas. The entrepreneurs were not at all co-operative because they assumed that the researcher was a Government agent and tried to extract facts from them about their enterprise. Only after pursuation they were convinced that the basic value of the interview was academic one and it had nothing to do with the Government/ administration. Even then some of the entrepreneurs were reluctant to answer our queries. Similar was the case of the DSIDC officials. Whenever the researcher tried to contact them, they were busy. It was really a hard time for the researcher to catch hold of the DSIDC officials for interview purpose. Some of the entrepreneurs as well as the DSIDC's officials asked to leave the schedule with them with a provision that after filling up, the schedules will be returned by post. In certain cases we had no option except to concede to their request. But inspite of several telephonic reminders they did not return back the schedule either in filled up form or without filling it up. In such a situation, we had to go for some other entrepreneurs for interview purpose. Inspite of such difficulties the researcher was able to complete the field work.

Aspects of the Study

The present study has been coached in nine chapters. The first chapter i.e. Introduction, has been divided into two parts. A brief historical outline of SSIs, importance of SSIs and the concept of SSIs is presented in the first part. The second part sets forth the parameters of the research of the present study i.e. it deals with the statement of the problem, review of earlier research works on SSIs, objectives of the study, hypotheses and methodological aspects of the study.

In the second chapter, we have discussed the role of the State in industrial development in the Indian context. The chapter has been divided into three parts. The first part deals with the State and industry. The second part deals with the role of the State and the third part deals with the industrial evolution of India.

In the third chapter, an attempt has been made to discuss the Industrial Policy pursued by the Government since Independence. Apart from this, we have also discussed the progress of SSIs through the successive plans.

Promotion and growth of the SSIs sector has always been a corner-stone of the India's Industrial Policy. As such in the fourth chapter, we have discussed about the various agencies/institutions that has been established both at the Central and the State levels for the promotion of the SSIs. Apart from the organisations/

institutions at the Central and State level, we have also discussed the specialised institutions and the industry associations which play an important role in the promotion of SSIs.

A detailed industrial profile of Delhi has been provided in the fifth chapter. It also deals with the facilities made available to the small scale entrepreneurs by the Government of NCT, Delhi and different other agencies of the Government of NCT, Delhi.

A brief description of the genesis of the DSIDC has found place in the sixth chapter. Besides, the objectives of the DSIDC and the administrative structure have also been dealt with. Finally, the functions of the DSIDC have been discussed.

Seventh and eighth chapters provide the empirical view of the problem in which attempt has been made to provide the perception of the small scale entrepreneurs and the officials of the DSIDC respectively on different aspects of the problem, for example, marketing, procuring raw material, export, registration, etc.

The ninth and the final chapter is devoted to the summary of findings and conclusions in regard to the functioning of the DSIDC.

Endnotes

1. Government of India, *India's Industrial Policies from 1948 to 1991*, Development Commissioner (SSIs), Department of SSIs and Agro and Rural Industries, Ministry of Industries, New Delhi,1997, p.3.
2. Government of India, *Twenty-Five Years of Progress*, Ministry of Industrial Development (SSI), New Delhi, 1971, p.1.
3. Rao, R.V., *Small Industries and the Development Economy in India*, Concept Publishing Company, New Delhi, 1979, p.12.
4. Government of India, *Report of the Indian Industrial Commission*, 1918, p.160.
5. Government of India, *Report of the Fiscal Commission*, 1949-50, p.99.
6. *Report of the Committee on Finance for the Private Sector*, Reserve Bank of India, Bombay, April, 1954, pp.80-81.
7. Rao, R.V., *op.cit.*, p.13.
8. Government of India, *Report of the Village and Small Scale Industries Committee*, Planning Commission, New Delhi, 1956, p.115.

9. Government of India, *Small Scale Industries in India*, Development Commissioner, Small Scale Industries, New Delhi, 1968, p.53.

10. *Ibid.*

11. Hattangdi, Anil, *Banker's Handbook on Small Scale Industries*, IBH Publishing Company, Delhi, 1973, p.21.

12. Government of India, *Assistance to Small Scale Industries*, Ministry of Civil Supplies, Small Scale Industries Board, Delhi, 1975.

13. Dawar, Ram, *Institutional Finance to Small Scale Industries*, Deep and Deep Publications, New Delhi, 1986, p.17.

14. Government of Tamil Nadu, *Small Scale Industries - Second SSI Census*, Directorate of Industries and Commerce, Tamil Nadu, 1988, p.3.

15. "Investment Limit for SSIs, Hiked", *IIPA Newsletter*, Vol.XLII, No.1, January 1998, p.4.

16. Government of India, *SIDBI Report on Small Scale Industries Sector 2000*, Small Industries Development Bank of India, New Delhi, 2000, p. 29.

2

Role of the State in Industrial Development : The Indian Context

In the present chapter, an attempt has been made to discuss the role of the State in industrial development in the Indian context. The chapter has been divided into three parts. The first part deals with the State and Industry. The second part deals with the role of State and the third part deals with the industrial evolution of India.

I

The State and Industry

In the early days of the British rule the East India Company was mainly a trading concern whose chief business was to exchange the manufactured goods of England for the agricultural products of India. When the company attempted to improve the existing industries of the country by organisational and financial assistance, their policy was strongly opposed by manufacturers in England which insisted that the company should concentrate on the export from India of the raw materials necessary for manufacturers in England.

The British administration in India was apathetic to industrial growth. The acceptance of the policy of laissez-faire in England kept the Government of India aloof from the industrial development of the country. It was assumed that what was good for England was also good for India, though the stages of development of the two countries were different. The decline of traditional industries and the pressure of population on land pointed to the need for a change in policy. A series of famines visited India during the last quarter of the 19th century in which millions of Indians died. As such in 1880, the Famine Commission was appointed to look into this matter. The Commission directed the attention of the Government to a policy of diversification of occupations as a remedy against the recurrence of famines. At that time Indian opinion insisted that the State should take a positive role in promoting the industrial development of the country. The first measure adopted by the Government assumed a two-fold form: (i) establishment of the Commercial Museum at Calcutta and (ii) a provision of technical education.[1]

Soon Lord Curzon realised the need for a systematic policy of promoting industries. As such in 1905 the Department of Commerce and Industry was created. But in 1910 its activities were curtailed by the Secretary of State for India. Some of the Provincial Governments took initiative in the industrial field. The Madras Government initiated an experiment with certain selected industrial crafts. The Government of the United Provinces also took up the pioneering example of the Madras Government.[2] However, Lord Morley disapproved this policy and his decision checked the initial attempts made by the Government for the improvement of industries.

The Industrial Conferences organised by a body of leading Congressmen and industrialists attracted the attention of the country upon the immense possibilities of industrial development of the country. But the policy of the Government of India continued to be one of non-interference. For the first time it was felt by the Government that the development of at least some industries was essential from the military point of view during the First World War. As a result an Industrial Commission was appointed in 1916 under the chairmanship of Sir Thomas Holland to assess the possibilities of industrialisation of India and make suitable recommendations with that objective in view. The Commission urged the Government to adopt a vigorous policy for India's industrial development. It pointed out that the formulation of a definite industrial policy hinges upon the principle that in future the Government must play an active part in the industrial development of the country. The Commission further suggested that the State assistance to industries might be given in various forms, *e.g.*, research, technical advice, educational facilities, commercial intelligence, financial assistance, local purchase of stores, etc. In the meantime Government had set up the Munitions Board for the purpose of buying army requirements as far as possible in India. This gave a stimulus to the growth of industries, especially those catering for war materials. Following the recommen-dations of the Industrial Commission, different provinces started separate Department of Industries and passed the State Aid to Industries Acts in 1923 under which the Government granted loans for the development of small industries under certain conditions.

As a sequel to the fiscal autonomy convention, the first Fiscal Commission was appointed in October 1921 to consider the protectionist policies for developing modern industries in India. In its report (1923), it recommended a policy of discriminating protection. It favoured grant of fiscal protection to deserving industries in the initial stages of development or in cases when they were suffering from unfair competition. In order to qualify for grant of fiscal protection, the industry must satisfy the following criteria.[3]

1. The industry must be one possessing natural advantages, such as an abundant supply of raw material, cheap power, a sufficient supply of labour, and a large home market.
2. The industry must be one which without the help of protection is not likely to develop at all or as rapidly as is desirable in the interest of the country.
3. The industry must be one which will eventually be able to face world competition without protection.

This so-called 'Triple Formula', which was not very unreasonable in itself, overlooked the fact that in the case of strategic and basic industries, and also in cases of extreme unemployment and under employment, departures from it might be necessary and justified. The experience of Japan's industrialisation abundantly illustrates that the handicap in respect of one or two factors, for example, the lack of an abundant domestic supply of raw materials, need not be an inseparable barrier to the growth of an industry. It was necessary to apply the formula flexibly and sympathetically. The colonial administration, however, thought otherwise. The policy of discriminating protection was greatly whittled down in implementation through rigid and unsympathetic interpretation of the formula. The requests for protection were turned down on slight grounds. The Fiscal Commission had recommended a permanent Tariff Board to consider the applications for protection, but the Government instituted a system of temporary Tariff Boards. As soon as a Tariff Board had disposed off the case for which it had been constituted, it was dissolved. The system "militated against indepen-dence of judgement, accumulation of experience in the examination of cases, uniformity of approach, and a co-ordinated development of different industries".[4] Industries had to be established without prior assurance of grant of protection because the application was entertained only after the industry had been established. Despite the above limitations, the policy of discriminating protection did provide some stimulus to industrial development.

The provincial Governments were conferred wide powers in regard to industries, with the introduction of provincial autonomy under the Government of India Act, 1935. Many provinces took active measures to help the growth of indigenous industries.

It was during the Second World War period that the British Government became more conscious of the necessity for industrial expansion, research and training. As a result, conditions were created for the emergence of many new industries as foreign supplies were curtailed. In 1940, the Board of Scientific and Industrial Research was established. The Government of India assured the new industries that they should be granted protection against foreign competition. In April 1945, the Government announced a full-fledged policy of industrial development with the following objectives:[5] (i) Rapid industrialisation of the country; (ii) Balanced regional distribution of industries; (iii) Balanced development of the economy as a whole; and (iv) Equitable distribution of the national income.

The industrial pattern before independence can be characterised as (i) low capital intensity, (ii) limited development of medium-sized factory and industries, and (iii) imbalance between consumer goods and capital goods industries.[6]

The attainment of independence in 1947 changed the entire position and a new era began with regard to State in relation to industry.

II

Role of State

In a mixed economy like India where both the public and private enterprises are supposed to play an important but complementary role, the intervention of State is far reaching and spreads over a wide area of its economy. Particularly responsible for this has been the objective set before the public sector to attain a commanding height in the economy with the ultimate object of setting up a socialistic–or rather a socialist, as it was changed to later on–pattern of society.[7]

A modern welfare State is expected to take care of the citizens' needs from cradle to the grave. There is hardly any country in the world, the economy of which remains uninfluenced by State activities. The type and extent of State intervention may vary very widely depending upon several factors, *e.g.*, the stage of development of an economy, the political ideology, the political parties and the Government of a country, the behaviour of the private sector and so on.

In India, the basic guiding principles of State functioning are clearly laid down in the Preamble of the Constitution, Part III of the Constitution, i.e., the Fundamental Rights, and Part IV of the Constitution, i.e., the Directive Principles of State Policy. The economic responsibilities earmarked for the State are enormous and call for significant State interference in the functioning of the economy. The Preamble of the Constitution, for instance, requires attainment of social, economic and political justice; equality of status and of opportunity, etc., for all citizens of India. Similarly, Fundamental Rights have economic significance in as much as there cannot be any discrimination on ground of religion, race, caste, sex, etc. The State may, of course, impose reasonable restrictions on such rights in public interest. The power to impose reasonable restrictions has again led to remarkable increase in statutory control over business.

The Directive Principles of State Policy is a unique feature of the Indian Constitution. They are economically very significant and the State is expected to exercise its authority in such a manner that these principles are ordinarily observed. This again provides enormous scope for State intervention in functioning of the economy, including private business and industry.

State intervention in industry has been continuously increasing. State has been empowered to impose restrictions on the right of citizens to carry on any trade, business, industry or service with a view to enabling the State to undertake any scheme of nationalisation or prescribing professional or technical qualifications necessary for practising any profession or carrying on any occupation, trade or business. In other words, State has been acquiring more and more powers to control the private activity and to enlarge its own ownership and management of the economy. This has been primarily to ensure justice to all sections of the society and prevent undue concentration of economic power in a few hands.

A number of different sorts of relationships exist between the Government and industry, e.g., (i) Government raises revenue by taxing industry; (ii) Government buys goods and services from industry; (iii) Government provides numerous services to industry; (iv) Government and industry compete for the available resources; (v) Government exercises control over, and provides incentives to industry; (vi) Government provides capital for, and in some cases comes to act as a partner in, or owner of, certain sectors of industry; and so on.[8] In short, it can be said that State seeks to regulate the commercial and physical environments in which industry operates.

In view of the aforesaid relationships, State is in a position to play a significant role in the creation of proper atmosphere for rapid industrial development. It is more so because of its advantageous position vis-a-vis the private sector in overcoming various hindrances. In the words of R.B. Sutcliffe:

"State has always played some role either positive or negative in every industrialisation, though it may not have been a decisive one; the State may put obstacles in the way of industrialisation; it may refrain from putting obstacles in the way; it may remove obstacles; it may provide incentives to others to industrialise; it may partake in the industrial growth itself; or it may assume a completely dominant role in an industrialisation. In all cases its role is important".[9]

It is the responsibility of the State to provide suitable institutional facilities to encourage industrial development. State may help in allaying fears and apprehensions in the minds of indigenous industrialists and foreign investors. It may encourage and facilitate behavioural and institutional changes, for example, abolition of the Zamindari system, fixation of a ceiling on land, etc., by promoting skill and capital formation, by acquainting people with development potentials, and by creating general conditions for development.

Increasing intervention by the State in the industrial development has been a characteristic feature of this century, particularly during the recent past. Very few areas of industry remain free of State regulation or control. Industrialists and managers now recognise the significance of numerous roles which the State is obliged to play. Let us examine in detail some of the numerous roles played by the State in industrial development.

Regulatory Role of State

The first and foremost role which the State plays in industrial development is that of a regulator. As a regulator, the Government's aim is to apply rules so that industry does not conduct itself in a manner which is prejudicial to the interests of the society. State regulation and control of the private business is being increasingly accepted as legitimate and inevitable. The pre-requisite for creation of a favourable climate of confidence is consistency in State policy towards industry. Since industry is very much sensitive to Government's moves for its regulation and control, the ever increasing controls have to be flexible and reasonable so as to motivate industry to adjust itself without much problem. Government regulation of industry may be through: (i) direct controls and (b) indirect controls.

One of the most important direct control measures for regulation of industrial development is industrial licensing. It is in conformity with the national socio-economic objectives. For the major industries, Government's permission is required in the form of a licence for setting up an industrial undertaking, for expansion of capacity or for shifting the location. Industrial licensing policy may be called an operational counterpart of the Industrial Policy Resolutions (IPRs). The legal authority is derived basically from the Industries (Development and Regulation) Act, 1951, and is supported by statutes like the Companies Act, 1956, the MRTP Act, 1969, the FERA, 1973, etc. Constitutional validity is derived from the fact that both the Preamble of the Constitution of India and the Directive Principles of State Policy authorise the State to regulate and control economic activities.

An industrial licence or permission is required for all industries mentioned in the First Schedule to the Act, which go by the name 'Schedule industries'.[10] It is a written permission from the Union Government to an industrial undertaking to manufacture specified articles. A licence is necessary (i) for establishing a new industrial undertaking, (ii) taking up a new article (other than those already mentioned in the licence) in an existing firm, (iii) for substantial expansion of capacity in an existing line of manufacture, (iv) for carrying on business (with a COB licence) in the lines of production is scheduled industries which had started before the Act, or in lines outside the scheduled industries or those made specially exempt but subsequently brought under the Act, or (v) for changing the location.[11]

Apart from industrial licensing, there is import licensing through which State regulates the industrial development. Whenever imports of capital goods, raw materials and components are involved, entrepreneurs have to take Government's permission and should take note of the current import licensing policy and procedures. Such occasions may arise while setting up a new undertaking or effecting a substantial expansion or diversification of existing undertakings.[12]

The indirect controls are usually exercised through various fiscal and monetary incentives and disincentives or penalties. For instance, a high import duty may discourage imports. On the other hand, fiscal and monetary incentives may encourage the development of export - oriented industries and foreign collaborations.

Promotional Role of State

Next to regulatory role is the promotional role of the State. State may promote industrial development by providing numerous incentives. The incentives are regarded as positive measures and supplementary to the regulatory role of the State. Incentives may be broadly classified as: (a) Direct incentives, such as cash subsidies, tax concessions, building of infrastructure, provision of financial assistance, etc., and (b) Indirect incentives, like provision of an environment conducive for investment in the industrial sector.[13]

Apart from the general incentives, State may provide certain special incentives for development of industrially backward areas. It may liberalise import policy and provide numerous facilities and incentives for SSS.

Another aspect of promotional role of the State is the policy of reservation of some items for exclusive production in the SSIs sector. This policy was initiated in 1967 with the objective to protect some goods produced in the SSIs from competition from large scale industries producing similar goods and eventually make their production in SSIs technically feasible and economically profitable. Under this policy of reservation, capacity of large scale industries and units therein is pegged down with reference to their best production achieved within the last three years; and no new large or medium scale units are to be allowed to be set up for the production of that reserved item, except where such industrial units undertake to export 75 per cent of their additional output. It is hoped that future increase in demand for goods in the reserved category would be met by SSIs and thus this sector would get a boost for further growth and development.[14]

Yet another aspect of promotional role of State in industrial development is the Government's store purchase policy. The Government is for long the single largest buyer of various items produced in the SSIs sector. With a view to facilitate and help to solve the marketing problem of this sector, the Central Government decided to reserve certain items for the exclusive purchase from the SSIs sector. In 1988, the number of such items was 404: in the case of another 12 products purchases are made by the Government to the extent of 75 per cent; and in the case of another 25 items, Government purchases from this sector are made to the extent of 50 per cent. In addition, the SSIs sector receives a price preference of 15 per cent in the case of products from that sector which have to face competition from large scale industries.[15]

The establishment of financial institutions is also one of the aspects of promotional role of the State. They may act as catalytic agents in promoting development by taking initiatives in certain spheres like discovery of investment projects, preparation of project reports, provision of technical advice, and management services, provision of management training to prospective entrepreneurs, etc.

The financial institutions provide long and medium term credit to industry and co-ordinate and augment the facilities for industrial growth. There are a number of financial institutions which provide finance to small and medium sized industries. Some of them are discussed below.

The Industrial Finance Corporation (IFC) was set up in 1948 and its main object was to make medium and long term credit more readily available to industrial concerns in India especially when normal banking or other financial sources were not open or the issuance of shares through the internal capital market was not possible. In addition to providing finance, it also plays a promotional role whereby the IFC renders assistance to medium and small-scale industrial entrepreneurs in the country in the form of much needed guidance through its specialised agencies in project identification, project formulation and implementation, promotion of ancillary and SSIs and encouraging indigenous technology.[16]

The State Financial Corporation (SFC), modelled more or less on the pattern of the IFC, were set up between 1953 and 1967 to provide finance to medium and small sized industries within their area. Besides, there are State Industrial Development Corporations (SIDC) in most of the States to assist the small industries.

The Industrial Credit and Investment Corporation of India (ICICI) was established in 1955, with the following objectives in view:[17]

1. To provide financial assistance in promoting, expanding and modernisation of industrial undertakings;
2. To encourage and promote participation of private enterprise, both Indian and foreign, in industrial enterprises in India; and
3. To encourage and promote industrial investment and expansion of investment market.

The Industrial Development Bank of India (IDBI) was established in 1964 to function as an apex institution of integrated federal structure of long term financing and other financial facilities like underwriting, refinancing, etc.[18] The IDBI is empowered to provide financial assistance to all types of industrial establishments engaged in activities like, manufacturing, processing and preservation of goods, shipping and transport, mining, fishing, hotelling, setting up of industrial estates, etc.

The Unit Trust of India was also set up in 1964 in order to facilitate small investment in industrial securities.

The Life Insurance Corporation (LIC) was set up in 1956 to undertake and encourage investment in shares and debentures of industrial undertakings. With its huge resources mobilised out of the savings of the people all over the country, the LIC has been the largest institutional investor in industry and has lent considerable support to the capital market as well.

The Industrial Reconstruction Corporation of India (IRCI) was set up in 1971 on IDBI's initiative, with the object of rehabilitating closed industrial units or those facing the risk of closure by way of reconstruction of capital, strengthening management, diversification of products, improvement in technology and labour relations and advancing finances on soft terms.

Establishment of non-financial institutions is another significant promotional role of State. These institutions do not provide finance, but their role is crucial and sometimes more significant than the role of the financial institutions. For instance, they may work for collecting and analysing international commercial intelligence or for locating suitable foreign parties for collaboration. Some of the important institutions directly related to the business and industry are India Investment Centre, institutions working for promotion of foreign trade, *e.g.*, Indian Institute of Foreign Trade, State Trading Corporation, etc.

Protective Role of State

The State also plays the role of protector of industries. The protective role of the State may be divided into two parts. Firstly, the State protects industry from external competition, internal disturbances, war and the consequence thereof. Protection against foreign competition is perhaps the oldest device to stimulate private investment. In past, protection has suited the interests of most nations of the world. But it has lost much of its glamour in recent times. If the number of plants involved is small, subsidies are considered to be a better course to follow. Protection against internal disturbances and wars is a significant role of the State. A sense of insecurity can prohibit the free growth of industry and trade. In this regard, State policies may provide for a sense of security and thus, accelerate the rate of growth of the industry.

Secondly, State protects people from their exploitation either as consumers or workers. In this category may fall acts like legislation concerning contracts of employment for employers to observe; there are laws on the safety, health and welfare of employees, on the protection of shareholders' funds and the consumers' interest. There appears to be some overlapping of this role with the regulatory role, but the approach here tends to stress protection of those who are least equipped to deal with the problems and the negative aspects of the industrial system.

Stabilising Role of State

The stabilising role of the State has strongly been advocated by John M. Keynes. Under the stabilising role, the State controls the prices and distribution of goods produced by industry. Such control may be formal or informal imposed either by comprehensive legislation or exercised under executive orders/ notifications issued under some general enabling statute. Pricing of many industrial goods and services were regulated by Government in a variety of ways such as fixation of maximum prices, minimum wage or bonus regulation etc. Beginning with the Industries (Development and Regulation) Act following the IPR, some major legislations were put through affecting investment in spelling out that under planning "controls on production and on movement and physical allocations to consumers become inescapable".[19] The rationale of such controls is that scarce national resources should go first to sectors given priority in the Plans and public policy; the prices should be such that the basic requirements of the people, particularly the poorer section, can be met, and at the same time development needs of the industry in respect of replacement, modernisation and expansion be provided, say from retained earnings.

As a result of these long term planning objectives, promotional controls came into being. Besides, there were the corrective controls in the sense of imposing these with the short term objective of achieving relative price stability in periods of wide fluctuation in prices of industrial goods and demands. Most of the price control belong to the latter category of corrective nature. The wartime controls on cotton cloth, sugar, iron and steel were of this nature.[20]

For the successful implementation of the planning in a mixed economy, the crucial role of effective price policy has been well recognised in the plans.[21] The developing economies have before them two main objectives of price policy: (i) the policy of price stabilisation in order to maintain the volume of the development expenditure; and (ii) the policy of price support and incentives to stimulate the investment and production efforts, especially of the farmers.

In India, pricing of industrial production has been given less importance as compared to control of agricultural prices. Approach in respect of industrial prices has been protectionist one. Efforts have been made not only to avoid depression but also to provide all possible incentives for higher production in accordance with national priorities. With this aim in view, all monetary, fiscal and direct control measures have been used.

Participative Role of State

Today there is hardly any country in which State is not engaged actively and directly in the setting up and management of economic and industrial enterprises. These include transport systems, generations and distribution of power, etc., to the industrial establishments of all kinds, such as integrated steel plants, fertilisers and chemicals; manufacture of ships, aircrafts, locomotives; etc. State may directly participate in such activities through: (a) nationalisation, (b) establishment of public enterprises, *i.e.*, entering into business and industry like any other entrepreneur, in specific areas for special considerations, and (c) partnerships and joint ventures in the existing or new enterprises.

Nationalisation may be resorted to as a matter of principle, or for the sake of expediency, or as a result of a combination of the two.[22] In India, public sector not only occupies a pivotal position in the economy but is all pervasive. It has grown substantially both vertically and horizontally as is evident from Table 2.1. Public enterprises are controlling a major part of the total production of basic materials.

Finally, establishment of joint sector is an alternative method of extension of the public ownership and control over industry. Joint sector indicates joint ownership of the equity shares and participation in management by the Government and the private entrepreneurs. Such ventures are expected to check concentration of economic power in the private hands and ensure the fulfilment of social responsibilities of business.

Table 2.1 : Growth of Public Enterprises

	No. of enterprises	*Total investment (in crores)*
At the commencement of the Ist Plan (1-4-1951)	5	29
At the commencement of the IInd Plan (1-4-1956)	21	81
At the commencement of the IIIrd Plan (1-4-1961)	47	948
At the end of the IIIrd Plan (31-3-1966)	73	2410
At the commencement of the IVth Plan (1-4-1969)	84	3897
At the commencement of the Vth Plan (1-4-1974)	122	6237
At the end of the Vth Plan (31-3-1979)	169	15534
At the commencement of the VIth Plan (1-4-1980)	179	18150
At the commencement of the VIIth Plan (1-4-1985)	251	42673
As on (31-3-1989)	238	85627
At the end of the VIIth Plan (31-3-1990)	244	99329
As on (31-3-1991)	246	113896
As on (31-3-1992)	246	135445
As on (31-3-1993)	245	147587
As on (31-3-1994)	246	164332

Source: Government of India, *Public Enterprise Survey*, 1993-94, Vol.I, Department of Public Enterprises, Ministry of Industry, New Delhi, p.91.

Assistance Role of State

The loan capital structure of the small scale industrial units coupled with their weak bargaining power emphasises the need for assistance from State. In view of the strategic importance of the small scale industrial sector in the national economy, State assistance had been advocated by various committees and commissions. On the recommendations of various committees in general and the International Planning Team and International Perspective Planning Team in particular, a number of assistance programmes to provide direct and indirect financial assistance were undertaken by several agencies sponsored by the Central and State Governments. The schemes for providing direct financial assistance were:[23] (i) Assistance under State Aid to Industries Act/Rules; (ii) Participation in capital structure of small scale industrial sector; (iii) Central grant or subsidy scheme for establishment of units in backward areas; and (iv) Interest-free loan through refund of sales tax.

All these points are briefly discussed below :

Firstly, it was the princely State of Mysore which accepted Government responsibility of providing financial assistance to industry as early as 1913. The first State Aid to Industries Act was enacted in Madras in 1922. Later on, such Acts were enacted in other States also.

All classes of small scale industrial units are eligible to receive assistance under State Aid to Industries Rule. However, cases of industrial units like flour, pulses and rice mills falling under 'Food Processing Group' are not entertained. Further, conventional industrial units such as chaff cutting, carding, ginning, saw mills and printing presses are to be given a low priority.

Secondly, the lack of access of the SSS to the organised capital market and the consequent operation of these units with a thin capital base reflect the need of the scheme for participation in the capital structure of the small scale units through State agency. Besides strengthening the capital base of the units, this scheme fortifies their position to raise long and short term borrowings. The maiden attempt to initiate a scheme of capital participation in the SSS in the country was made by the Government of Orissa in 1957-58.[24]

Thirdly, with a view to promote the development of industries in the backward areas the Government of India introduced a scheme under which 15 per cent subsidy (originally 10 per cent and revised to 15 per cent with effect from 1st April, 1973) on fixed capital investment would be granted to industrial units to be set up in selected backward districts on or after 1st October, 1970.[25] The subsidy under this scheme has been available only to those industrial units whose total fixed capital investment is below Rs. 1 crore (Rs. 50 lakhs before April, 1973 and increased to Rs. 1 crore from that date).[26] Besides new units, old units planning substantial expansion may also have the benefit of subsidy. Substantial expansion has been defined as an increase in the value of fixed capital investment of an industrial unit by not less than 25 per cent for the purpose of expansion of capacity, modernisation etc.

Finally, the grant of interest free loan through refund of sales tax has also become a popular medium for extending financial assistance to industrial units. This type of financial assistance was first extented by the State of Maharashtra through SICOM to the units set up in the backward pockets of the State.[27]

Apart from direct assistance, the State also provides indirect assistance to the industries. The State provides indirect assistance to industries by establishing industrial estates. One of the core problems of small scale industrial units is the lack of suitable factory space. Due to the lack of suitable factory space, small scale industrial units operate in congested surroundings and unsuitable buildings. As a result, their further expansion is blocked and their productivity is adversely affected. The small scale industrialist find very difficult to arrange for adequate land and building, more so according to municipal regulations. Thus, with a view to solve the problem of small scale industrial entrepreneurs, the scheme of industrial estates was envisaged. Under this scheme, factory sheds are constructed in a specified area according to health and municipal regulations. Further the colony is equipped with all amenities like water, power, sewage, rail and roads.

The industrial estate serves the purpose of providing long term financial assistance to small scale entrepreneurs. Dr. Eugene Staley and Richard Morse regard the provision of suitable factory premises on rental or hire purchase basis as good as a loan, particularly when an enterprise has to finance its own building.[28] By bringing a number of units together, it assists in the establishment of common service centres, introduction of modern techniques of production and formation of collective purchase and sales organisation etc. Further the agency of industrial estates helps in decentralisation of industries and thereby in diffusion of economic power.

The State provides indirect assistance also by way of supplying machinery on hire purchase basis. One of the problems facing small industrial units is their outmoded and old types of equipment which adversely affect their competitive power. The shortage of finance has been a major limiting factor to equip their factories with modern machines. The National Small Industries Corporation (NSIC) was set up in 1955 to arrange the most of modern equipment for SSIs at reasonable rates. The NSIC supplies machinery on hire purchase basis.

Under this scheme, the assistance is provided to the entrepreneur in kind, and the possibility of misutilisation of funds is ruled out. The NSIC, providing this finance, also lends its expertise in procurement of machinery. It also relieves an entrepreneur from a lot of botheration involved in case of imported machinery, in arranging foreign exchange etc.

Conciliatory Role of State

State cannot be a silent spectator to the happenings in industry. Whenever there is any conflict in the industry, e.g., conflicts between management and labour, industry and consumers, or between special interest groups, state intervenes. When the normal mechanism breaks down, for instance, in an industrial dispute, Government services for conciliation, arbitration, etc. may be activated. Similarly, suitable forums may be provided for consumer protection, protection of the interests of shareholders, creditors, etc.

Educative Role of State

Government is a major compiler and publisher of statistics: on population, trade, production, employment, wages, prices, finance and so on. By virtue of its unique position as trustee of information concerning a large number of institutions and individuals, there cannot be any other comparable publisher.

State helps business organisations in making accurate forecasts concerning their respective fields of activities.

Managerial Role of State

The State performs its most obstructive and least understood role, as a planner and manager of economy. The spectrum is wide, concerning rates of economic growth, the distribution of wealth, overall levels of employment, the balance of payments, interest rates, and so on. State has to strive to continuously increase plan outlays and ensure fair share for the various sectors. The volume and the allocation of the outlay have to be with regard to the socio-economic policies of the State and the aspirations of the people.

What we have discussed in the preceding pages are instances of direct intervention by the State in industry. Besides, there are two other methods by which Government is directly involved in industrial development of the country.

Firstly, public sector industries direct Government participation in industrial production either by setting up industrial capacity and manufacturing goods in core and strategic sectors of industry or by taking over industrial units in the private sector even in the field of consumer goods when these are found mismanaged or falling sick for any reason.

Secondly, Government may use other weapons of control of industry and directing them in desired channels. These include legislation for the control of monopoly and restrictive practices, discriminatory fiscal or tight/easy monetary policy.

Various roles of the State may overlap and at places come in conflict with each other. An incomes policy, imposed by Government as economic manager, can conflict with its responsibility to be a good employer. The role of employer itself may conflict with the conciliatory role when Government is involved with its own employees in an industrial dispute. In spite of these overlappings and conflicts in certain areas, the role of the Government which is so vast and varied has become inevitable for achieving any industrial or economic growth in a country.

III

Industrial Evolution of India

During the Mughal period, India had a considerable variety of arts and handicrafts which indicated a more advanced economic and financial organisation than the crafts of contemporary Europe. In several handicrafts specialisation of jobs had advanced to such an extent that particular classes of artisans undertook distinct processes in the chain of production. The products commanded wide foreign markets. Artisans worked on their own account as well as in Karkhanas under master artisans, dealers and financiers. In the 17th century, India was hub of world trade and commerce. At that time no European country could produce enough that could be imported in India in exchange for her cotton and silk goods which they demanded. They had to pay bullion in exchange for Indian exports. "At a time when the west of Europe, a birth place of modern industrial system, was inhabited by uncivilized tribes, India was famous for the wealth of her rulers and for the high artistic skill of her craftsmen; and even at a much later period, when the merchant adventurers from the West made their first appearance in India, industrial advancement of this country was, at any rate, not inferior to those of the more advanced European nations".[29]

Even during the 18th century, India was on par with Europe in industrial production and her finished products found a ready market in many foreign countries. In the middle of the 18th century two main types of industry existed in India - (i) rural industry and (ii) urban industry. Most of the rural industries were carried on in the cottages of workers and served the day-to-day requirements of the agriculturists in the village. They served mostly local needs, that is, they manufactured utility goods such as the earthen wares, coarse cloth, baskets, etc. The artisans plied their traditional occupations uninfluenced by the outside world. There was no specialisation and the economic organisation was of a most primitive and crude character.

On the other hand, urban industries were engaged in producing luxury and semi-luxury goods and served the townsfolk and wider foreign markets. The most important of them were the silk and woollen fabrics, calicoes, gold and silver wares. In addition to the above industries, there were quite a few others which were also well-known for other goods during the pre-British days. Thus, "Artistic glassware was produced in India and found its way abroad". Different types of toys were made out of metals, wood and backed clay. It was said, "these products have delighted the people of this country and have been admired by those of other lands".[30]

During the pre-British days urban industries in India were well-organised. The urban industries were organised in the guilds or by middlemen who made advances to the craftsmen. Many of the products of these industries were of high artistic value though the output was small in quantity by modern standards. These industries were first to feel the impact of foreign competition. The handicrafts were practised on a fairly large scale and they gave rise to big towns and cities. Different parts of the country were specialised in different varieties of manufacturers.

Decline of Indian Handicrafts

The handicrafts in India could be classified as follows.[31] (i) Village handicrafts turning out goods of daily requirements of villagers; (ii) urban handicrafts producing goods for the daily use of towns folks, the work of production being carried out in the family house, mainly with the help of family members and some hired hands; (iii) urban handicrafts carried out on a comparatively large scale, employing hired hands with requisite skills. The third class of handicrafts practised a certain amount of division of labour and specialisation. The class of urban handicrafts generally produced luxury and semi-luxury goods of exquisite quality, goods such as Dacca muslin, metalwares, woollen shawls, wood-carving works, etc.

The supremacy of Indian handicrafts could no longer be maintained. Perhaps this glory of India's industry, trade and commerce represented the last flickers of the flame which was to die out almost completely by the middle of the 19th century. The arrival of the European traders in the Asiatic waters in the 16th century brought with them the germs of decay which slowly penetrated deep into the organism of the Indian industry and trade and finally led to its decay and death. Perhaps it would be correct to say that the decay and destruction of the excellent industrial and commercial organisation began from the farthest end.[32]

There are numerous causes for the decline of Indian Handicrafts. Some of them are - Industrial Revolution in England; decline of demand from Nawabs, Princely Rulers and Court officials prohibitory duties on Indian goods; establishment of an alien rule; exploitation by the company agents, the changed nature of demand from new educated Indian classes, etc.

The adverse impact of the above factors was first felt by the urban handicrafts producing luxury and semi-luxury goods. Their decline started by the beginning of the 19th century and got accelerated after 1850. By 1880, the decline of handicrafts was nearly complete and the mass of the handicraftsmen had no new industrial means of livelihood. Free trade was adopted in India while the railway alignment and the railway rates policy completed the work of killing the indigenous handicrafts.

The causes of decline of handicrafts have been nicely summed up by Sir William Hunter:

"Many circumstances conspired to injure the Indian industry in the last century. England excluded these fabrics not by fiscal duties, but by absolute prohibition. A change of fashion in the West Indies on the abolition of slavery took away the best customers left to India. Then came the cheapness of production in Lancashire, due to improvements in machinery. Lastly, the high price of raw cotton during the American War, however, beneficial to the cultivators, fairly broke down the local weaving trade in the cotton growing tracts. And whilst on the one hand the downfall of the native courts deprived the skilled workman of his chief market, on the other hand the English capitalist has enlisted in his service forces of nature against which the village artisans in vain try to compete. The tide of circumstances has compelled the Indian weaver to exchange his loom for the plough and has crushed away many of the minor handicrafts".[33]

Evolution of Modern Industry

Before 1850, there was neither any factory nor any Industry in India.[34] Since then, a small modern industrial sector has slowly emerged in the Indian economy out of sheer necessity arising from the First and Second World Wars. The establishment of British rule in India, the Industrial Revolution in England, the opening up of the railways and the development of towns all combined to change the shape of Indian industry. Along with the disappearance of all indigenous industries, attempts were made to start new forms of industry at that time.

Towards the end of the 18th century, European planters, mainly British, began manufacturing indigo in India. Their activity took two forms, namely, plantation system and factory system.

The plantation was the first to be introduced in India. It was from the very beginning owned, managed and controlled by the ex-employees of the East India Company and it was the beginning of European exploitation of Indian resources. Europeans were interested in indigo, tea and coffee plantation because they provided quick and high return on the investment.

The factory industry which took the place of handicrafts had its beginnings since the beginning of the 19th century. Real and satisfactory progress in the factory industries began only after 1875.

During the next two decades, cotton textiles and jute manufactures were in a fairly flourishing condition. But as M.G. Ranade pointed out: "It was, however, only after the late nineties that industrial progress all over the country began; and in the first decade of the twentieth century, many mineral industries and some small miscellaneous industries came into prominence. It was also during these later years that their spread in India, the use of small machines and small engines and that there was generally a tendency to make a greatly increased use of mechanical appliances everywhere".[35]

A number of factors were responsible for the development of modern industries in India until the outbreak of World War I. The destruction of capitalistic urban handicraft and village artisan's industry paved the way for the transformation of India into a single economic unit and the Indian people into a nation composed of classes existing on a national scale. It unified the entire people into a system of exchange relations. The problems confronting the new classes transcended a mere town or village and became really national in character.

Gradually a mercantile class emerged in India. Also, the growth of towns like Bombay and Ahmedabad, where for the time being the enterprising merchant class was concentrated contributing greatly to the development of cotton textile industry. Calcutta to the development of jute mills, and Kanpur to the development of leather goods and woollen industry.

The introduction of Indian language in 1835 in the Indian educational system resulted in the training of Indians in sciences and in the various technical branches of the knowledge which was essential for the development of modern industries and business organisations along modern lines that was being adopted in Western countries. Spread of English education gradually brought into existence professional classes of people in India who were required if a country was to have a modern industrial system.

Another factor that contributed to the development of industries in India was the abolition of the trading monopoly of the East India Company in India in 1833. It resulted in the inflow of British capital and industrial enterprises into India, leading to the development of a number of industries. Thus inflow of British capital and industrial enterprise into India laid the foundation of subsequent modern industrial development in the country.

The improvement of the oceanic and inland transport system encouraged the establishment of factories in the country by providing facilities for procuring machines and skill from foreign countries. Though railways were developed more with an idea of commercial penetration of the country, for the movement of foodgrains in periods of famine, and the consolidation of the British power in India, they affected favourably the development of modern industries.

The American Civil War (1860-65) gave a great impetus to the development of cotton textile industry in India; the Crimean

War gave an impetus to the development of jute industry; and the World War I (1914-18) to that of the iron and steel industry.

However, as S.C. Kuchhal has rightly pointed out : "the development of industries in India was not only slow but lop-sided in its character. The results of industries up to World War I were disappointing. With abundant supplies of raw materials; with a redundant population often starving because of lack of profitable employment, a hoard of gold and silver second perhaps to none in the world; and with access through the British Government to a money market which was providing large quantities of capital to the entire world; with an opening for British business leaders who were developing both at home and abroad all sorts of capitalistic industries; with an excellent market within her own border, India after a century was supporting only about 2 per cent of her population by factory industry".[36]

The World War I and Indian Industries

The World War I (1914-18) and the years immediately following that war (1919-20) experienced a sort of industrial boom in the country. It was also during the period of the World War I that, for the first time, the Indian Industrial Commission came to be appointed in 1916 to assess the possibilities of industrialisation of India and make suitable recommendations with that objective in view.

The war-time demand together with the Nationalist Movement provided a great fillip to the development of Indian trade and industry. The prices of manufactured goods as a whole, rose, while the rise in the price of raw materials was comparatively less and wages rose little, if at all, during the war period. Further, the difficulties of importing machinery strengthened the position of existing producers and manufacturers in all industries made phenomenal profits. The change in the State policy following the Montague Chelmsford Reforms helped the growth of the industry. A change in Government's tariff policy in 1923 and the development of the banking system did much to help the growth of Indian industry.

World War II (1939-45) and Indian Industries

Indian industry suffered serious dislocation due to the World War II and thereafter due to the partition of the country in 1947. The Second World War created conditions for the maximum utilisation of existing capacity in Indian industries. From 1942 onwards, India having become a base for the supply of men and materials to the Allies, there was a phenomenal increase in the demand for all types of goods, including essentials of life like cloth. This was the major factor responsible for the increase in industrial production. The Government's policy towards industry became more active and the Government not only encouraged private enterprise but also became interested in starting industries itself. However, conditions were not favourable for setting up of large scale equipment and plant for new industries. Several industries such as mechanical industries (bicycles, machine-tools, etc.), chemical industries (caustic soda, chlorine, etc.), non-ferrous metals (copper wires, copper cables, etc.) and ferro alloys (ferro-manganese, ferro-silicon, etc.) were started on a modest scale during this period, but the major impetus of the war was felt in the sector of medium and SSIs such as light engineering, pharmaceuticals, etc.

The impact of the Second World War on Indian industries was far too great compared to that of First World War. Thus, by 1945, the total number of companies had risen from 11,114 to 14,859 during 1939 to 1945, and the paid up capital of the companies from Rs. 290 crores to Rs. 389 crores during the same period.[37]

While the Second World War did give encouragement to a number of industries in India and did help bring about their development, the war also had some adverse impact on the industrial economy of India. It generated inflationary pressures in the Indian economy as the war came to be financed through deficits year after year. Many products like iron and steel, cotton textiles, sugar and cement, etc. were brought under statutory control, Government having practically commandered all the commodities.

The Second World War left the legacy of quick and enormous profits to the big industrialists due to the ever-rising prices, regime of controls with its inevitable off-spring of corruption and black market, rising profits and declining real wages of workers resulting in estranged relations between employers and workers, and a sense of uncertainty in the country regarding the future of Indian industries once peace returned. It created a number of problems in the industrial sector of India with which India had to graple even long after she became independent. The major emphasis in industrial development during the Second World War, had been on consumer goods industries.[38]

Post-World War II Crisis (1945-47)

In the immediate post-war years, several new units e.g. automobiles, ball and roller bearings, ring frames etc. were started and existing units expanded their activity. For the first time, engineering industries began to produce spare parts and semi-manufactured goods which were formerly imported. Industrial development during the war and the post war period was influenced largely by the prevailing inflationary conditions and scarcities, with the result that long-term factors such as the most advantageous location or scale of operation, the availability of raw materials, the size of the market and adequacy of financial and technical organisation for successful operation under competitive conditions did not receive the attention they deserved.

In April 1945, the Government announced an industrial policy. It was realised that if India was to make a rapid headway and if the standard of living of the masses was to be effectively raised, a vigorous and sustained effort was necessary in which the State, no less than private industry, must take a part. Government had decided to take positive steps to encourage and promote rapid industrialisation of the country to the fullest possible extent. They attached particular importance to the development of those industries which constituted the foundation of modern industrial life such as the iron and steel industry, the heavy engineering industries, the machine-tool industry, the chemical industry and so on. But while the development of these industries must take high priority, it must form part of a balanced plan in which due place should be given to consumption goods industries. It was clear that if progress was to be achieved, the development of industry must be planned by Government in co-operation with industry and every effort should be made to make the plan effective.

Post-Partition Period (1947 to 1951) and Recovery

During the immediate post-partition period, industrial production continued to be hampered by lack of confidence among industrialists because of various pronouncements of political leaders during the period of national struggle, and also partly due to non-availability or scarcity of machinery and equipment, shortages of raw materials (especially, cotton and raw jute), transport bottlenecks and industrial disputes and disturbed industrial relations as a result of the prevalence of inflationary conditions and the possible fear of unemployment due to stoppage of war demand for several types of goods and services. With a view to rehabilitate the disrupted Indian economy, several steps came to be taken affecting the Indian economy by the national leaders who commanded great respect among all sections of the Indian society.

In December 1947, the Tripartite Industries Conference was called to consider the problem of labour-capital relations at length. The Conference passed a resolution calling for a three-year industrial truce between capital and labour and for determination of fair wages and conditions of work as also fair returns to capital. The Government also took other measures to provide incentives to industry like (i) the grant of tax concessions to industry in the budget for 1948-49, (ii) the assurances given by the authorities of their intention not to reverse their cheap money policy, and (iii) the passage of a Bill to establish the IFC in 1948.[39]

Excepting steel and coal industries which registered a decline in production compared to the previous year, almost all other industries showed in 1948 a definite trend towards improvement over their previous year's production. This general trend towards improvement in industrial production in 1948 was due to several factors such as improved capital - labour relations, better utilisation of the existing installed productive capacity in textile industry; expansion of the existing units in cement industry, establishment of new units in some industries such as diesel engines, caustic soda, electric motors, batteries, electric fans and so on. Though there was this general trend in the direction of improved industrial production, in some industries like cement, cotton textiles and steel, production registered in 1948 was much below the installed capacity. This was mainly due to shortages of raw materials, spare parts for machines and so on.

Recovery in industrial production marked in 1948 continued during 1949. Most of the industries recorded higher production with the exception of cotton and jute. Progress in recovery was mainly due to a distinct improvement in transport and in labour relations. Improvement in rail transport enabled a removal of control of priorities. Labour-management relations were improving since the industrial truce of December 1947.

During 1950, the rising trend in industrial production was on the whole well-maintained and most of the industries recorded substantial increase in their output. However, cotton and jute textiles and sugar industries registered a decline. The rise in the output of cement, steel, electrical goods, and diesel engines was particularly substantial. Other industries like paper and paper board, chemicals, power alcohol, power transformers also showed increase in their output. Improvement in production was due to the installation of additional production units, expansion of existing units, harmonious labour relations, and an improvement in the transport system. From 1952 onwards, however with the return of the buyer's market all over the world and the disappearance of inflationary potential in the country, competition became acute and many medium and SSIs began to experience difficulties.

These were of various kinds, to the fact that many of these industrial undertakings, when exposed to market competition, were unable to function as economic units. This led to fall in production much below the installed capacity sometimes because of the poor quality of products or lack of demand. In some cases, the demand fell either absolutely or relatively as a result of a shift in consumer's demand or import policy. In others, industrial units suffered from various handicaps, which tended to raise their cost of production and thereby undermine their competitive position. Investigations showed that in some regions shortage of power was the main reason, while in others, there was transport and raw material difficulties. Most of them experienced difficulties regarding marketing and finance for purposes of working capital. This situation persisted till the end of the First Five Year Plan.[40]

CONCLUSION

The above analysis shows that there was neither any factory nor any industry in India before 1850. It was only after 1850, that a small modern industrial sector has slowly emerged in the Indian economy out of sheer necessity arising from the First and Second World Wars. Indian industry suffered serious dislocation due to the World War II and thereafter due to the partition of the country in 1947.

In the immediate post war years, several new units were started and the existing units expanded their activity. Industrial development was influenced largely by the prevailing inflationary conditions and scarcities, with the result that long-term factors such as the most advantageous location or scale of operation, the availability of raw materials, the size of the market and the adequacy of financial and technical organisation for successful operation under competitive conditions did not receive the attention they deserved.

It was in this background that the Statement of Industrial Policy (SIP) of 1945 was issued by the Planning and Development Department. The SIP of 1945 was the first comprehensive proposal for industrial development strategy issued by the Government. It brought a new, explicit approach towards economic policy. It called for Government control over twenty key industries.[41]

The SIP of 1945 was a declaration of the Government's determination to take positive steps toward rapid industrialisation. It stated that basic industries whose promotion were regarded as essential to the national interest would be nationalised if adequate private capital was not forthcoming. Apart from stressing the need for State control over heavy and basic industries, the SIP of 1945 called for controls over capital issue, controls over industrial enterprises through licensing, and controls over regional industrial concentration. It also proposed the setting up of a system of targets to determine the volume of capital flowing into excessive profits.

Thus, it was clear that if progress was to be achieved, the development of industry must be planned by Government in co-operation with industry and every effort should be made to make the plan effective. However, with the return of the buyer's market all over the world and the disappearance of inflationary potential in the country, competition became acute and many medium and SSIs began to experience difficulties.

This situation created a proper environment in which some industrial reform could be brought by the Government. Accordingly, the Government of India elaborated the objectives and the approach embodied in the SIP of 1945 and issued the Industrial Policy Resolutions of 1948 and 1956, which has been discussed in greater details in the next chapter.

Endnotes

1. Ghosh, Biswanath, *The Changing Profile of India's Industrial Economy*, The World Press Private Limited, Calcutta, 1974, p.30.
2. *Ibid.*
3. As quoted by Ghosh, Alak, *Indian Economy, Its Nature and Problems*, 20th Edition, The World Press Private Limited, Calcutta, 1976, p.301.
4. Padhy, K.S., and Behara, A.K., *Industrial Policy of India*, Discovery Publishing House, Delhi, 1988, pp.52-53.
5. Ghosh, Biswanath, *op.cit.*, pp.31-32.
6. Padhy and Behara, *op.cit.*, p.53.
7. Mukherji, A.K., *Economics of Indian Industry*, S. Chand and Company Ltd., New Delhi, 1985, p.185.
8. Maheshwari, R.P., and Gupta, A.N., *Business, Government and Society: A Study of Business Environment*, Vikas Publishing House, New Delhi, 1985, p.39.
9. Sutcliffe, R.B., *Industry and Underdevelopment*, Addison-Wesley, London, 1971, p.284.
10. Mukherji, A.K., *op.cit.*, p.234.
11. *Ibid.*
12. *Ibid.*, p.242.
13. Maheshwari and Gupta, *op.cit.*, pp.40-41.

14. Desai, S.S.M., *Industrial Economy of India*, Himalaya Publishing House, Bombay, 1988, p.352.
15. *Ibid.*, p.353.
16. *Ibid.*, p.426.
17. *Ibid.*, pp.434-435.
18. Mukherji, A.K., *op.cit.*, p.275.
19. *Ibid.*, p.280.
20. *Ibid.*, p.281.
21. United Nations, *World Economic Survey*, Department of International Economic and Social Affairs, New York, 1965, p.55.
22. Hanson, A.H.(ed.), *Nationalisation: A Book of Readings*, George Allen and Unwin Ltd., London, 1963, p.22.
23. Pareek, H.S., *Financing of Small Scale Industries in a Developing Economy*, National Publishing House, New Delhi, 1978, p.104.
24. *The Economic Times*, October 30, 1969, p.3.
25. Pareek, H.S., *op.cit.*, p.104.
26. *Ibid.*
27. *Ibid.*
28. Staley, Eugene and Morse, Richard, *Modern Small Industry for Developing Countries*, McGraw Hill Book Company, New York, 1965, p.373.
29. Government of India, *Report of the Indian Industrial Commission*, 1916-18, p.6.
30. Desai, S.S.M., *op.cit.*, p.39.
31. *Ibid.*
32. Sharma, Tulsi Ram, and Chauhan, S.D., *Indian Industries (Development, Management, Finance and Organisation)* 2nd Ed., Shiva Lal Agarwala & Co. (P) Ltd., Agra, 1965, p.6.
33. Ghosh, Biswanath, *op.cit.*, pp.18-19.
34. Ghosh, Alak, *op.cit.*, pp.7-8.
35. Desai, S.S.M., *op.cit.*, p.42.
36. Kuchhal, S.C., *The Industrial Economy of India*, VIIIth Ed., Chaitanya Publishing House, Allahabad, 1970, pp.36-37.
37. Desai, S.S.M., *op.cit.*, p.46.
38. Gupta, N.S., and Singh, Amarjit, *Industrial Economy of India*, Light and Life Publications, New Delhi, 1978, pp.113-14.
39. Kuchhal, S.C., *op.cit.*, p.46.
40. Society fór Social and Economic Studies, *Capital for Medium and Small Industries*, Asia Publishing House, Bombay, 1959, p.16.
41. Inove, Kyoko, *Industrial Development Policy of India*, Institute of Developing Economies, Tokyo, 1992, p.5.

3

Industrial Policy of the Government of India : Retrospect and Prospect

In the preceding chapter we have discussed in detail the role of the State in industrial development in the Indian context. We have also discussed the Industrial Policy of the Government during the colonial rule. As such in the present chapter, an attempt has been made to discuss the Industrial Policy pursued by the Government since Independence. Apart from this we have also discussed the progress of SSIs through the successive plans.

Industry is the keynote of economic development of a country. No country can progress and prosper without its industrial development and no abound and balanced industrial growth is possible without an industrial policy. Consequently all industrially advanced countries have a national industrial policy of their own. It determines a reasonable relationship between the State and the private enterprise, between industry and industry and between regions and regions.[1]

Industrial policy is a comprehensive concept. It covers all those principles, policies, procedures, rules and regulations which control the industrial undertakings; and provides necessary direction and pattern to the industrial development of a country. Industrial policy in its broader sense includes matters concerning industrial labour, industrial legislation, industrial finance, industrial organisation and management and so on which have a direct bearing on large-scale, medium-scale and SSIs in the country and their future development. The policy underlines national priorities and the means and ways to achieve the same. It lays down the Government policies towards foreign capital and knowhow, labour, tariff, etc., which have a significant role to play in the industrial sector. In a nutshell, Industrial policy of a country is a major and, perhaps, the most significant aspect of the overall economic policy.

Industrial Policy in India

During the pre-Independence days, India hardly had its own Industrial policy in the above sense. It was only after the country became independent and sovereign in 1947 that we notice a systematic evolution of comprehensive Industrial policy for the country as a whole.

After Independence, the Directive Principles of State Policy enunciated in the Constitution of India and the adoption of a socialist pattern of society by the Parliament, have provided the general guidelines for social and economic policies. Several Industrial Policy Resolutions/Statements have been pronounced by the Government since then. The Industrial policy in India is expected to help achieve certain specific objectives.

The basic objectives of the Industrial policy that got evolved since 1947 to the present day may be said to be as follows:[2]

(i) To bring about rapid economic development of the country by accelerating the growth of industries and industrialisation of the country;

(ii) To provide increasing opportunities for gainful employment and skill formation of various types required for modernising society;

(iii) To help establish the goal of socialist pattern of society as accepted by the Indian Parliament;

(iv) To bring about the expansion of the public sector as a dominant sector of Indian economy;

(v) To prevent undue concentration of economic power and emergence and functioning of industrial monopolies in the private sector;

(vi) To bring about reduction in regional disparities especially, by establishing public sector industries in economically backward regions of the country and also promoting industries in backward regions of the country;

vii) To bring about development of basic and heavy industries with a view to reduce dependence of the country on foreign countries in the case of essential and vital goods and services such as defence production and various metals, heavy chemicals, heavy and light engineering goods, etc., and to make the country self-reliant in all such matters;

(viii) To give encouragement to small-scale, cottage and village or rural industries and handicrafts as also to co-operative industrial sector of the Indian economy;

(ix) To take steps to promote exports of industrial goods so that India can have its due share in world export trade; and

(x) To bring about the development of modern industrial culture by establishing scientific, technical and professional institutions of education as all such skills are essential and basic to modem type industrialisation.

Industrial Policy Resolution (IPR), 1948

The first Industrial Policy Resolution in independent India was enunciated in 1948 in which the State took the major responsibility in the development of industries. It contemplated a mixed economy for the country in which both the public sector and private sector would play an important and effective role in the industrial sphere. It emphasised the importance to the economy of securing a continuous increase in production and its equitable distribution, and pointed out that the State must play a progressively active role in the development of industries. It laid down that besides arms and ammunition, atomic energy and railway transport, which would be the monopoly of the Central Government, the State would be exclusively responsible for the establishment of new undertaking in six basic industries except where, in the national interest, the State itself found it necessary to secure the co-operation of private enterprise. The rest of the industrial field was left open to private enterprises though it was made clear that the State would also progressively participate in this field. The chief objects of this policy were:[3] (i) the establishment of a social order wherein justice and equality of opportunity shall be secured to all the people; (ii) the provision of educational facilities and health services on a much wider scale and the promotion of a rapid rise in the standard of living of people by exploiting the latent resources of the country; (iii) the increase in production both agricultural and industrial; (iv) the offering of opportunities to all for employment in the service of the community; (v) the need for careful planning and integration of effort and the necessity for the establishment of a National Planning Commission; (vi) the determination of the extent of State responsibility and the limits of private enterprise; and (vii) the regulation of the private enterprise.

The IPR of 1948 categorised industries into four groups:[4]

The first group included such strategic industries as the manufacture of arms and ammunition, the production and control of atomic energy and the ownership and management of railway transport. Further, the Government reserved for itself the power to take over, in an emergency, any industry vital for national defence.

The second category included such basic and key industries as (i) coal, (ii) iron and steel, (iii) ship building, (iv) aircraft manufacture, (v) manufacture of telephone, telegraph and wireless apparatus, and (vi) mineral oils. For these industries it was laid down that the State would be exclusively responsible for the establishment of new undertakings while existing units would be allowed to operate for a period of ten years at the end of which the position was to be reviewed. Since the responsibility of inviting new concerns was assumed by the State, private enterprise lost interest in this category of industries.

In the third category there were 18 basic industries, such as automobiles and tractors, salt, prime movers, electrical engineering, heavy machinery, machine tools, heavy chemicals and pharmaceuticals (including fertilizers), rubber manufacturers, cotton and woollen textiles, cement, sugar, paper and newsprint, air and sea transport, minerals and industries related to defence. These industries would be ordinarily operated by private enterprise but would be subject to central regulation and control, since their locations must be governed by economic factors of all India importance or they require considerable investment and a high degree of technical skill.

The rest of industries would be in the fourth category. These industries would be normally opened to private enterprise, individual as well as co-operative. But even here the State would also participate progressively in this field and would not hesitate to intervene whenever the progress of an industry under private enterprise was unsatisfactory.

The **IPR** of 1948 assigned a significant role to the cottage and SSIs because they offer a great scope to vast masses of people, especially in rural and semi-urban areas and to co-operatives; they help rehabilitate displaced people, and they help bring about decentralisation of industries and of economic power. It emphasised the need for their healthy expansion by making suitable provision of raw material, cheap power, technical advice, organised marketing of their produce, and where necessary, safeguarding against excessive competition by large-scale manufacturers. A cottage and SSIs Directorate was proposed to be set up within the Directorate General of Industries and Supplies.

Appraisal of the IPR, 1948

The Resolution tried to give a definite direction to the process of industrialisation in India. It laid the foundation of a mixed economy. It gave cottage and SSIs their due place and importance in the economy of the country and also as a means of decentralisation of industrial structure and power. Labour was made an important partner in the process of industrialisation of the country. It emphasised the importance of foreign capital and enterprise and gave them due place in the process of industrialisation. It aimed at greater production and the proper utilisation of wealth so produced in order to establish a society wherein justice and equality of opportunity would prevail.

The Industries Development and Regulation Act (IDR), 1951

This Act was passed with the objective of enabling the Government to carry out its industrial policy and to regulate private enterprise in line with the IPR of 1948. The important provisions of the Act were:[5] (i) all the existing industrial undertakings in the scheduled industries have to be registered; (ii) no new industrial unit can be established or substantial extension to existing units made without a licence from the Central Government; (iii) the Government can order an investigation in respect of any scheduled industry or undertaking if there has been a fall in production or a marked deterioration in quality or an unjustified increase in price; and (iv) in the event of an industry or unit not carrying out the directions issued after such an investigation, the Government can take over its management. By 1953, this Act was amended for detailed specification of the groups or greater elaboration in separate heads of the industries in the schedule.[6]

Industrial Policy Resolution, 1956

A second IPR was adopted by Parliament on April 30, 1956. The need for a fresh statement of industrial policy was necessitated by a number of significant developments which took place since the adoption of the Resolution of 1948.

It was considered appropriate by the Government to frame the new policy keeping in view the principles laid down in the Constitution, the objective of socialism, and the experience gained during the past eight years. As a result, the Indian Parliament adopted the IPR of 1956.

The industries were classified into three categories, having regard to the role which the State would play in each of them. These three categories resembled to a great extent the classification of industries in the IPR of 1948. But the IPR of 1956 defined the three categories more sharply. Keeping in view the basic principles and objectives the door was kept open for the State to undertake any type of industrial production.

The first category shown in Schedule A [7] consists of industries the future development of which will be the exclusive responsibility of the State. All new units in these industries would be set up only by the State. It was made clear that whenever operation with private enterprise was necessary, the State would ensure, either through majority participation in the capital or otherwise, that it had the requisite powers to guide the policy and control the operations of the undertaking.

The second category comprised of those industries which were listed in Schedule B.[8] With a view to accelerating their future development, the State was to establish new undertakings in these industries. At the same time, the private enterprise will be allowed to develop in this field, either on its own or with State participation.

The third category included all the remaining industries, and it was expected that their development will be undertaken ordinarily through the initiative and enterprise of the private sector, though it will be open to the State to start any industry even in this category. Thus, no field was safe from Government encroachment. It would be the policy of the State to facilitate and encourage the development of these industries in the private sector, in accordance with the programmes formulated in successive Five Year Plans, by ensuring the development of transport, power and other services, and by appropriate fiscal and other measures. In special cases, the State might grant financial assistance to the private sector.

The Resolution stressed the role of cottage and village and SSIs in the development of the national economy. The distinct advantages which such industries offered were explicitly recognised by the Resolution in these words:

"They provide immediate large-scale employment; they offer a method of ensuring a more equitable distribution of the national income and they facilitate effective mobilisation of resources of capital and skill which might otherwise remain unutilised. Some of the problems that unplanned urbanisation tends to create will be avoided by the establishment of small centres of industrial production all over the country".[9]

The State followed a policy of supporting these industries by restricting the volume of production in the large scale sector by differential taxation or by direct subsidies. It further envisaged that the State policy should be to ensure that the decentralised sector acquires sufficient vitality to be self-supporting and its development is integrated with that of the large-scale industry. As such the State sought to concentrate on measures designed to improve the competitive strength of the small-scale producer. It was decided to improve and modernise the technique of production and to remove their handicaps of technical and financial assistance, of suitable working accommodation and of repair and maintenance facilities. To remove these deficiencies, a beginning was made with the establishment of industrial estates and rural community workshops. The extension of rural electrification, and the availability of power at prices which the workers can afford would also be of considerable help. The organisation of industrial co-operatives in this sphere was appreciated and the Government was envisaged to give constant attention to the development of these industries.

The Resolution recognised that with the growing participation of the State in industry and trade, the manner in which these activities should be conducted and managed has assumed considerable importance. Speedy decisions and a willingness to assume responsibility are essential if these enterprises are to succeed. For this, wherever possible, there should be decentralisation of authority and their management should be along business lines. The Resolution expected that the public enterprise would augment the revenues of the State and provide resources for further development in new fields. Sometimes such enterprises may incur losses. Public enterprises should be judged by their total results and in their working they should have the largest possible measure of freedom.

Appraisal of the IPR, 1956

The Resolution recognised that industrial progress had not been satisfactory; and aimed at speeding the pace by being less ambiguous about the particular roles of public and private sectors. It gave primacy to the role of the State to assume a predominant and direct responsibility for industrial development and emphasised the right of the State to acquire any industrial establishment. As a result, doubts were expressed about the ability of the private sector to bring about by its own efforts alone, accelerated industrial development of the country.

The Resolution greatly reduced the scope for private industry. Flexibility was envisaged but it was to operate primarily in favour of the public sector because the State was free to enter into any industry or trade it chose. The private enterprise was expected to play only a supplementary role in industries listed in 'Schedule B', and even in the category of industries where the development would be undertaken ordinarily through the initiative and enterprise of the private sector, it would be open to the State to start any industry. Hence no field was safe from Government encroachment. In a sense the private sector was relegated into the background. As Venkatasubbiah pointed out, "The so-called private sector became a sort of residuary legatee. Economic development was more explicitly equated with State enterprise".[10]

The Resolution not only expanded the list of subjects reserved for State venture, but also enlarged the powers and role of the Government in the industrial sphere. This policy statement was a beginning which would ultimately lead to the extinction of entrepreneurial activities in the country. There is no doubt that the IPR of 1956 has had a great and long-lasting impact and influence, both favourable and unfavourable, on India's industrial expansion and its structure.

Industrial Policy During 1975-1977

After the proclamation of emergency in June 1975, the Government of India contemplated several measures in favour of the private sector and to relax restrictions on big business and foreign enterprises. In order to promote industrial growth, it was considered necessary to free a growing number of industries from industrial licensing. In October 1975, 21 industries were delicensed and in 30 other industries larger industrial houses and foreign concerns were permitted unlimited expansion provided the additional production was either exported or sold in accordance with Government directions.[11]

The official definition of SSI has changed from time to time. Accordingly in 1975 also, the definition of small-scale enterprises was changed to include all industrial units with an investment in plant and machinery of not more than Rs. 10 lakhs. The entire policy toward village and SSIs was conditioned by the political ideology or slogan at the time, viz., "removal of poverty". Village and SSIs were made to serve the purpose, mainly because of the comparatively decentralized character of the sector. The Government's commitment to the removal of poverty placed the direct responsibility to provide job opportunities, raising income levels, and developing backward areas on the village and SSIs, and the facilities were arranged for the purpose.

Industrial Policy Statement, 1977

Janata Government, after assuming power at the Centre, presented to the Parliament a Statement on Industrial Policy on December 23, 1977. In his Industrial policy statement the Minister for Industries strongly criticised the previous industrial policies followed by the Congress Governments. He strongly denounced the poor performance of the previous Governments. A major point of criticism against the 1956 Resolution was that it meant all things to all men and that it was too flexible and under it anything that the Government wanted to do could be done. The Janata Government also pointed out that the operation of the IPR of 1956 had paid only lip service to the development of SSIs, while concentrating only on the development of large-scale industries.

The new Industrial policy was sought to be directed towards removing the distortions of the past, so that the genuine aspirations of the people could be met by promoting cottage and SSIs within a time-bound programme of economic development. It was, however, admitted that some of the elements of the 1956 Resolution still remained valid, particularly in regard to the desirable pattern of industrial development.

The main thrust of the new Industrial policy had been on effective promotion of cottage and SSIs widely dispersed in rural areas and small towns. The policy statement observed: "The emphasis of Industrial policy so far has been mainly on large industries, neglecting cottage industries completely and relegating SSIs to a minor role".[12] The policy of the Government would be that whatever can be produced by small and cottage industries must only be so produced. For this purpose an exhaustive analysis of industrial products was made to identify those items which are capable of being established or expanded in the SSS. The list of industries which would be exclusively reserved for the SSS was significantly expanded and included more than 500 items as compared to about 180 items earlier.[13] The policy emphasised that the list of industries reserved, for the SSS should be continually reviewed so that capacity creation does not lag behind the requirements of the economy. Apart from this, an annual review of reserved industries was to be undertaken in order to ensure that reservation accorded to the small scale is efficient and is also continually expanded as new products and new processes capable of being manufactured in the small scale are identified.

Since there was no special protection for cottage and household industries sector, Government considered introducing special legislation for protecting the interest of cottage and household industries with a view to ensuring that these activities which provide self-employment in large numbers get due recognition in our industrial development.

It emphasised that the focal point of development for small scale and cottage industries will be taken away from big cities and State capitals to the district headquarters. In other words, in each district there will be one agency i.e. District Industries Centre (DIC), to deal with all requirements of small and village industries. DIC was to provide under one roof all the services and support required by small and village entrepreneurs.

In order to provide effective financial support for promotion of small, village and cottage industries, a specially created special wing of the Industrial Development Bank of India (IDBI) was to look after the credit needs of small and cottage industries and co-ordinate, guide and monitor the entire range of credit facilities offered by other institutions to these industries. It was also expected that banks will earmark a specified proportion of their total advances for promotion of small, village and cottage industries. Government's policy was to see that no worthwhile scheme of small or village industry was given up for want of credit. The marketing of goods of these sectors with its concomitant of product standardisation, quality control, marketing surveys needed special attention. As such, the Government was to provide the maximum support for these activities on a priority basis. To support the marketing of these products measures such as purchase preference and reservation for exclusive purchase by Government Departments and Public Sector Undertakings was to be used.

Since the development and application of technology appropriate to our socio-economic conditions had not received adequate attention so far, it became an integral part of the policy and Government was to ensure that this important area got adequate attention and special arrangements was to be made to ensure an effective and co-ordinated approach for the development and widespread application of suitable small and simple machines and devices for improving the productivity and earning capacity of workers in small and village industries.

The policy statement also defined a clear role for large scale industries in India. However, the Government was not to favour large scale industries merely for demonstration of sophisticated skills or as monuments of irrelevant foreign technology. The role of the large scale industries was to be related to the programme for meeting the basic minimum needs of the population through wider dispersal of small scale and village industries and strengthening of the agricultural sector. In general, areas for large scale industries was to be: (a) basic industries which are essential for providing infrastructure as well as for development of small and village industries, such as steel, non-ferrous metals, cement, oil refineries; (b) capital goods industries for meeting the machinery requirement of basic industries as well as SSIs; (c) high technology industries which require large scale production, and which are related to agricultural and small scale industrial development such as fertilizers, pesticides, and petro-chemicals etc.; and (d) other industries which are outside the list of reserved items for the SSS, and which are considered essential for the development of the economy such as machine tools, organic and inorganic chemicals.[14]

Funds of the public sector financial institutions were to be made available mainly to SSIs sector. Previously, this fund was utilised by large industrial houses. It was stated that encouragement would be given to the public sector industries to develop a wide range of ancillary industries, and contribute to the growth of decentralised production by making available its expertise in technology and management to small scale and cottage industry sectors. It would also be the endeavour of the Government to operate public sector enterprises on profitable and efficient lines in order to ensure that investment in these industries pays an adequate return to society.

Appraisal of the Policy Statement, 1977

The main thrust of the policy statement was the emphasis on the establishment of small-scale and cottage industries. The DICs were set up to provide all kinds of support needed by the SSIs. If the objectives of the new Industrial policy of accelerating the pace of industrial growth, rapid increase in levels of employment, productivity and income of industrial workers and a wide dispersal of small and village industries have to be achieved, the willing co-operation of industrial worker, trade unions, managers, entrepreneurs, financial institutions and various Governmental authorities responsible for implementing schemes of assistance will be essential.

The statement of 1977 gave greater importance to reservations for small-scale and village industries rather than demarcating the spheres of public and private sectors, limiting the production capacity of large-scale industries. But all these measures for encouragement of SSIs sector were already suggested by the IPR, 1956. The only radical thing which the policy of 1977 did was to expand the number of exclusively reserved articles for SSIs.

On the whole, it can be said that the policy statement had a new look and was satisfactory. However, due to the fall of the Janata Government after a very short tenure, no significant achievement is on record, as far as the implementation of the policy is concerned.

Industrial Policy Statement, 1980

The Industrial policy announced in 1980 by the new Government of Mrs. Indira Gandhi fully supported the 1956 policy in all its essentials. It renewed its emphasis on public sector to make it "the pillars of the country's economic infrastructure", while not forgetting to accept the private sector as an important component of national economy which should develop in consonance with targets and objectives of national plans and policies.[15]

The major socio-economic objectives of the new Industrial policy were–(i) optimum utilisation of the installed capacity; (ii) maximising production and achieving higher productivity; (iii) higher employment generation; (iv) faster promotion of export-oriented and import substitution industries: (v) promoting: economic federalism with an equitable spread of investment and the dispersal of returns amongst widely spread over small but growing units in rural as well as urban areas; and (vi) consumer protection against high prices and bad quality.[16]

The policy statement is a significant milestone in the policy of SSIs which emphasised *inter-alia* strengthening of the encouragement for credit facilities, creating buffer stock of critical raw materials, easy flow of technology above all harmonising the growth of SSIs with large and medium scale sector.

In order to boost the development of SSIs and to ensure their rapid growth, the Government decided to increase the limit of investment–(i) in the case of tiny units, from rupees one lakh to rupees two lakhs ; (ii) in the cast of small-scale units, from rupees ten lakhs to rupees twenty lakhs; and (iii) in the case of ancillaries, from rupees fifteen lakhs to rupees twenty-five lakhs.[17] The Government also extended the area of reservation to 834 industries for the SSS keeping in view its performance and potentialities.[18]

To sort out the financial difficulties experienced particularly by industrial entrepreneurs in small, cottage and rural sectors, Government would evolve a system of co-ordination to ensure the flow of credit to the growing units in the decentralised sector at the right time and on appropriate terms. The Government proposed to strengthen the existing arrangements of providing finance, both short-term and long-term, by making such changes as may be necessary to facilitate the availability of credit to the growing units in the SSS.

In order to assist the growth of SSIs it proposed to introduce a scheme for building up of buffer stocks of essential materials which are often difficult to obtain. For this the existing set-up such as Small Industries Development Corporations in the Centre will also be utilised Priority will be given to the special needs of States which rely heavily on a few essential raw materials. It proposed to continue the policies regarding marketing support to the decentralised sectors and reservation of items for SSIs, in the interest of growth of the SSIs.

The policy statement proposed to promote small-scale industrial units in rural areas to make rural communities economically viable, to generate higher employment and higher per capita income for the villagers in the country without disturbing the ecological balance. Handlooms. handicrafts, khadi and other village industries were to receive greater attention to achieve a faster rate of growth in the villages.

The proposed nucleus plants in industrially backward districts would generate a spread out network of small-scale, units, or the existing network of small-scale units in an area would acquire a faster growth by the coming up of a nucleus plant in the area. Such a two way traffic would create an ancillarisation effect in terms of larger employment and more equitable distribution of the benefits of industrialisation in the shape of higher per capita income.

One of the important features of the Industrial policy statement of 1980 was the introduction of the concept of economic federalism which helps give shape to the integrated industrial development. The main purpose in adopting this was to set up some nucleus plants in each district identified as industrially backward, to generate as many ancillaries and small and cottage industries as possible. These nucleus plants would concentrate on assembling the products of the ancillary units falling within its orbit on producing the inputs needed by a large number of smaller units and making adequate marketing arrangements. These nucleus plants will also ensure a widely spread pattern of investment and employment and will distribute the benefits of industrialisation to the maximum possible and would also work for upgrading the technology of small units. Thus, economic federalism can be realised in the dispersal of industries throughout the length and breadth of the country.

The policy statement emphasised that the Indian industry

must earmark substantial resources for Research and Development (R&D) to constantly up-date technologies with a view to optimal utilisation of scarce resources, better service to consumers and achieving greater exports. Greater emphasis was to be laid on bringing the benefits of the latest R&D to the medium and small units. Further it was emphasised that Government will take active measures to facilitate the transfer of technology from efficiently operating units to new units. Companies which have well established R&D organisation, and have demonstrated their ability to absorb, adapt and disseminate modern technology will be permitted to import such technology as will increase their efficiency and cost effectiveness. This would not only lead to saving of foreign exchange but would also ensure self-sufficiency and higher exchange earnings.

The policy statement proposed to evolve modernisation packages that would suit the requirements of each industry. The Government endeavoured to ensure that the process of modernisation percolates down to small units and the villages. With this end in view, the Government was to review the present arrangements in terms of special facilities and incentives such as soft loans, establishing of power linkages in the field of marketing and strengthening the credit facilities particularly for the decentralised sector.

Appraisal of Industrial Policy Statement, 1980

The Policy statement recognised the various deficiencies of public sector industrial enterprises in the country and recommended various corrective measures to improve their efficiency and thus help restore faith of the public in India's public sector industrial establishments. It recommended several measures to make public sector industrial units play effectively their assigned role and thus help accelerate rapid indus-trialisation of the country.

Some of the positive features of the policy statement were– it enhanced the investment limits in the tiny, small-scale and ancillary units; it emphasised the distribution of the fruits of industrialisation in such a way that largest possible segment of the country's population is benefitted and economic concentration in a few hands is avoided; it assured a close examination of public sector undertakings on a unit-by-unit-basis to facilitate corrective steps; it proposed to recognise and endorse additional capacities in specific cases; it promised evolution of modernisation packages to suit the requirements of each industry; it proposed to introduce checklist to serve as an early warning system for identifying symptoms of industrial sickness; it assured appropriate steps in regard to transfer of technology, promotion of R&D; it streamlined licensing procedures; and so on.

Thus, the policy statement pointed an optimistic picture. However, keeping in view the complacency in the implementation of policies in the past, it was not certain as to how far the provisions of the statement will be given effect to.

Industrial Policy, 1990

The Industrial policy, 1990 was announced by the Minister for Industries, Shri Ajit Singh in the Parliament on 31st May, 1990. The investment ceiling in plant and machinery for SSIs (fixed in 1985) was to be raised from the present rupees 35 lakhs to rupees 60 lakhs and correspondingly, for ancillary units from rupees 45 lakhs to rupees 75 lakhs. In order to enable SSIs to play an important role in the total export effort, such of the small scale units which undertake to export at least 30 per cent of the annual production by the third year was to be permitted to step up their investment in plant and machinery to rupees 75 lakhs.[19]

As many as 836 items were reserved for exclusive manufacture in the SSS.[20] Efforts were to be made to identify more items amenable to similar reservations. It proposed to effectively deal with encroachment and violation by large scale units into areas reserved for SSS.

It proposed to implement a new scheme of central investment subsidy exclusively for the SSS in rural and backward areas capable of generating higher level of employment at lower capital cost. With a view to improving the competitiveness of the products manufactured in the SSS, programmes for modernisation and upgradation of technology would be implemented. A number of technology centres, tool rooms, process and product development centres, testing centres, etc. were to be set up under the umbrella of an apex Technology Development Centre in Small Industries Development Organisation (SIDO).

A new apex Bank known as SIDBI has already been established to ensure adequate and timely flow of credit for the SSIs. One of the major tasks of SIDBI and other commercial banks/financial institutions would be to channelise need-based, higher flow of credit, both by way of term loan and working capital, to the tiny and rural industries.

It proposed to review the existing regime of fiscal concessions both to provide sustained support to the units in the SSS and to remove the disincentives for their graduation and further growth. It also proposed to undertake an exercise to identify locations in rural areas endowed with adequate power supply and intensive campaigns were to be launched to attract suitable entrepreneurs, provide all other inputs and foster small scale and tiny industries. Similarly, industries which were not energy-intensive were to be identified for proliferation in rural areas where power supply is presently a constraint.

The Government proposed to lay particular emphasis on training of women and youth under the Entrepreneurial Development Programme in order to widen the entrepreneurial base. To assist women entrepreneurs, a special cell was proposed to be established in SIDO and State Directorates of Industries.

On the whole, it can be said that the Industrial policy, 1990 had a new look so far as SSIs was concerned. It proposed to raise the investment ceiling of the SSIs and made various provisions for the promotion of the SSIs. However, due to the fall of the National Front Government led by Shri V.P. Singh after a very short tenure, no significant achievement is on record, so far as the implementation of the policy is concerned.

New Industrial Policy, 1991

The Industrial policy statement of 1991 was designed to achieve the following objectives:[21] (i) to build on the gains already made in the industrial sector; (ii) to correct the distortions or weaknesses in the pattern of industrial growth; (iii) to maintain a sustained growth in productivity and gainful employment; and (iv) to attend technological dynamism and international competitiveness.

The primary objective of the SSIs policy proposed to impart more vitality and growth impetus to the sector to enable it to contribute its mite fully to the economy, particularly in terms of growth of output, employment and exports. The sector was substantially delicensed. Further efforts were to be made to deregulate and de-bureaucratise the sector with a view to remove all hurdles on its growth potential, reposing greater faith in small and young entrepreneurs. It proposed to review and modify, wherever necessary, all statutes, regulations and procedures, to ensure that their operations do not militate against the interests of the small and village enterprises.

So far as the investment limits in plant and machinery of SSIs, ancillary units and export-oriented units was concerned, Government had already announced increase in these limits to rupees 60 lakhs, 75 lakhs and 75 lakhs respectively. Similarly, in respect of tiny enterprises, such limits was to be increased from the rupees 2 lakhs to rupees 5 lakhs, irrespective of location of the units.

The main thrust of Government's new policy was that a separate package for the promotion of tiny enterprises was being introduced. While the SSS (other than tiny enterprises) would be mainly entitled to one-time benefits (like preference in land allocation/power connection, access to facilities for skill/ technology upgradation), the tiny enterprises would also be eligible for additional support on a continuing basis, including easier access to institutional finance, priority in the Government Purchase Programme and relaxation from certain provisions of labour laws.

It was decided to widen the scope of the National Equity Fund Scheme to cover projects upto rupees 10 lakhs for equity support (upto 15 per cent). Single Window Loan Scheme was also enlarged to cover projects upto rupees 20 lakhs with working capital margin upto rupees 10 lakhs. Composite loans under SWS, available through State Financial Corporations (SFCs) and twin function SSIDCs, was also to be channelised through commercial banks. This would facilitate access to a larger number of entrepreneurs.

Financial Support Measures

So far as financial support measure was concerned, it proposed that emphasis would henceforth shift from subsidised/ cheap credit, except for specified target groups, and would be made to ensure both adequate flow of credit on a normative basis, and the quality of its delivery, for viable operations of this sector. It also proposed to set up a special monitoring agency to oversee that the genuine credit needs of the SSS are fully met.

To provide access to the capital market and to encourage modernisation and technological upgradation, it was decided to allow equity participation by other industrial undertakings in the SSI, not exceeding 24 per cent of the total shareholding. This would also provide a powerful boost to ancillarisation and sub-contracting, leading to expansion of employment opportunities. Regulatory provisions relating to the management of private limited companies were being liberalised. It proposed to introduce a limited partnership Act to enhance the supply of risk capital to the SSS. Such an Act would limit the financial liability of the new and non-active partners/entrepreneurs to the capital invested.

To solve the problem of delayed payments to small industries, factoring services were set up through SIDBI. Network of such services were to be set up throughout the country and operated through commercial banks. To ensure prompt payment of Small Industries Bill, a suitable legislation was to be introduced.

Infrastructural Facilities

A new scheme of Integrated Infrastructural Development (including Technological Back-up Services) for SSIs was to be implemented with the active participation of State Governments and financial institutions, to facilitate location of industries in rural/backward areas and to promote stronger linkages between agriculture and industry. To provide technology inputs to improve productivity and competitiveness of the products of the SSS, a Technology Development Cell (TDC) was to be set up in the SIDO. The TDC was to co-ordinate the activities of the Tool Rooms, Process-cum-Product Development Centres, existing as well as to be established under SIDO, and would also interact with the other industrial research and development organisations to achieve its objectives.

It proposed to ensure adequacy and equitable distribution of indigenous and imported raw materials to the SSS, particularly the tiny sub-sector. It proposed to design the policies in such a manner that they do not militate against entry of new units. Tiny/Small Scale units were to be given priority in allocation of indigenous raw materials on the basis of the capacity needs. A proper and adequate arrangement for delivery of total package of incentives and services at the District level will be evolved and implemented.

Marketing and Exports

In spite of the vast domestic market, marketing remains a problem area for small and tiny enterprises. In order to solve this problem, it proposed to provide tiny/SSS such markets where the products are marketed by the organised sector. In addition to the existing support mechanism, it proposed to undertake market promotion through co-operative/public sector institutions, other specialised/professional marketing agencies and consortia approach, backed up by such incentives, as considered necessary. NSIC would concentrate on marketing of mass consumption items under common brand name and organic links between NSIC and SSIDCs would be established.

Government recognised the need to widen and deepen complementarity in production programmes of large/medium and small industrial sectors. Parts, components sub-assemblies, etc. required by large public/private sector undertakings would be encouraged for production in a techno-economically viable manner through small scale ancillary units. Industry associations would be encouraged to establish sub-contracting exchanges, in addition to strengthening the existing ones under the SIDO. Emphasis would also be laid on promotion of a viable and competitive 'component' market. The SIDO was recognised as the nodal agency to support the SSIs in export promotion. Apart from this, an Export Development Centre was to be set up in SIDO to serve the SSIs through its network of field office to further augment export activities of the sector.

Modernisation, Technological and Quality Upgradation

A greater degree of awareness to produce goods and services conforming to national and international standards would be created among the SSS. It proposed to encourage and support industry associations to establish quality counselling and common testing facilities. Technology Information Centres to provide updated knowledge on technology and markets would be established.

It proposed to pursue a re-oriented programme of modernisation and technological upgradation aimed at improving productivity, efficiency and cost effectiveness in the SSS. Specific industries in large concentrations/clusters would be identified for studies in conjunction with SIDBI and other banks. Such studies will establish commercial viability of modernisation prescriptions, and financial support would be provided for modernisation of these industries on a priority basis.

It emphasised that the persistent complaint of small scale units of being subjected to a large number of Acts and Laws, being required to maintain a number of registers and submit returns and face an army of inspectors, would be attended to within a specified time frame of three months. To enable the entrepreneurs to concentrate on production and marketing functions, procedures were to be simplified, bureaucratic controls effectively reduced, unnecessary interference eliminated and paper work cut down to the minimum.

Promotion of Entrepreneurship

It emphasised significant expansion of Entrepreneurship Development Programmes (EDP), and for this large number of EDP trainers and motivators would be trained. Industry Association would also be encouraged to participate in this venture effectively. It stated to built EDP into the curricula of vocational and other degree level courses.

It proposed to simplify the definition of "Women Enterprises".

Women entrepreneurs were to be given support through special training programmes. The present stipulation with regard to employment of majority of women workers were to be dispensed with and units in which women entrepreneurs have a majority shareholding and management control, would be defined as "Women Enterprises".

Appraisal of the New Industrial Policy, 1991

Consequent to the unveiling of the new economic policies, a separate set of policy measures were introduced for the promotion and strengthening of SSIs in August, 1991. This new policy statement was a clear re-affirmation of the commitment of the Government towards the importance of this sector in economic growth objectives. The investment limits in plants and machinery of SSIs, was increased to rupees 60 lakhs. The main thrust of Government's new policy was that a separate package for the promotion of tiny enterprises was being introduced. A special monitoring agency was to be set up to oversee that the genuine credit needs of the SSS are fully met. A TDC was to be set up in the SIDO to provide technology inputs to improve productivity and competitiveness of the products of the SSS. The SIDO was recognised as the nodal agency to support the SSIs in export promotion. Apart from this, an Export Development Centre was to be set up in SIDO to serve the SSIs through its network of field office to further augment export activities of the sector.

The new policy measures have exhibited continuation of many tenets of the earlier policies pursued for the SSS, which in brief are:

- (i) Priority sector lending to SSI.
- (ii) Fiscal concessions in the form of excise reliefs.
- (iii) Uniform policy framework for the entire spectrum of SSI.
- (iv) Reservation of products for exclusive manufacture in SSI sector.
- (v) Price and purchase preference to products manufactured in SSI in Government purchase programmes.[22]

Recent Policy Initiatives

As a sequel to the new policy initiative, a number of administrative reforms have been introduced. Licensing restriction in production in SSS has been removed, locational restrictions have been reduced to minimum, industry-related services have been brought within the fold of small-scale development programme, registration procedure has been simplified, steps have been taken to transform the enforcement of labour laws for SSIs from a regime of regulation to an era of self-discipline and voluntary compliance, environmental clearance procedures for SSIs have been rationalised and simplified, and major procedural simplifications in the administration of the excise tax regime.

Nayak Committee

To look into the credit need of the SSS, a committee (known as 'Nayak Committee after the name of its Chairman) was constituted. The committee recommendations envisaged sanction of working capital on the anticipated turnover (*i.e.* providing working capital to the extent of minimum 20 per cent of the annual turnover by the banking sector); giving preference to the credit need of the village, tiny and small industries in that order; drawing up annual credit budget for SSS by banks; prescribing quick and time-bound procedure to dispose off loan applications, and setting up dedicated bank branches for SSIs in places of their concentration.[23] The RBI has accepted these recommendations and other banks have been advised to implement these recommendations.

Seven-Point Action Plan

Time-bound implementation of these recommendations has been operationalised by a Seven-Point Action Plan for improving credit to SSS in 1995-96. They are as follows:

(i) Time-bound action for setting up specialised SSI branches in 85 identified districts; at least 100 such dedicated branches to be opened before the end of 1995-96;

(ii) Adequate delegation of powers at the branch and regional levels;
(iii) Banks to conduct sample surveys of their performing SSI accounts to find out whether they are getting adequate credit;
(iv) Steps to be taken to see as far as possible composite loans (covering both term loans and working capital) are sanctioned to SSI entrepreneurs;
(v) Regular meetings by banks at zonal and regional levels with SSI entrepreneurs;
(vi) Need to sensitise bank managers and reorient them regarding working of the SSI sector, and
(vii) Simplification of procedural formalities by banks for SSI entrepreneurs.[24]

Liberalisation and SSIs

Liberalisation has posed certain challenges as well as opportunities to the SSS. Liberation exert pressure on industry through import competition, competition from internationalized firms, changing customer requirements, changing corporate character and the need to conform to a growing number of international commitments. SSIs have so far functioned in a protected environment, enjoying the benefits of product reservation, market reservation, price preference, priority sector lending, fiscal concessions and exemptions. They are now challenged to higher levels of professionalism and performance efficiency, to improve their competitiveness in the new environment, which envisages a steady dismantling, of many of the existing protective support - systems.[25] The SSIs cannot grow by default any more. The large Indian companies and multinationals now have the advantage of greater access to capital markets, superior business services and technology. SSIs can continue to grow in such an environment if they are fortified with positive strengths. As such, large and small industries will have to go hand in hand. A provision has been made to allow equity investment in SSI by other industrial undertakings to the extent of 24 per cent so that the technology upgradation can be encouraged and capital flows into the SSS. This will especially be beneficial to ancillary type of small-scale enterprises.

The nature of SSI sector is diversified and as a result, the impact of liberalisation, is felt by individual SSI units and sub-sectors and depending on their size, finances, location, product and market. The SSIs are exposed to new pressures from imports and competition from foreign brands, manufactured in India. Besides, the success of SSI units to institutional credit has been restricted by the financial sector reform. As a result of delicensing of industries, on the one hand, the support agencies fall short on giving effective services to SSI units and on the other hand, instead of providing better services and infrastructure to the SSIs, the State Government seem to be more keen on attracting big business to their respective areas.[26]

In short, the challenges have come in the form of competition, reduced protection in the form of lower tariff, lack of attraction for moving into backward areas, limited access to banks, fund and relative higher rate of interest. On the other hand, opportunities have come in the form of better technology, availability of variety of raw materials and components, impetus to quality, efficiency opportunity to restructure and diversify.

As a result of liberalisation, the focus of the Government is on enhancing the capabilities and competencies of SSIs, to take advantage of opportunities in the form of access to capital for productive investment, better technology, development of entrepreneurial skills, availing ISO 9000 etc. To meet the financial needs of SSIs, commercial banks were opened in identified areas of SSI clusters. In 1998, a special package of facilities and incentives was announced for the tiny sector. Further, a separate Ministry for SSIs and Agro and Rural Industries was created in 1999. The investment ceiling has been reduced from Rs.300 lakhs to Rs. 100 lakhs. The SSI sector has been described as "the Growth sector for the Millenium by the Ministry of SSIs and AKI, Government of India. The Ministry's "Agenda for the Millenium" recognizes the need to evolve a new policy framework, emphasising improved supply of credit, better infrastructure facilities and giving an impetus to modernisation and technological upgradation in SSIs.[27] More and more items are being dereserved since 1991. Following the recommendation made by the Abid Hussain

Committee on SME, in April 1997, 15 items were further dereserved. The overall performance of the SSI sector inspite of dereservation of some items, is satisfactory which is clear from Table 3.1. The number of SSI units in India has increased from 20.8 lakh in 1991-92 to 28.6 lakh in 1996-97. The output at current prices has increased from Rs. 1,78,699 crores to Rs. 4,12,636 crores and employment from 129.8 lakh to 160 lakh during the same period [28]

Table 3.1 :Overall Performance of SSI Sector after Liberalisation

Year	*No. of units as on 31 Dec. in Rs. lakh*	*Output (at current prices) (Rs. crore)*	*Employment (Lakh Nos.)*	*Export (at current prices) (Rs.. crore)*
(1)	(2)	(3)	(4)	(5)
1991-92	20.8	1,78,699	129.8	13,883
	(6.7)	(15.0)	(3.6)	(43.7)
1992-93	22.5	2,09,300	134.1	17,785
	(8.2)	(17.1)	(3.3)	(28.1)
1993-94	23.8	2,41,648	139.4	25,307
	(5.8)	(15.5)	(4.0)	(42.3)
1994-95	25.7	2,93,990	146.6	29,068
	(8.0)	(21.7)	(15.2)	(14.9)
1995-96	27.2	3,56,213	152.6	36,470
	(5.8)	(21.2)	(4.1)	(25.5)
1996-97 (P)	28.6	4,12,636	160.0	39,249
	(5.2)	(15.8)	(4.8)	(7.6)

Note: P. Provisional
Figures in brackets show percentage growth
Source: Government of India, *Economic Survey* 1997-98.

An elaborate set of policies, programmes and institutions has evolved over the past four decades for providing Government support for the promotion of small industries in India. Small enterprises in many barriers of the service sector has emerged as provider of employment and contributors to export development which necessitates reconsideration of the view that the policies for small enterprise development should concentrate on the manufacturing sector. As such, it becomes necessary to address the need for reforms in the existing policies and design new policies for Small and Medium Enterprises (SME) development which will facilitate the growth of viable and efficient enterprises that can adjust to technology change and remain internationally competitive.

The positive impact of the New Economic Policy in India, according to a case study[29], has become visible. Entrepreneurs of small and tiny industries have become more quality conscious, are looking for technological upgradation and investing in human resource development. The study concludes that the SSS in India has come of age and is gearing up to face competition with vigour.

Abid Hussain Committee

As a result, Government constituted an "Expert Committee on Small Enterprises" under the chairmanship of Abid Hussain (former member of Planning Commission), which was to go into these issues in depth and make its recommendations to the Government. The Committee submitted its report in January, 1997.

The major recommendations of Abid Hussain Committee are:[30]

(i) The guiding principle of the future course of small scale enterprise (SSE) development policy should be their accelerated growth and competitiveness.

(ii) The policy of protection be replaced by promotion as the cornerstone of future policy. Adequate supply of credit, services, technology assistance, infrastructure and low transaction costs are the hallmarks of the proposed strategy for promotion of SSEs. This can be achieved by developing a variety of linkages between enterprises and their support institutions, partnerships between the private sector and the Government, greater information flows and by streamlining the legal and institutional framework.

(iii) The Sate Governments should identify the existing SSE clusters and then promote new types of organisations which are joint ventures between the State Governments or local authorities and business associations in these clusters.

(iv) A completely new look to be given on the functioning of the DICs in order to make them more promotional rather than regulatory. DICs need to be redesigned as autonomous District Enterprise Promotion Agencies (DEPAs) with participation from business associations, Government agencies, banks, etc.

(v) Abolition of reservation of items for exclusive manufacture in the SSS and providing annual resources of the order of rupees 2,500 crore for the next five years to the industries affected by dereservation.

(vi) Raising of investment limit for SSI units from rupees 60 lakh to rupees 300 lakh and for tiny units from rupees 5 lakh to 25 lakh.

(vii) Enactment of a separate law for small enterprises with the objective of defining the small enterprise sector and outline the broad framework for the promotion of the sector.

On the basis of the recommendations of the Abid Hussain Committee, some action has been taken by the Government. They are:[31]

(i) The Advisory Committee on Reservation constituted under the Industries (Development and Regulation) Act considered the recommendation of total dereservation. It was of the view that complete dereservation is not desirable at this stage as it would affect quite a large number of units and may be done in a phased manner.

(ii) The investment limit for SSI and tiny sector has been raised from rupees 60 lakh to rupees 3 crores and rupees 5 lakh to 25 lakh respectively. This has been done to meet the growing needs of technology upgradation and modernisation, investment for anti-pollution measures and offset the erosion in the value of rupee or account of domestic inflation.

(iii) To ensure availability of credit to all segments of the enlarged SSI sector, RBI has issued instructions to banks for ensuring that out of the funds available to all segments of the SSI sector, 40 per-cent is made available to units with investment in plant and machinery upto rupees 5 lakh; 20 per-cent for units with investment upto rupees 5 lakh and rupees 25 lakh and 40 per-cent for other SSI units.

(iv) The existing ceiling on composite loan by SIDBI has been increased to rupees 200,000 from the existing limit of rupees 50,000.

(v) The scope of the TDMF scheme of SIDBI has been enlarged to cover non-exporting units. Units graduating out of SSI sector will also be covered under the scheme.

In short, these new policy measures are in consonance with the new economic policies, considering that the industrial, trade and fiscal policies have undergone significant changes in the economic reforms process. The changes are of fundamental nature and will result in pervasive and irreversible industrial restructuring. The new measures are designed to enable the SSS to take advantage of the opportunities thrown open by liberalisation process. On the other hand, it would also be essential to promote, protect, nurture and guide the SSS, to consolidate the gains achieved over the years.

Small Scale Industries and the Five Year Plans

In view of the overwhelming importance of SSS, Government of India has sought to help, promote and develop this sector since independence. Planned development of SSS was undertaken with the help of Five Year Plans.

First Five Year Plan (1951-56)

The First Five Year Plan acknowledged the need for development of cottage and SSIs. It drew a distinction between village and modern SSIs and indicated the need for such industries, particularly village industries from employment considerations.

Small industries were divided into three groups, namely

(i) those in which small-scale production has certain advantages and is not affected by large-scale industry to any great extent;

(ii) those in which SSI is concerned with the manufacture of certain parts or with certain stages of production in a manufacturing process in which the predominant role is that of Large-Scale Industry (LSI); and

(iii) those in which SSI has to meet the competition of the corresponding LSI.

The three types of industries could perhaps be described respectively as industries which exist independently or as units integrated with or as units competitive to LSIs.[32]

Since the First Plan was mainly devoted for the development of agriculture, only a sum of rupees 5.20 crores was allocated for the development of SSIs. Table 3.2 and chart 3.1 presents the plan expenditure and outlays under central plan on SSIs sector over the various Five Year Plan periods.

Table 3.2
Plan Expenditure and Outlay on Small-Scale Industries Programme in Five Year Plans

(Rs. in cores)

Plan	*Period*	*Outlay*	*Total Public Sector Outlay*	*Total Expenditure*	*% of SSI to Total Public Sector Outlay*
First Plan	1951-56	5.20	1960	48.00	0.26
Second Plan	1956-61	56.00	4672	187.00	1.20
Third Plan	1961-66	113.06	8577	248.00	1.32
Annual Plan	1966-69	53.48	6625	126.00	0.80
Fourth Plan	1969-74	96.19	15779	242.00	0.60
Fifth Plan	1974-79	221.74	39426	610.00	0.56
Annual Plan	1979-80	104.81	12177	1780.45	0.86
Sixth Plan	1980-85	616.10	109292	3232.80	0.56
Seventh Plan	1985-90	1120.51	180000	-	0.62
Eighth Plan	1992-97	2812.14	434100	-	0.65

Source : Compiled from Plan Documents for Various Plan Periods, Government of India, New Delhi.

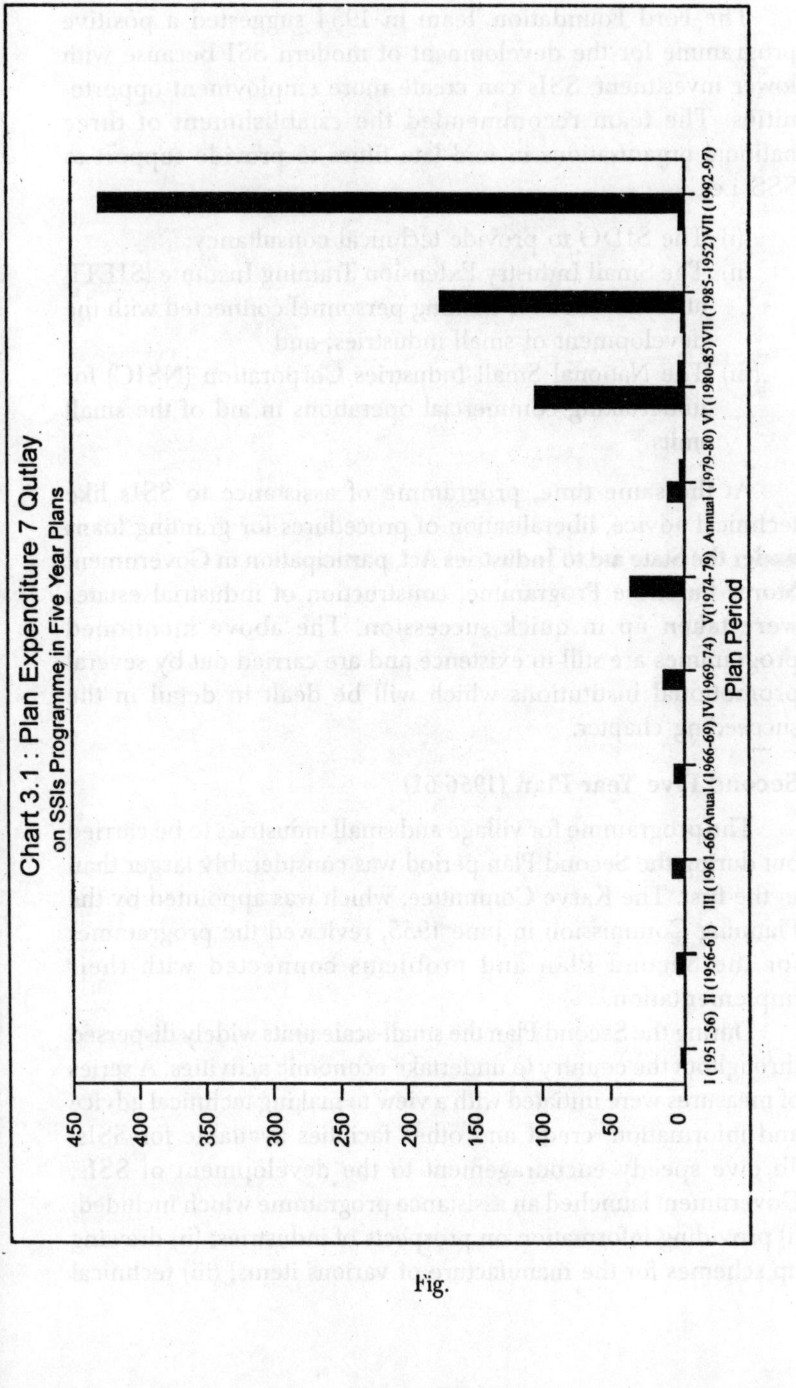
Chart 3.1 : Plan Expenditure 7 Qutlay
on SSIs Programme in Five Year Plans
450
400
350
300
250
200
150
100
50
0
I (1951-56)
II (1956-61)
III (1961-66)
Anual (1966-69)
IV (1969-74)
V (1974-79)
Annual (1979-80)
VI (1980-85)
VII (1985-1952)
VII (1992-97)
Plan Period

Fig.

The Ford Foundation Team in 1954 suggested a positive programme for the development of modern SSI because with lower investment, SSIs can create more employment opportunities. The team recommended the establishment of three national organisations in mid late fifties to provide support to SSS i.e.,

(i) The SIDO to provide technical consultancy;
(ii) The Small Industry Extension Training Institute (SIETI) at Hyderabad for training personnel connected with the development of small industries; and
(iii) The National Small Industries Corporation (NSIC) for undertaking commercial operations in aid of the small units.[33]

At the same time, programme of assistance to SSIs like technical advice, liberalisation of procedures for granting loans under the State aid to Industries Act, participation in Government Stores Purchase Programme, construction of industrial estates were taken up in quick succession. The above mentioned programmes are still in existence and are carried out by several promotional institutions which will be dealt in detail in the succeeding chapter.

Second Five Year Plan (1956-61)

The programme for village and small industries to be carried out during the Second Plan period was considerably larger than in the first. The Karve Committee, which was appointed by the Planning Commission in June 1955, reviewed the programmes for the Second Plan and problems connected with their implementation.

During the Second Plan the small-scale units widely dispersed throughout the country to undertake economic activities. A series of measures were initiated with a view to making technical advice and information, credit and other facilities available for SSIs. To give speedy encouragement to the development of SSIs, Government launched an assistance programme which included: (i) providing information on prospects of industries; (ii) drawing up schemes for the manufacture of various items; (iii) technical assistance; (iv) assistance in procurement of machinery on hire purchase basis; (v) training; (vi) factory space in industrial estate; (vii) credit facilities on liberalised terms; (viii) participation in Government stores purchases; and (ix) modernisation in technological development.[34]

As a result of the assistance measures given by the Government, SSIs rapidly developed during the Second Five Year Plan period. The SSS started producing articles requiring higher degree of technical skills, and those which were being previously imported. The SSS also took up the production of items like radio amplifiers, transistor radios, various types of radio components, tape recorders, simple type of optical lenses including microscopic lenses, simple camera lenses, etc. The number of SSI units rose to 0.36 lakh from 0.16 lakh in the First Plan providing direct employment to 10.61 lakh persons. The value of purchases made by the Central Government from cottage and SSIs rose from rupees 75 lakhs in 1953-54 to nearly rupees 6 crores in 1960-61.[35]

Third Five Year Plan (1961-66)

In the Third Plan period, intensive development of village and SSIs was taken up in selected project areas, known as Rural Industries Projects. Development programmes in the SSS was to be oriented and strengthened so as to enable small units to take the fullest advantage of these opportunities. With regard to SSIs it was specifically mentioned in this plan that "these will need to be developed further in line with the large tasks set in the Third Plan".[36] Apart from this, it was stated that there should be close integration between small scale and large scale units over a wide range of industries and development of SSIs as ancillarly industries.

The main objectives of the small industries programme, in the Third Plan, were to improve the productivity of the worker, to enlarge the availability of institutional finance, and to pay special attention to the growth of small industries in rural areas and towns.

The progress of SSIs was encouraging during the first two years of the Third Plan; then slowed down for various reasons including the shortage of raw materials following the hostilities of 1962 and 1965.[37] The total number of SSI units stood at 1.32 lakh at the end of Third Plan, providing employment to 13.52 lakh persons. The value of output stood at rupees 3918 crores. The definition of SSIs had undergone changes over the years in terms of investment limits[38] which can be illustrated by Table 3.3.

Table 3.3
Evolution of Investment Limits for SSIs

Year	*Investment Limits*	*Additional Condition*
1950	Upto Rs. 5 lakh in fixed asset	Less than 50/100 persons with or without power
1960	Upto Rs. 5 lakh in fixed asset	No condition
1966	Upto Rs. 7.5 lakh in plant and machinery	No condition
1975	Upto Rs. 10 lakh in plant and machinery	No condition
1980	Upto Rs. 20 lakh in plant and machinery	No condition
1985	Upto Rs. 35 lakh in plant and machinery	No condition
1991	Upto Rs. 60 lakh in plant and machinery	No condition
1997	Upto Rs. 3 crore in fixed assets in plant and machinery	No condition

Source : *Report of the Expert Committee on Small Enterprises, New Delhi, January 27, 1997, p. 48.*

Annual Plans (1966-69)

During annual plans, growth of SSS once again showed signs of revival. Upto the end of 1968-69, about 140, 000 small scale units had been registered with the States Industries Directorates, as compared to about 36,000 units at the beginning of 1962.

Fourth Five Year Plan (1969-74)

The objectives of the programmes in the Fourth Plan were:

to improve progressively the production techniques of small industries so as to enable them to produce quality goods and to bring them to a viable level; to promote decentralisation and dispersal of industries; and to promote agro-based industries.

The Fourth Plan insisted on formulation of a small scale industrial policy, modernisation of the SSS, intensive development of selected industries including ancillaries and industrial co-operatives and, subject to criteria of feasibility, promotion of industries in semi-urban, rural and backward areas, incentives for selected SSIs, marketing and export promotion, close link between LSIs and SSIs, encouragement to entrepreneurs with technical and managerial background, key statistics for the SSIs. Efforts were to be made to encourage the production of itmes which were being imported and other items required by priority industries including agro-industries. The Fourth Plan further envisaged schemes for training and financial assistance to technically qualified persons so as to enable them to set up industries. This plan also pleaded for suitable modifications from time to time in the existing policy reservations, to protect SSIs from undue competition from large industries.[39] Hence the reservation policy is constantly reviewed. The policy of reservation was primarily initiated in 1967 as a promotional and protective measure for the SSS *vis-a-vis* large scale sector. The total number of items/products reserved for exclusive manufacture in SSS stood at 846 as on March 31, 1994. The number of reserved items de-reserved and net number of items in the reserved list at different points of time are shown in Table 3.4.

Table 3.4

Progressive Reservation of Items for Exclusive Manufacture in the Small Scale Sector

Date of Notification	*No. of items Reserved*	*No. of items De-Reserved*	*Cumulative Net No. of items Reserved*
Phase I			
1 April 1967	47		47
19 February 1970	8		55
24 February 1971	73		128

conti.

11 November 1971		4	124
26 February 1974	53		177
5 June 1976	3		180
26 April 1978	324		504
Total Number of Items (excluding De-reserved Items)	504		
Phase II			
26 April 1978*	807		807
30 Dec. 1978		1	806
12 May 1980	27		833
19 February 1981	1	1	833
3 August 1981	9		842
23 December 1981	2	13	831
14 October 1982		3	882
19 October 1982	9		837
3 September 1983	35		872
18 October 1984	1	1	873
30 May 1986	7	14**	869
30 October 1986	1	7	863
13 February 1987		13	850
20 July 1987		3	847
18 March 1988		1	846
3 March 1989	3	14	835
31 July 1989	1		836
Total Number of Items (excluding De-reserved Items)	836		

* In 1978 it was decided to recast the reserved list by following codes adopted in the National Industrial Classification and in this process the list of reserved items expanded from 504 to 807 items.

** Since it include three sub-items, the effective number comes to 11 only.

Source : *Hand Book of Statistics–Small Scale Industries India, Development Commissioner, SSI, Government of India, New Dehi, p. 66.*

It could be observed from the above table that net number of reserved items reached the highest at 873 in October 1984 and thereafter it started declining. After July 1989 to December 1996 *i.e.* for over seven years, reservation policy has remained stagnant even though the number of products manufactured in the SSS has gone up from 2,400 to 8,000 from 1972 to 1996.[40]

Fifth Five Year Plan (1974 -79)

In the Fifth Plan, schemes to develop entrepreneurial skills, growth centres in semi – urban and rural areas were initiated. The plan aimed at removal of poverty and inequality in consumption standards of persons, creations of large scale opportunities for fuller and additional productive employment and improvement of their skills so as to improve their level of earning.[41] Thus, the SSIs were encouraged wherever possible by the Government.

To achieve the above objectives, following measures were proposed - protection, encouragement, and reservation for the SSS, adequate availability of credit and raw materials, provision for "seed" capital and "margin" money, technical assistance, special promotional steps for traditional and small industries like handlooms, handicrafts, and sericulture, etc. Other measures such as imposition of differential excise duties, rebate grants on sales of the products of a few small industries, and reservation of a number of items to be purchased by the Directorate General of Supplies and Disposals (DGS & D) exclusively for the SSS were also adopted in order to protect, support and promote SSIs during the plan period.[42] Development of 124 industries was already reserved for the SSS.[43] Subsequently the number of items reserved for the SSS was expanded to 180.

The entire policy toward village and SSIs was conditioned by the political ideology or slogan at the time, viz., "removal of poverty". Village and SSIs were made to serve the purpose, mainly because of the comparatively decentralized character of the sector.[44]

Annual Plan (1979-80)

The centrally sponsored scheme of Rural Industries Projects was merged with the new scheme of DICs. It was decided that the loan assistance provided under the DICs would be utilised as margin/seed money to avail of institutional finance and would not be used for direct loaning.

Certain steps were taken to liberalise institutional credit for small industries. Under the Reserve Bank scheme of finance for the handloom industry, the limits of credit for production and marketing for handloom weavers in the co-operative sector were also enhanced substantially.

The anticipated levels of production and exports to be achieved in 1979-80 are indicated in Table 3.5.

Table 3.5
Anticipated Level of Production and Exports During 1979-80 Production

1. Handloom Cloth (million metres)	2600
2. Powerloom Cloth (million metres)	3400*
3. Khadi and Rural Industries (Rs. crores)	490.33
4. Raw Silk (million kgs.)	5.24
5. Handicrafts (Rs. crores)	660
6. Small Scale Industries (Rs. crores) (Both registered and non-registered units)	15.20
Exports	
7. Cotton Handloom Fabrics and Manufactures (Rs. crores)	300
8. Silk Fabrics and Waste (Rs. crores)	45
9. Handicrafts (Rs. crore)	550
10. Coir Products	
Quantity ('000 tones)	50
Value (Rs. crores)	30

* Includes Art Silk Fabrics.

Sources: Government of India, *Annual Plan (1979-80)*, Planning Commission, New Delhi, 1979, p. 51.

Sixth Five Year Plan (1980-85)

The Sixth Plan also aimed at development of existing as well as new viable small industries. The targets of production and exports set for SSS and the employment to be generated during the 1980-85 plan period are indicated in Table 3.6.

The new programmes initiated during the Sixth Plan period comprised entrepreneurial development, establishment of sub-contracting exchanges and modernisation of selected industries. The policy measures included.[45]

a) increase in the number of items reserved for

(i) exclusive production in the small industry sector to 807 items;

and

Table 3.6

Targets of output, employment and exports for different village and small industries

Industries	*Output value (in Rs. crores) Unit*	*1979-80*	*1984-85*	*Employment Coverage* (in lakh persons) 1979-80*	*1984-85*	*Exports (Rs. crores) 1979-80*	*1984-85*
A. Traditional Industries							
1. Khadi	Million Sq. m.	81	165	11.24	15.40	-	-
	Value	98	200				
2. Village Industries	Value	314	1000	18.21	35.10	-	-
3. Handlooms	Million Metres	2900	4100	61.50	87.00	261	370
	Value	1740	2460				
4. Sericulture	Lakh Kgs. of raw silk	48	90	16.00	21.50	49	100
	Value	131	245				
5. Handicrafts	Value	2050	3200	20.30	28.00	835	1315
6. Coir	Lakh Tonnes of Fibre	1.85	2.63	5.59	8.00	30	50
	Value	86	122				

Sub-total (A)	Value	4419	7227	132.84	195.00	1175	1835
B. Modern Small Industries							
7. Small Scale Industries	Value	21635	32873	67.00	89.00	1050	1850
8. Powerlooms	MillionMetres	3450	4300	11.00	14.00	-	-
	Value	3250	4100				
Sub-total (B)	Value	24885	36973	78.00	103.00	1050	1850
C. Others	Value	4206	5035	25.00	28.00	-	-
Total : VSI (A+B+C)	Value	33510	49235	235.84	326.00	2225	3685

Note : Data for items 1 and 2 above relate to units under the purview of the KVIC, and for item 7 relate to units under SIDO, with reference to revised definition of SSI Units of July, 1980. Data for 'Others' (Under C) relate to units not covered under the above specified industry groups.

* Employment coverage includes both full time and part time.

Source : Government of India, *Sixth Five Year Plan, 1980-85,* Planning Commission, New Delhi, 1980, p. 189.

(ii) exclusive purchase from the sector by the Government and related organisations to 257 items.

b) identification of 'tiny' units with investment upto rupees 1 lakh in plant and machinery and located in towns with population less than 50,000 for offering special incentives;

c) liberalisation of procedures and conditions of financial assistance from commercial banks and other institutions;

d) special facilities for import of raw material and components;

e) intensification of extension services through the SISI, Branch Institutes and Extension Centres apart from Tool Rooms and Regional Testing Centres; and

f) the value of import licences issued to SSIs were increased so that they can import their requirements easily.

Seventh Five Year Plan (1985-90)

Major objective of the Seventh Plan was upgradation of technology and modernisation to improve the competitiveness of SSIs by strengthening/creation of tooling and workshop facilities for development of prototype design, new products and processes and revamp the organisational structure. Ancillarisation was given greater emphasis. Steps were taken to provide product design development and testing facilities to clusters of units, in industries such as locks, builders hardware, metal finishing, general engineering, food processing and sports goods.

The DICs programme was to continue in the Seventh Plan. Efforts by the State Governments were to be stepped up for providing the required services to entrepreneurs at district and sub-district levels through DICs in co-ordination with other State level agencies and Central Bodies like Handlooms and Handicraft Board, KVIC etc.

Emphasis was to be laid on giving integrated and comprehensive marketing support to small units through marketing, counselling, research and special studies, assistance to marketing consortia, participation in the trade fairs and exhibitions. SSIDCs were to play an increasing role in providing market support and technology package to SSI units. Programme of State Corporations were to be dovetailed with those of NSIC in Hire-Purchase of equipment and marketing.

Table 3.7
Share of Small Scale Industries in Total Exports

Year	*Total Exports*	*%age increase*	*Exports from Small Scale Sector*	*%age increase*	*%age share of SSI*
1971-72	16080.0		1549.9		9.6
1972-73	19710.0	22.57	3057.9	97.29	15.5
1973-74	25234.0	28.03	3931.6	28.57	15.8
1974-75	33328.8	32.08	5407.1	37.53	16.2
1975-76	40442.5	21.28	5321.1	(-) 1.59	13.2
1976-77	51422.5	27.21	7658.3	43.92	14.9
1977-78	54042.6	5.09	8448.2	10.31	15.6
1978-79	57262.6	5.06	10692.4	26.56	18.7
1979-80	64587.6	12.79	12263.1	14.69	19.0
1980-81	67107.1	3.90	16432.0	33.99	24.5
1981-82	78059.0	16.32	20706.1	26.01	26.5
1982-83	89077.5	14.11	20450.3	(-) 1.23	22.9
1983-84	98721.0	10.83	21639.8	5.82	21.9
1984-85	114937.2	16.43	25407.8	17.41	22.11
1985-86	108945.9	(-) 5.45	27691.1	8.99	25.42
1986-87	125666.2	15.34	36436.7	31.58	28.99
1987-88	157412.0	25.26	43729.6	20.01	27.78
1988-89	202952.0	28.93	54896.3	25.54	27.05
1989-90	276814.7	36.39	76257.4	38.91	27.55
1990-91	325533.4	17.60	96641.5	26.73	29.68
1991-92	440048.1	35.29	138834	43.03	31.52
1992-93	533505.4	21.14	177848	28.10	33.34

Sources: Government of India, *Small Scale Industries in India : Opportunities in the Small Sector*, Development Commissioner (SSI), Department of SSI and ARI, Ministry of Industry, New Delhi, 1994, p. 31.

Exports from SSS (at current prices) also witnessed a notable increase. Share of SSIs in total exports is presented in Table 3.7 Table 3.8 presents the growth of SSI sectors under different plans.

Table 3.8
Progress of SSI Sector Under Different Plan Periods

Plan	*No. of Units (In Lakhs)*	*Value of Output (Rs. Crores)*	*Average Value of Production (Rs. Lakhs)*	*No. of Persons Employed (in Lakhs)*	*Average No. of Employees Per Unit*
First Plan (1951-56)	0.16	40	2.50	-	-
Second Plan (1956-61)	0.36 (125)	1,170 (28.25)	3.25	10.61	30
Third Plan (1961-66)	1.32 (266)	1,969 (68.29)	1.49	13.52 (27.42)	11
Annual Plan (1966-69)	1.99 (50.75)	3,918 (98.98)	1.97	29.30 (116.71)	15
Fourth Plan (1969-74	3.18 (59.80)	6,500 (65.90)	2.04	41.40 (41.30)	13
Fifth Plan (1974-79)	8.00 (151.6)	20,934 (222.06)	2.61	69.10 (66.91)	9
Sixth Plan (1979-85)	12.8 (60.25)	50,520 (141.33)	4.00	90.00 (30.25)	7
Seventh Plan (1985-90)	18.27 (42.51)	1,32,320 (161.91)	7.24	119.60 (32.89)	7
Annual Plan (1990-91)	19.48 (6.62)	1,53,340 (15.88)	7.87	125.80 (5.18)	6
& (1991-92)	20.82 (6.87)	1,78,699 (16.53)	8.58	129.80 (3.17)	6

Note: Figures in brackets indicate % age increase over the previous plan.

Sources: (1) *Five Year Plan Documents,* Planning Commission, New Delhi.

(2) *SIDO Relevant Annual Reports.*

Annual Plans (1990-91 and 1991-92)

The SSS experienced a severe set back during 1990-92. The reasons for lower growth rate were import restrictions, credit squeeze, costlier funds due to higher margin money requirements etc., imposed during 1991.[46]

Due to the combined effects of these factors, SSIs, experienced serious difficulty in obtaining the requisite raw materials in time which adversely affected their production and capacity utilisation. The constraints continued during 1991-92.

Eighth Five Year Plan (1992-97)

The Eighth Plan envisaged establishment of 70 Growth Centres. It proposed to earmark a certain percentage of developed industrial area for SSIs. It envisaged to increase the share of credit available to the SSI sector from commercial banks from the present 16-18 per-cent.

It was also envisaged that the industry associations will be encouraged to come forward and evolve a suitable distribution mechanism so that the interest of SSI sector is protected. It has also initiated a bigger programme of development of appropriate technology and technology upgradation. Industry associations were to be encouraged to form marketing organisations which, besides marketing, will go into the quality aspect of products.

Estimates of likely achievement of employment, production and export for the SSS during the annual plans (1990-91 and 1991-92) and their respective targets during Eighth Plan (1992-97) fixed as above are shown in Table 3.9.

Table 3.10 presents figures of annual growth rates of the SSS (adding together the unregistered sector of the National Accounts and the SSI sector obtained from the ASI) for the year since 1980-81. Table 3.11 presents state wise growth of SSS in the last 5 years. The number of units registered with various States/UTs have shown a phenomenal increase over the years. As at the end of December 1992, the total number of registered units with various States/UTs was 16.37 lakhs.

Table 3.9
Targets During Eighth Plan Period in Small Scale Sector

Item of Information	*At the end of 7th Plan (1989-90)*	*At the end of Annual Plans*	*Target During VIII Plan Period*					
		1990-91 (Achievement)	*1991-92 Likely Achievment*	*1992-93*	*1993-94*	*1994-95*	*1995-96*	*199-97*
1. Employment (Lakh Nos.)	119.60	124.30 (P)	126.0	128.9	133.0	138.6	144.4	150.5
2. Producton at (1990-91) Prices (Rs. Crores)	143170	155340 (P)	160000	168000	179760	196118	213965	233436
3. Exports at (1990-91) Prices (Rs., Crores)	7626 (P) (At current Prices)	9100 (P) 12658*	13820*	15178*	16695*	18364*	20201*	

* An inflation factor of 1.30 has been used for taking into account devaluation of rupees during 1991. (P) Provisional.

Sources : Government of India, *Eighth Five Year Plan, Vol.II, (1992-97)*, Planning Commission, New Delhi, 1992. pp. 150-151.

Table 3.10
Growth Rates of Small Scale Sector (Unregistered Sector of the National Accounts and the SSI Sector from the Annual Survey of Industries)

Year	Gross Value Added (Rs. crores)	Growth Rate (%)
1980-81	11,973	
1981-82	11,477	(-) 4.14
1982-83	13,319	16.05
1983-84	14,271	7.15
1984-85	14,469	1.39
1985-86	15,999	10.57
1986-87	16,932	5.83
1987-88	18,157	7.23
1988-89	19,402	6.86
1989-90	20,898	7.71
1990-91	21,440	2.59
1991-92	22,525	5.06
1992-93	23,370	5.15

Source : *Report of the Expert Committee on Small Enterprises,* New Delhi, January 27, 1997, p. 79.

Table 3.11
Cumulative No. of SIDO Units Registered on Permanent Basis with States/UTs

States/UTs	*1988*	*1989*	*1990*	*1991*	*1992*
1. Andhra Pradesh	69789	78051	85470	93281	107372
2. Assam	9374	11518	11366	12805	14354
3. Bihar	59886	65192	71804	76779	83782 (E)
4. Gujarat	65553	71299	78441	85220	94879
5. Haryana	61229	65166	69365	74360	79953
6. Himachal Pradesh	9929	10565	11107	11653	12165

conti.

7.	Jammu and Kashmir	17935	19080	19877	21677	22653
8.	Karnataka	62534	68300	74182	80292	88513
9.	Kerala	43900	49574	57738	78420	86595
10.	Madhya Pradesh	139700	149239	160896	1725545	184245(E)
11.	Maharashtra	54610	53955	56837	59953	68003
12.	Manipur	2890	3719	4152	4059	4310(E)
13.	Meghalaya	1003	1114	1233	1368	1616(E)
14.	Nagaland	509	547	580	615	642
15.	Orissa	16061	15251	15736	16004	16505(E)
16.	Punjab	96519	106526	115003	124453	134337
17.	Rajasthan	56761	58367	59931	62393	64437
18.	Tamil Nadu	86499	96501	107503	116940	133807
19.	Tripura	3252	4054	4411	4967	5665
20.	Uttar Pradesh	145797	161017	185566	217376	247907
21.	Sikkim	109	131	185	209	224
22.	Arunachal Pradesh	365	451	474	525	571
23.	West Bengal	131656	134619	137526	139878	142508 (E)
24.	Mizoram	1694	2087	2245	2478	2638
25.	Goa	4494	4794	4947	5146	5381
26.	Andaman & Nicobar	537	586	653	795	852
27.	Chandigarh	2401	2512	2656	2765	2844
28.	Dadar & Nagar Haveli	272	278	284	282	306
29.	Delhi	23817	24804	25774	26228	26606(E)
30.	Lakshadweep	Nil	Nil	104	144	184
31.	Pondicherry	2380	2631	2893	3190	3517
32.	Daman and Diu	228	259	344	385	440(E)

Note : (E) - Estimated position as on 20th July, 1993.

Sources: Government of India, *Small Scale Industries in India: Opportunities in the Small Sector*, Development Commissioner (SSI), Department of SSI and ARI, Ministry of Industry, New Delhi, 1994, pp. 47-48.

Ninth Five Year Plan (1997-2002)

The main highlights of the Ninth Plan strategy for the village and SSIs sector will be:[47]

i) The small scale and village industries will be provided incentives and support to facilitate their growth and employment. It will be ensured that foreign investment does not displace such industries.

ii) The list of items reserved for SSIs will be reviewed with a view to achieve the benefits of economies of scale, technological upgradation, export capabilities, etc.

iii) Credit flow to SSI will be augmented. The financial institutions will be motivated to offer factoring services to SSI in addition to the present system of discounting bills.

iv) The coverage of programmes such as the Prime Minister's Rozgar Yojana (PMRY) will be enlarged to create new employment opportunities.

v) The KVIC will be organisationally and financially strengthened to be able to generate more job opportunities under the 2 million jobs programme in KVIs.

vi) Technology department and upgradation in the VSI sector, especially in the case of SSIs, handlooms, powerlooms, coir, handicrafts, wool, etc.will receive special attention.

The growth of the SSS and its contribution to exports has been impressive. However, this sector requires even further encouragement to be able to grow by tapping both domestic as well as international markets. New initiatives need to be taken in this regard. The Ninth Plan will encourage the formation of SSIs consortia for attaining the required volume and financial strength to compete effectively both at home and abroad.

CONCLUSION

Since the launching of planning in the country, the SSI sector has made remarkable progress. Consequent to the priority assigned to small industry by the Government, the SSI sector has shown impressive growth in terms of number of units, output, employment and exports. The key planks of India's policy for the development of small industry have been reservations, fiscal concessions by way of lower excise duties, extension of business services by the Government and preferential procurement by Government. Small industry was sought to be protected from the competition of big companies. As such, a large number of products was earmarked for exclusive manufacture by them. At present, 850[48] products are reserved for exclusive manufacture by the SSIs. The units which are not in the SSS can manufacture reserved items only if they undertake to export 75 per cent of their production (50 per cent in case of garments). It has been observed that about 30 per cent of these items are not produced by SSIs at all.[49]

The new industrial and economic policies were initiated in full earnest in the middle of 1991. These new policy measures are in consonance with the new economic policies, considering that the industrial, trade and fiscal policies have undergone significant changes in the economic reforms process. The main thrust of Government's new policy was that a separate package for the promotion of tiny enterprises was being introduced. The new measures are designed to enable the SSS to take advantage of the opportunities thrown open by the liberalisation process. The new policies for the SSS have exhibited a continuity in the various promotional measures undertaken for this sector. It would therefore be relevant to look at the promotional aspect of the SSIs i.e. institutions promoting SSIs. This has been discussed in greater detail in the next chapter.

As a sequel to the new policy initiative, a number of administrative reforms have been introduced. Licensing restriction in production in SSS has been removed, locational restrictions have been reduced to minimum, industry – related services have been brought within the fold of small-scale developmental programme, registration procedure has been simplified, environmental clearance procedures for SSIs have been rationalised and simplified, and major procedural simplifications in the administration of the excise tax regime. Newly started SSIs have been exempted from payment of excise duties by the Government of India while State Governments have exempted these units from payment of sales tax.

In order to provide adequate and timely credit, at the instance of Government of India, Reserve Bank of India constituted a Committee (Nayak Committee) in December 1991. Most of the recommendations of this Committee have been accepted and have been followed by directives from Reserve Bank of India.

Liberalisation has posed certain challenges as well as opportunities to the SSS. The challenges have come in the form of competition, reduced protection in the form of lower tariff, lack of attraction for moving into backward areas; limited access to banks, fund and relative higher rate of interest. The reservation policy lost its relevance with the dawn of liberalisation era because delicensing and decontrol were introduced.[50] Previously, the Government was able to implement the policy of reservation by licensing. On the other hand, opportunities have come in the form of better technology, availability of variety of raw materials and components, impetus to quality, efficiency and opportunity to restructure and diversify.

At a Conference organised by the Laghu Udyog Bharati in the capital, the Prime Minister, Shri Atal Behari Vajpayee said that Government will work out ways to ensure easy credit to the SSS, irrespective of the size of the loan. He further said that he will request the larger players to pay their ancillary units on time.[51]

On the issue of SSI funding, the Prime Minister announced that the NABARD and the SIDBI will be strengthened to ensure easy flow of credit to these units. The Prime Minister rejected the Abid Hussain Committee recommendations for total dereservation of items for the SSI and said that potential for employment in the SSS needed to be strengthened rather than weakened. As such the reservation of items to be produced in the SSS will continue. He further said that his Government was committed to fulfilling the promise to end quota-permit raj.[52]

Thus, we hope that the SSIs will have a bright future in the background of the assurances made by our Prime Minister.

To conclude, it can be said that the successive Industrial Policy Resolutions of the Government of India and various plan documents have enunciated the broad objectives behind development of village and SSIs in India. These are:

i) Creation of employment (with particular emphasis on self employment);

ii) Growth of output ensuring regular supply of goods and services through use of local skills and resources;

iii) Diffusion of entrepreneurship through mobilisation of hitherto untapped entrepreneurial talents;

iv) Growth and regional dispersal of industries to promote regional balance; and

v) To counter the growth of monopoly and foster a techno-efficient balance in the growth of large and SSIs.[53]

Endnotes

1. Sharma, Tulsi Ram and Chauhan, S.D. Singh, *Indian Industries (Development, Management, Finance and Organisation)*, 2nd ed., Shiva Lal Agarwala and Co.(P) Ltd., Agra, 1965, p.70.
2. Desai, S.S.M., *Industrial Economy of India*, Himalaya Publishing House, Bombay, 1988, pp.65-66.
3. Government of India, *India's Industrial Policies From 1948 to 1991*, Office of the Development Commissioner (SSI), Department of SSIs and Agro and Rural Industries, Ministry of Industry, New Delhi, 1997, p.l.
4. Maheshwari, R.P. and Gupta, A.N., *Business, Government and Society*, Vikas Publishing House, New Delhi, 1985, pp.84-85.
5. Ghosh, Biswanath, *The Changing Profile of India's Industrial Economy*, The World Press, Calcutta, 1974, p.274.
6. Mukherji, A.K., *Economics of Indian Industry,* S.Chand and Company Ltd., New Delhi, 1985, p.225.
7. Schedule A listed the following 17 industries: (1) Arms and ammunition and allied items of defence equipment, (2) Atomic energy, (3) Iron and steel, (4) Heavy castings and forgings of iron and steel, (5) Heavy plant and machinery required for iron and steel production, for mining, for machine tool manufacture and for such other basic industries as may be specified by the Central Government, (6) Heavy electrical plant including large hydraulic and steam turbines, (7) Coal and lignite, (8) Mineral oils, (9) Mining of iron ore, manganese ore, crome-ore gypsum, sulphur, gold and diamond, (10) Mining and processing of copper, lead, zinc, tin, molybdenum and wolfram, (11) Minerals specified in the Schedule to the Atomic Energy (Control of Production and Use) Order, 1953, (12) Aircraft, (13) Air transport, (14) Railway

transport, (15) Ship building, (16) Telephones and telephone cables, telegraph and wireless apparatus (excluding radio receiving sets), and (17) Generation and distribution of electricity. (Quoted from Government of India, India's Industrial Policies from 1948 to 1991; *op.cit.*, p.12).

8. Schedule B included the following 12 industries: (1) All other minerals except 'minor minerals' as defined in Section 3 of the Minerals Concession Rules 1949, (2) Aluminium and other non-ferrous metals not included in Schedule A, (3) Machine Tools, (4) Ferro-alloys and tool steels, (5) Basic and intermediate products required by chemical industries such as the manufacture of drugs, dye-stuffs and plastics, (6) Antibiotics and other essential drugs, (7) Fertilisers, (8) Synthetic rubber, (9) Carbonisation of coal, (10) Chemical pulp, (11) Road transport, and (12) Sea transport. (Quoted from Ibid.).
9. Ibid., p.10.
10. Desai, S.S.M., *op.cit.*, p.72.
11. Padhy, K.S. and Behera, A.K., *Industrial Policy of India*, Discovery Publishing House, Delhi, 1988, p.93.
12. Government of India, *India's Industrial Policies from 1948 to 1991*, *op.cit.*, p.14.
13. *Ibid.*, p.14.
14. *Ibid.*, p.16.
15. Padhy and Behera, op.cit., p.97.
16. Government of India, India's Industrial Policies from 1948 to 1991, *op. cit.*, p. 24.
17. Ibid., p. 26.
18. Padhy and Behera, op.cit. p. 98.
19. Government of India, India's Industrial Policies from 1948 to 1991, *op. cit.* p. 33.
20. *Ibid.*
21. Kumar, Sharad, *Industrial Organisation and Management*, Discovery Publishing House, New Delhi, 1997, p. 128.
22. Government of India, *Small Scale Industries in India: Opportunities in the Small Sector*, Development Commissioner (SSIs), Department of SSI and Agro and Rural Industries, Ministry of Industry, New Delhi, 1994, p. 43.
23. Prasad, C. S., "Policy for Small-Scale Industries in India", *The* Indian Journal of Public Administration, Vol. XLIII, No.3, July-September, 1997, p. 544.
24. Ibid., pp. 545-46.

25. Vas, Loretta M., *SSIs and the Challenge of Liberalisation*, APPPA Dissertation, Indian Institute of Public Administration, New Delhi, 2001, p. 37.
26. Ibid, pp. 37-38.
27. Ibid, pp. 14-15,
28. Samal, Kishor C., Liberalisation and its Adverse Impact on Informal Sector Workers", Man and Development, Vol. XXI, No.2, June 2000, p. 140.
29. Krishna, K. V. S. M. and Awasthi, D. N., "Responsiveness of Small and Tiny Enterprises to Policy Reforms in India", *The Journal of Entrepreneurship,* Vol. 3, No.2, July-December, 1994, pp. 163-89.
30. Report of the Expert Committee on Small Enterprises (Chairman: Abid Hussain), New Delhi, January 27, 1997, pp. 1-9.
31. Prasad, C. S., op.cit., p. 551.
32. Government of India, *First Five Year Plan,* 1951-56, Planning Commission, New Delhi, 1951, p. 330.
33. Government of India, Report of the *International Perspective Planning Team on Small Scale Industry in India,* Delhi, 1954, p.8.
34. Gupta, N. S. and Singh, Amarjit, *Industrial Economy of India,*Light and Life Publications, New Delhi, 1978, pp. 187-88.
35. Government of India, *Third Five Year Plan,* 1961-66, Planning Commission, New Delhi, 1961, p. 448.
36. Gupta and Singh, *op.cit.* 188.
37. Government of India, *Fourth Five Year Plan*, 1969-74, Planning Commission, New Delhi, 1969, p. 284.
38. Report of the Expert Committee on Small Enterprises, *op. cit.* p. 48.
39. Government of India, Fourth Five Year Plan, *op.cit.*, p. 291.
40. Report of the Expert Committee on Small Enterprises, *op. cit.*, p. 176.
41. Government of India, *Draft Fifth Plan*, Vol. II, Planning Commission, New Delhi, p. 164.
42. Chellaswami, T., "*Policy Relating to Small Scale Sector*", in Mongia, J. N. (ed.), *India's Economic Policies*, 1974-77, Allied Publishers, New Delhi, 1980, p. 227.
43. Government of India, *Draft Fifth Five Year Plan,*Vol.I, Planning Commission, New Delhi, 1974, p. 162.
44. Inove, Kyoko, Industrial *Development Policy of India*, Institute of Developing Economies, Tokyo, 1992, pp. 84-85.
45. Government of India, *Sixth Five Year Plan*, 1980-85, Planning

Commission, New Delhi, 1980, p. 199.

46. Government of India, *Eighth Five Year Plan*, Vol. II, 1992-97, Planning Commission, New Delhi, 1992, p. 132.
47. Government of India, *Draft Approach Paper to the Ninth Five Year Plan*, 1997-2002, Planning Commission, New Delhi, 1997, pp. 59-60.
48. *ICSI Herald*, Vol. IX, No.5, May, 1998, p. 24.
49. Raju, B. Yerram, "Small Scale Industries in India: A Policy Perspective", ASCI *Journal of Management*, Vol. 25, No.2, March 1996, p. 49.
50. Ibid.
51. "Package to Boost SSIs", in *The Economic Times*, New Delhi, April 29, 1998.
52. *Ibid.*
53. Prasad, C. S., *op.cit.*, p. 541.

4

Institutions Promoting Small Scale Industries

Promotion and growth of the Small Scale Industries (SSIs) sector has always been a corner-stone of the Indian Industrial Policy. The Government of India has always accorded a high priority to this sector on account of the vital role it plays in balanced and sustainable economic growth. To achieve the objective of a proportional and continuous small industry development programme as declared in the Industrial Policy Resolutions (IPR) and the successive Five Year Plans, various agencies have been established both at the Central and State levels. Under the Indian Constitution, the development of SSIs is primarily the responsibility of the State Governments. But in view of the fact that, various issues involved in the small industry development programme have an all India bearing and cuts across the national economic fabric requiring policy formulation at the national level, and also because of the magnitude on which efforts have to be made, it was considered necessary and desirable for the Central Government to assume the responsibility for co-ordinating the basic programme of development.[1]

After independence, the specific role of SSIs was recognised by the IPR of 1948. After the formulation of First Five Year Plan, a Committee was appointed by the Planning Commission under the chairmanship of Professor D. G. Karve to study the development of small industry. The Committee recommended that any development programme for small industry should be decentralised, should aim at gradual improvement in techniques without reducing job opportunities, should assure marketing through co-operatives, and aim at positive promotional support.[2] Another landmark in the small industry development programme was the visit of International Perspective Planning Team in 1954 to study the prospects of small industry in India. The Committee recommended among others, creation of many institutions for promotion of SSIs. Accordingly, the Government have set up organisations at the Central and State levels. The Centre as well as State Governments have put in place an impressive institutional support structure to cater to the needs of SSIs. There are a number of institutions and agencies engaged in the areas of credit lending, technology support services, infrastructural services and a host of marketing and support related services.[3]

Chart 4.1 depicts the support agencies and specialised services for SSI. The specialised training institutes along with their major activities have been given in table 4.1. The role and func-tions of these organisations are outlined in the succeeding pages.

Table 4.1

Specialised Training Institutes

Name of Institutes	*Location*	*Major activities*
National Institute of Small Industry Extension Training	Hyderabad	Training Research and consultancy activities
National Institute for	New Delhi	Co-ordinating &

conti.

Entrepreneurship & Small Business Development		overseeing activities of various institutes agencies engaged in entrepreneurship development.
Indian Institute of Entrepreneurship	Guwahati	Training and entrepreneurship development with focus on North East
Integrated Training Centre (Industries)	Nilokheri	Integrated training in different trades
Institute for Design of Electrical Measuring Instruments	Mumbai	Render services to the Instrument Industry
Central Institute of Hand Tools	Jalandhar	Aims at rapid growth of the Hand Tool Sector
Hand Tool Design Development and Training Centre	Nagaur	Assistance for improvement in productivity, betterment in quality, high value addition.
Central Tool Room	Ludhiana	Provide services in the area of consultancy, tool design & manufacture and technical training.
Central Tool Room & Training Centre	Calcutta	Training, design & manufacture of complicated precision tools for the telecom industry and other Common Facility Services
Central Institute of Tool Design	Hyderabad	Training, CAD/CAM Centre for post graduate trainees, automatic

		process control units etc.
Product-cum-Process Development Centre for Sports Goods	Meerut	Training, process & product development of sports goods, R & D.
Product-cum-Process Development Centre for Essential Oils	Kannauj	Modernise and upgrade technology status for the essential oils & perfumery industry.
Product-cum-Process Development Centre	Agra	Provide better technology to small scale foundry & forging units, process & product development, provision of design for melting equipment, testing units facilities
Electronic Service & Training Centre	Ramnagar	Training, technical & consultancy services
Centre for the Improvement of Glass Industry	Firozabad	Development & adoption of new technologies & products
National Small Industries	New Delhi	Supply of machinery, marketing assistance, training.

Source : Government of India, SIDBI Report on Small Scale Industries Sector, 2000, Small Industries Development Bank of India, New Delhi, 2000, p. 96.

Chart 4.1 : Support Agencies and Specialised Services for SSIs.

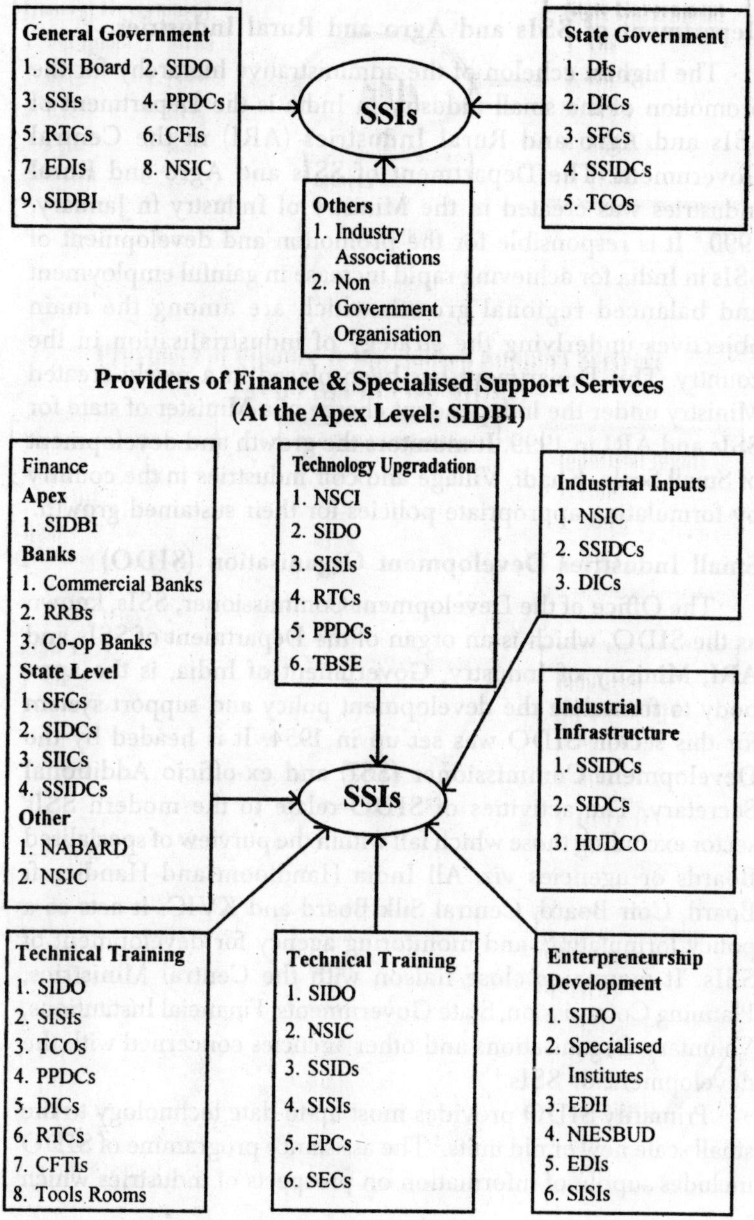

Central Level Organisations

The Central level organisations are the following:

Department of SSIs and Agro and Rural Industries

The highest echelon of the administrative hierarchy for the promotion of the small industry in India is the Department of SSIs and Agro and Rural Industries (ARI) in the Central Government. The Department of SSIs and Agro and Rural Industries was created in the Ministry of Industry in January, 1990.[8] It is responsible for the promotion and development of SSIs in India for achieving rapid increase in gainful employment and balanced regional growth which are among the main objectives underlying the strategy of industrialisation in the country. This Department has been placed in a newly created Ministry under the independent charge of a Minister of state for SSIs and ARI in 1999. It monitors the growth and development of Small Scale, Khadi, Village and coir industries in the country by formulating appropriate policies for their sustained growth.

Small Industries Development Organisation (SIDO)

The Office of the Development Commissioner, SSIs, known as the SIDO, which is an organ of the Department of SSIs and ARI, Ministry of Industry, Government of India, is the apex body to formulate the development policy and support system for this sector. SIDO was set up in 1954. It is headed by the Development Commissioner (SSI) and ex-officio Additional Secretary. The activities of SIDO relate to the modern SSIs sector excluding those which fall within the purview of specialised Boards or agencies *viz.* All India Handloom and Handicraft Board, Coir Board, Central Silk Board and KVIC. It acts as a policy formulating, and monitoring agency for development of SSIs. It maintains close liaison with the Central Ministries, Planning Commission, State Governments, Financial Institutions, Voluntary Organisations and other agencies concerned with the development of SSIs.[4]

Primarily SIDO provides most up-to-date technology to the small scale new or old units.[5] The assistance programme of SIDO includes supply of information on prospects of industries which could be taken up in the SSS, drawing up technical schemes for the manufacture of various itmes, technical consultancy services, common facilities and extension services, training in management and technical trades, economic service assistance in modernisation and technological development and guidance in the procurement of machinery, factory space, finance, marketing, participation in Government Stores Purchase Programmes.

SIDO co-ordinates the work relating to the development of SSIs on an all-India basis by :

i) Evolving an all-India policy and programmes for development of SSIs;
ii) Co-ordinating the policies and programmes of various State Governments;
iii) Maintaining liaison with different States, Central Ministries, Planning Commission, RBI and Financial Institutions;
iv) Co-ordinating the programme of DIC and development of Industrial estates and ancillaries all over the country; and
v) Co-ordinating the programme for the development of large and small industries.[6]

An important function of the SIDO is to suggest a pattern of SSIs development for the country as a whole. This involves responsibilities for indicating the lines of manufacture which are suitable for the SSS and giving it all assistance in the form of promotion, procurement of raw materials and machinery and other technical advice from time to time.

Apart from the co-ordinating and policy formulating functions, SIDO also provides a comprehensive range of extension services to the SSS through the network of 28 Small Industries Service Institutes (SISI), 30 Branch Small Industries Service Institutes, 4 Regional Testing Centres, 15 Field Testing Stations, 2 Footwear Training Centres and One Production Centre.

As a policy measure, 37 extension centres were closed down w.e.f. 31st March, 1992. 30 extension centres stopped functioning whereas 6 extension centres were granted stay order by the Courts against closing down and one extension centre at Pondicherry was to be upgraded to Branch SISI.

SIDO provides a comprehensive range of industrial extension services ranging from identification of a suitable line of production to the marketing of the product. The magnitude of these services could be judged by the fact that on an average, every year SIDO provides guidance and assistance on technical, economic, managerial and other general matters to over 2 lakh units and entrepreneurs all over the country, besides about 20,000 jobs are undertaken by various workshops attached to the SISIs. Table 4.2 presents the details of the extension services provided to SSI units since 1986-87 to 1992-93 and Table 4.3 presents the budget of SIDO under various functions.

Table 4.2
Break-up Extension Services

Year	*Technical*	*Managerial*	*Economic and Statistical*	*Assistance to start new units*	*Other*	*Total*
1986-87	83053	6511	47540	36510	64911	238525
1987-88	81863	6836	44521	49961	59540	242721
1988-89	86151	5432	51743	39790	65274	248390
1989-90	76991	5894	48430	34524	59719	225558
1990-91	68332	7704	47161	41029	48211	212437
1991-92	81736	7429	40353	39162	37417	206097
1992-93	43894	4795	32851	22208	70374	174122

Source : Government of India, *Report on Functions and Activities,* SIDO (1992-93), Development Commissioner (SSIs), Department of SSI and ARI, Ministry of Industry, New Delhi, 1994, p. 7.

In addition, there are also specialised institutions like Central Institute of Tool Design (CITD), Hyderabad, Central Tool Room and Training Centre at Ludhiana, Nagaur and Calcutta, Central Institute of Hand Tools (CIHT), Jallandher, Institute for Design of Electrical Measuring Instruments (IDEMI), Bombay, Integrated Training Centre (ITC), Nilokheri, National Institute of Small Industry Extension Training (NISIET),

Hyderabad, National Institute for Entrepreneurship and Small Business Development (NIESBUD), New Delhi, Product cum Process Development Centres (PPDCs) at Agra and Meerut and Electronic Service and Training Centre, Ramnagar, which provide training, consultancy and technical services in specialised fields. Particular mention may also be made of the Indian Institute of Entrepreneurship at Guwahati which caters to the backward areas of the north-eastern part of the country.

Table 4.3
Budgetary Provision for SSI Promotion

	8th Plan	*1996-97*
Prime Minister's Rozgar Yojana	305.50	120.00
Integrated Infrastructure Development Scheme	50.50	17.59
Tool Rooms	105.05	22.11
Product and Process Development Centres	58.00	3.83
Collection of Statistics	29.00	6.48
Modernisation and Technology	15.80	0.05
Others	64.15	48.59
Total	627.50	218.65

Source: *Report of the Expert Committee on Small Enterprises* (Chairman: Abid Hussain), New Delhi, January 27, 1997, p. 64.

Services Being Provided by SIDO

SIDO provides a host of business services, ranging from quality control to consultancy, delivered by a network of institutions. A brief description of the services supplied by SIDO is given below.

Entrepreneurship Development and Training

Under the guidance of SIDO, various types of EDPs are run by the SISIs/Branch Institutes. Management inputs are provided to beginners/investors and specialised courses are organised for targetted groups of entrepreneurs to set up their units. The courses are conducted by the technical personnel available with the SISIs and Branch Institutions and a national institute called NIESBUD, set up in 1983.

Extension and Training Services

Under the aegis of SIDO, institutes like NISIET and Integrated Training Centre (ITC) provides technical training to artisans/workers. It also organises training of extension officers engaged in various developmental organisations. State Governments sponsor people for training at this centre.

Skills Development

Training in technical skills development is given to technicians and workers in various workshops attached to the SISIs and institutions such as Testing Centres and Tool Rooms. For example, Central Footwear Training Centre (CFTC) provides training to the workers in footwear trade.

Assistance to Entrepreneurship Development Institutes(EDIs)

A new scheme has been formulated to assist State Governments by way of capital and revenue grants not exceeding rupees 50 lakhs per State for strengthening and for setting up EDIs in the States. The Indian Institute of Entrepreneurship was established at Guwahati in March, 1993.

Preparation of Project Profiles

Project profiles on various product groups on a regular basis are prepared and updated by technical officers of SIDO at Central/State level. These are disseminated to entrepreneurs on a large and decentralised basis for use.

Plant Modernisation Studies

Detailed in-plant studies are undertaken in particular units located in industry clusters. Through these studies the present uses of processes/technology are identified and programmes for modernisation of the specified industry group based on the empirical studies. This is supplemented by efforts to encourage units to take up projects for modernisation.

Testing Services

Regional Testing Centres (RTCs), Field Testing Stations (FTSs) and the workshops attached to the SISIs provide testing facilities. Apart from testing, these institutions provide certification as well as third party assurance to purchasers who procure goods from SSI units.

Sub-contracting Exchanges

As many as 16 exchanges have been established for dissemination of information relevant to ancillaries. The functions of these exchanges are:

i) To register idle capacities available in SSI units;
ii) To identify the requirements of large units so as to utilise the idle capacities;
iii) To organise vendor development programmes and exhibitions and promotional programmes; and
iv) To promote interaction between small and large units.

Establishment of Tool Rooms and Product and Process Development Centres (PPDCs)

There are 10 Tool Rooms and 7 PPDCs. The Tool Rooms/ PPDCs generate revenue from the job work they undertake on behalf of the SSIs.

Marketing Support

The schemes being operated by SIDO for promoting market including exports consists of (i) Training in packaging, and (ii) Participation in Indian and International Trade Fairs.

Data Collection

SIDO has a vast programme for collection of statistics through a Central Scheme by involving both DICs and SISIs. SIDO meets the salary of the State Staff engaged in the task of data collection. It also conducts ad-hoc surveys and census.

Small Industries Services Institutes (SISIs)

Industrial Extension Service is rendered through the agency of SISIs, Branch Institutes and Extention Centres of the SIDO.

The SISIs and Branch SISIs are meant for providing services in a particular State/region. They have officers in technical, managerial, economic and statistics, marketing, ancillary development and other disciplines. The SISIs render techno-economic and managerial consultancies, disseminate trade and market information, undertake surveys, conduct training in various trades of activities and provide workshop facilities.

The workshops attached to the SISIs and Branch SISIs provide training to workers of small industrial unit in the use of modern machines, common facility services through machines installed in the workshops, develop prototypes of designs, make tools, dies, jigs, fixtures, etc., and carry out improvements in the use of raw materials and their substitutes. The officers provide both on-the-spot guidance in the premises of the industrial units and to entrepreneurs visiting the Institutes and also through correspondence.[8]

The main functions of the SISIs are:

- i) Interface between Central and State Governments;
- ii) Technical support services;
- iii) Entrepreneurial development programmes;
- iv) Developmental efforts;
- v) Promotional programmes; and
- vi) Export promotion liaison.

SISIs render assistance in following areas: (i) economic consultancy/information/EDP consultancy; (ii) trade and market informations; (iii) project profiles; (iv) State industrial potential survey; (v) district industrial potential surveys; (vi) modernisation and inplant studies; (vii) workshop facilities; and (viii) training in various trades/ activities.[9]

Through the network of SISIs, the SIDO organises various Entrepreneurship Development Programmes for different target groups such as (i) Educated Unemployed, (ii) Women, (iii) Weaker Section, (iv) Rural Artisans, (v) Physically Handicapped, (vi) Students, (vii) Defence Personnel, (viii) Self Employment Scheme and (ix) Technocrat.

SISIs organise EDPs exclusively for weaker sections including the persons belonging to SC/ST communities to motivate and equip them to set up small scale industrial units. They have also been given special powers in the selection of candidates for training in various programmes organised by SISIs.

Small Industries Services Institute-New Delhi

SISI, New Delhi with its jurisdiction of Union Territory of Delhi, District Faridabad in Haryana and Ghaziabad of Uttar Pradesh including Noida, caters to the needs of existing small scale units and prospective entrepreneurs with an objective to strengthen and develop SSIs. Besides, it provides common facilities including training, imparted to the delinquent children at its Extension Centre, Bal Sahyog, located at Connaught Place, New Delhi.

Workshop and Laboratories Services

The workshops attached to SISI, New Delhi and its Extension Centre, provides a wide range of common facilities like electroplating, ceramics, Heat-Treatment, Blue Print Reading, Tool and Die Making, machine shop practice and lens grinding.

Consultancy Services Provided

The Institute and its extension centre provide consultancy services to small scale industrial entrepreneurs in different fields and at different levels. Some of the important areas of consultancy services provided by the Institute during the year 1992-93 is presented in Table 4.4

Training

The Institute and its extension centre organise training courses to upgrade the technical skills of workers in the various trades like machine shop practice, tool die making, electroplating, heat treatment and lens grinding etc.

Management Development Programme

The Institute conducts management development courses in specialised fields like: financial management, marketing management, personnel management, material management, industrial and commercial laws, cost reduction, and packaging for exports.

Entrepreneurship Development Programme

To promote and develop entrepreneurship, the Institute conducts EDP-cum-Motivational campaign programmes of one month duration in different trades like food processing, computer software and hi-fashion garment.

Progress Made in Ancillary Development, Export and Marketing

In collaboration with women's wing of National Alliance of Young Entrepreneurs (NAYE), the SISI, New Delhi, organised a meet to discuss the opportunities towards subcontracting and ancillary development for women entrepreneurs.

Table 4.4
Consultancy Services Provided by the SISI, New Delhi during 1992-93

Sl. No.	*Types of Assistance*	*1992-93*	*1991-92*
1.	No. of entrepreneurs given technical assistance	4456	2392
2.	No. of entrepreneurs given technical assistance through correspondence	-	771
3.	No. of entrepreneurs given technical assistance at unit premises	375	364
4.	No. of units registered under the Government store purchase programme	105	-
5.	Technical assistance to start new units (i) Direct 237 (ii) Indirect 252 **489**	489	1309
6.	No. of entrepreneurs given managerial/ economical/ statistical assistance	-	882
7.	Miscellaneous assistance given to the existing/prospective entrepreneurs	75	715
Total		5500	6433

Source: Government of India, *Report on Functions and Functions, SIDO* (1992-93), Development Commissioner (SSIs), Department of SSI and ARI, Ministry of India, New Delhi, 1994, p. 149.

The Institute also organises a programme on packaging for export, to promote export from the SSS. As a part of marketing assistance programme, the Institute conducts market surveys for the benefit of existing and prospective entrepreneurs.

Special Assistance to Women/SC/ST and Weaker Sections

For development of entrepreneurship amongst the weaker section of society, namely, SCs, STs and Women, the Institute and its extension centre, organises a number of training courses for them.

Quality Control and Upgradation

The Institute organises programme on Quality Control and Upgradation through the use of modern machine tool accessories and attachment. The main objective of the programme is to motivate SSIs using machine tools to improve the quality of their products and productivity by adopting modern time saving attachments.

National Institute of Small Industry Extension Training (NISIET), Hyderabad

National Institute of Small Industry Extension Training (NISIET) is a premier national and international institution in training and research for small industry promotion and extension. The Institute conducts training programmes for our national and international participants in various inter-disciplinary modules. The Institute functions through seven departments. Each of these departments is involved in all the three major functions of training, research and consultancy.[10]

The Institute organises training programmes relating to development of entrepreneurs, ancillary development, planning for infrastructure, marketing management, financial management, economic investigation techniques, etc. Apart from this, the Institute organises outstation programmes of training on the specific requests of the State Governments, financial institutions, Central and State corporations. It also organises seminars and workshops on various aspects of small industries developments.[11] A documentation centre, known as a Small Enterprises National Documentation Centre , has been set up by the Institute.

Tool Rooms/Tools Design Institutes

The heart of Engineering Industry is the Tool Room. Small scale industrial units cannot afford to have their own tool rooms because of huge investments needed. As a result Government of India established these centres to help SSI units to obtain quality toolings.

The functions of the tool rooms/tools design institutes are– (i) Assistance in tool design, (ii) Manufacture of tools, jigs, fixtures, moulds, etc., (iii) Training facilities to tool makers, (iv) common service facilities, and (v) consultancy.

Tool rooms are located at several locations – (i) Central Tool Room and Training Centre, Calcutta, (ii) Central Tool Room, Ludhiana, (iii) Central Institute of Hand Tool, Jalandhar, (iv) Central Institute of Tool Design, Hyderabad, (v) Hand Tool Design, Development and Training Centre, Nagaur, (vi) Tool Room. Aurangabad, (vii) Tool Room, Ahmed-abad, (viii) Tool Room, Indore, (ix) Central Tool Room and Training Centre, Bhubaneshwar; and (x) Central Tool Room Centre, Jamshedpur.

After giving a brief account of the functions, facilities and locations of tool rooms/tools design institute, in the succeeding pages we have discussed in detail the aims and objectives; activities/achievements of various departments, etc. of two tool rooms viz. Central Institute of Tool Design, Hyderabad and Central Institute of Hand Tools, Jalandhar.

Central Institute of Tool Design (CITD), Hyderabad

The Central Institute of Tool Design (CITD) was established at Hyderabad in 1968 by the Government of India with the assistance of UNDP and ILO. The Institute is managed by the Governing Council with Additional Secretary and Development Commissioner (SSI) as Ex-officio Chairman and it has been functioning as an autonomous body from April 1, 1970. The Institute provides consultancy and common service facilities to small industrial units and training the entrepreneurs. Training is the main activity of the Institute and this work is carried on in the Design Department, Tool Room and the meteorology laboratory.

The aims and objectives of this Institute are following :

i) It gives training to technical personnel preferably of SSI in the design and manufacture of Tools, Jigs and Fixture, Dies and Moulds.

ii) It provides advisory, consultancy and common service facilities to SSIs.

iii) It promotes and exploits low cost automation techniques and takes up several projects which will assist and help SSI in achieving better productivity and technological upgradations etc.

Central Institute of Hand Tools (CIHT), Jalandhar

Central Institute of Hand Tools(CIHT) has been established as a National Institute at Jalandhar under the programme of Government of India which aim at rapid growth of hand tool sector in the country. The centre was established under the technical co-operation between Government of India, UNDP and Punjab Government. The management of the affairs of the Institute rests with the Governing Council appointed by the Government of India, with the Development Commissioner (SSIs), New Delhi, as the Ex-officio Chairman.

The aims and objectives of the Institute are as follows:

i) It gives technology support services such as improved design of hand tools;

ii) It gives assistance to SSIs in providing avenues of better markets, domestic and overseas in association with the Central and State level agencies;

iii) It trains personnel for the industry to adopt improved technology; and

iv) It establishes a technical-cum-documentation centre for rendering services to the industry, etc.

Product Cum Process Development Centre (PPDC)

Certain industries have a tendency to grow in a concentrated way in certain important centres. Such areas have emerged as important centres for specific type of industries like sports goods in Meerut, glass items in Firozabad, foundry in Agra etc. These units have been normally engaged in production of items in traditional manner and do not have much exposure to changing technology, designs and manufacturing process. Thus, to help meet the above requirements, SIDO has a programme of establishing PPDCs at such centres.

The functions of the PPDCs are -

(i) It serves as research and development institutions in areas of dense industry cluster;
(ii) product design and innovation;
(iii) product and process improvement and development of improved packaging techniques;
(iv) common facility centre; and (v) manpower development/ training.

The PPDCs are located at (i) PPDC, Ranchi for ceramic and glass industries; (ii) PPDC, Agra for foundry; (iii) PPDC, Meerut for sports goods; (iv) PPDC, Bombay for household electrical appliances; and (v) Electronic Service and Training Centre, Ramnagar (U.P.) for electronic industries. Apart from these five PPDCs, two new PPDCs have come which are under implementation. They are (i) Centre for the Improvement of Glass Industry , Firozabad (U.P.) for glass industry; and (ii) PPDC, Kannauj (U.P.) for essential oils and perfume industries.

PPDCs work basically as R and D institutes to carry out advanced developmental work and act as centres of excellence in the concerned fields. Steps to establish more PPDCs for pumps and diesel engines, food and bakery products, polymer and polymer based products are also being considered. The PPDCs get the financial assistance from international agencies.

National Institute for Entrepreneurship and Small Business Development (NIESBUD), New Delhi

The NIESBUD was set up in July, 1983 at New Delhi by the Government of India. The NIESBUD is serving as an apex body for the promotion and development of small scale entrepreneurship in the country. It co-ordinates and oversees the activities of various institutions/agencies engaged in entrepreneurship development in small industry and small business.

The NIESBUD discharges the following functions to

promote entrepreneurship in SSS: (i) it organises and conducts training programmes for motivators, trainers and entrepreneurs; (ii) it co-ordinates the training activities of various agencies and institutes involved in entrepreneurship promotion; (iii) it prepares model training syllabai for various organisations engaged in the entrepreneurial training activites; (iv) it organises seminars, workshops and conferences on entrepreneurship promotion; (v) it acts as a nodal agency in the field of entrepreneurship and small business development in the country; (vi) it conducts EDPs for the benefit of defence personnel SC/ST, women, engineers and technocrats to become viable entrepreneurs etc.

The Institute produces a bi-monthly newsletter. Besides this, the NIESBUD produces/developes video films on various topics related to entrepreneurship. The Institute also offers a well-managed information and documentation centre.

Institute for Design of Electrical Measuring Instruments (IDEMI), Bombay

The Institute for Design of Electrical Measuring Instruments (IDEMI) was set up at Bombay in 1969 by the Government of India with the assistance of UNDP and UNIDO. The Institute assists the electrical instrument industry in their designing, tooling and manufacturing problems and providing institutional services to the electrical measuring process control and electronic instrument industry. The main objective of the Institute has been to render services to the Instrument Industry in general and to the SSS in particular.

The major areas where IDEMI offers assistance to the industry are as follows :

i) Technical consultancy in various aspects of instrumentation;
i) Sponsored project in design and development of new electronic instruments;
iii) Testing and calibration of instruments and domestic appliances to the standards specified by standards laboratories;
iv) Tool design, tool making and other workshop facilities; and

v) Technical training for various professional in the electronics and instrumentation field.

The Institute has a design and development section which plays vital role in assisting small scale as well as LSIs. Services are provided on no profit basis with preference to SSIs units.

Integrated Training Centre (ITC), Nilokheri

Integrated Training Centre (ITC) was set up in 1965 under the Ministry of Industry, Department of Industrial Development to impart in-service training to Industrial Extension Officers and other functionaries of the State Governments both in modern SSIs and traditional village industries. The centre has been taken over by SIDO in 1983 and it now conducts the following training programmes :

i) Industrial consultancy training course for middle level functionaries of DICs. This is a full time residential course of 8 weeks duration.
ii) Basic course in Industrial Extension for Industries promotion staff of State Governments/Union Territories. This is a full time residential course of 1-1/2 months duration.[12]

The main objectives of the ITC are discussed below :

i) To train base level industrial extension and promotion staff of the State/UT Governments in industrial extension through the medium of base course in industrial extension of 12 weeks duration.
ii) To develop employment skill including self employment amongst entrepreneurs from weaker/under privileged sector of the society through condensed short term specialised courses in industrial technology of varying duration ranging from 2 to 4 months.
iii) In addition, the Centre is engaged in continuous follow up of the training programmes for technician entrepreneurs with a view to help them to overcome teething problems of their industrial ventures. This involves a close liaison with various development and financial institutions in the States.

SMALL SCALE INDUSTRIES BOARD (SSIB)

The SSIs depend on several departments/ministries and various organs of the Central/State Government to carry out its development work. As such, the Small Scale Industries Board (SSIB) has been constituted to facilitate co-ordination and inter institutional linkages.

The SSIB is an apex advisory body. Its main function is to give advice to the Government on various issues pertaining to the SSS.

The Chairman of SSIB is the Minister of Industries, Government of India. The Board consists of following members– State Industry Ministers, Some Members of Parliament, Secretaries of various departments of Government of India, Financial Institutions, Public Sector Undertakings, Industry Associations and Eminent Experts in the field.

The Board works through the Standing Committees. These committees look into the various issues relevant to the SSI sector. The Standing Committees too, have representation from the Central/State Governments, Financial Institutions, Promotional Agencies and Industry Associations. Since August 1992, there are nine standing committees of SSIB. The Committees are– (i) Committee on policies and programmes; (ii) Committee on credit and taxation; (iii) Committee on sickness; (iv) Committee on international co-operation, (v) Committee on development of industries in the north-eastern region and hill areas; (vi) Committee on ancillary development and marketing (including exports); (vii) Committee on upgradation of technology, modernisation quality improvement and environment, (viii) Committee on tiny industry; and (ix) Committee on development of women entrepreneurs.[13]

Khadi and Village Industries Commission (KVIC)

The Khadi and Village Industries Commission (KVIC) was established by an Act of Parliament in 1956. It is mainly a service organisation engaged in the development of Khadi and Village industries in rural areas. Besides Khadi, it has under its purview 96 village industries.[14] KVIC is the main promotional agency in the case of traditional industry.

The main objectives of the KVIC include (i) providing employment in rural areas; (ii) skill improvement; (iii) transfer of technology; (iv) wider objective of providing self reliance among the people and to build up strong rural community base/ spirit; and (v) rural industrialisation.

The development programmes of KVIC are implemented through 30 State/UT Khadi and Village Industries Boards which are statutory organisations established under State legislations, 3,690 institutions registered under Societies Registration Act, 1860 and 30,080 Co-operative-Societies registered under the State Co-operative-Societies Acts except in Hill Border, Tribal and Weaker Section areas, where KVIC directly shoulders the responsibility. KVIC also assists the individual artisans/entrepreneurs through State/UT KVI Boards.

The marketing of Khadi and products of village industries are effected through 10 Khadi Gramodyog Bhavans run directly by KVIC and 14,330 bhandars and sales points at production centres run by the implementing agencies.

So far training is concerned, during 1991-92 KVIC continued to impart various types of training for the artisans and supervisory technical personal through 24 departmental and 25 non-departmental training centres. Apart from this, there are 10 production-cum-training centres under different State offices.[15] There was an increasing trend in the participation of women candidates in KVIC's training programme.

National Productivity Council (NPC)

National Productivity Council (NPC) was established as an autonomous body under the Society's Act in 1958. The Council was reconstituted on 2nd November, 1992 for a term of 2 years. NPC has 12 Regional Directorates and two Regional Offices in addition to its Headquarters at Delhi. NPC has a network for 40 Local Productivity Councils to provide help in the furtherance of productivity related activities at the grass roots level.

The main objectives on NPC are as follows :

i) to increase productivity in all spheres of industries;
ii) to stimulate and promote productivity consciousness by disseminating information regarding productivity techniques and processe; and

iii) to stimulate and facilitate the establishment of regional/local and industry-wise productivity organisations.

NPC organises training programmes on various aspects of productivity, including management and technology. It also undertakes consultancy assignments in the public and private sector enterprises, covering manufacturing enterprises, public utilities, service and commercial organisations.[16] Besides, the NPC organises seminars, symposia, workshops and conferences for popularising and propagating extension of productivity techniques to relatively new areas of economic activity and newly developed concepts of management and productivity.

Small Industries Development Bank of India (SIDBI)

SIDBI is the apex bank set up for promotion, financing and development of industry in the SSS. The bank commenced operations on April 2, 1990. The main functions of SIDBI are as follows: (i) refinance of term loans extended to SSI by banks and State financial institutions; (ii) equipment refinance to SSI units; (iii) special refinance schemes for in-house quality control facilities, Diesel Gensets, pollution control equipment, energy saving systems; (iv) financial assistance to marketing organisations marketing SSI products; (v) loans to organisations/institutions to set up industrial estates for SSI; (vi) single window scheme (SWS) to provide both term loan and working capital to SSI through one agency; (vii) special refinance schemes for women entrepreneurs; (viii) resource support to factoring companies and other institutions promoting SSI; (ix) venture capital fund with a corpus of Rupees 20 crores; etc.

SIDBI liberalised the terms and scope of its existing schemes-in line with the policy measures announced by Government of India in August, 1991 for support to small, tiny and village enterprises. It reviewed the National Equity Fund (NEF) Scheme and SWS and in the light of the Government policy, the size of project eligible for assistance under NEF Scheme was raised from Rs. 5 lakh to Rs. 10 lakh and the quantum of equity assistance doubled from Rs. 75,000 to Rs. 1,50,500 per project.[17]

In order to meet the rising demand for larger variety of consumer/industrial products, SIDBI introduced a scheme of direct assistance designed to encourage ancillarisation. From a predominantly refinancing and bills rediscounting institutions, SIDBI has emerged as a major purveyor of a wide variety of financial services to the SSS. At present, financial assistance being provided by SIDBI covers direct equity participation, equity type loan on soft terms, term loan, working capital–bank rupee finance and foreign currencies, bills discounting, venture capital support and different forms of resource support to banks and other institutions. The proportion of direct assistance in the total portfolio of SIDBI has increased significantly.

Over the years, the scope of promotional and developmental activities has been enlarged to encompass several new activites. In such activities, SIDBI operates in collaboration with voluntary organisations, NGOs, technology firms, consultancy organisations and multilateral/international agencies to enhance the level of overall impact of such activities on the sector.

During the year 1994-95 the main thrust of SIDBIs policy initiative was on expanding the scope and coverage of major schemes of assitance, designing and introducing new schemes of assistance, and on strengthening collaborative relationship with other financial institutions, agencies of Government of India and international developmental agencies. Apart from this, special attention was given to the enhancement of the capabilities of the modern and export-oriented Small scale units.

SIDBI caters to the credit requirements of Small Scale units directly through tailor made schemes of assistance and indirectly through the vast network of primary lending organisations mainly in the form of refinance. Availment of refinance by the credit institutions has been on the decline since 1991-92. Whereas, SIDBIs operations under its schemes of direct assistance have been recording significant growth. The details of SIDBIs operations since 1990-91 to 1994-95 is being presented in Table 4.5.

Table 4.5
Scheme-wise Assistance of SIDBI

	1990-91		*1991-92*		*1992-93*		*1993-94*		*1994-95*	
	S	*D*	*S*	*D*	*S*	*D*	*S*	*D*	*S*	*D*
I. Direct Assistance										
a) Term Loans to -	2.9	-	13.3	3.1	16.7	3.4	91.8	35.0	468.5	112.3
Industrial concerns	5.5	0.7	26.0	7.2	51.3	32.6	237.0	205.6	535.5	427.0
Leasing companies										
b) Resource Support										
Factoring Companies	-	-	7.0	7.0	20.0	11.0	30.0	27.5	42.0	52.5
Other Institutions	75.0	72.1	25.8	17.1	30.0	31.6	144.3	96.3	311.4	104.6
c) Bill Financing										
Machinery	20.9	15.1	118.6	83.9	198.9	139.5	288.0	203.7	309.9	208.9
Components	5.1	5.0	66.7	63.8	300.9	288.6	583.3	560.8	1111.9	1073.6
d) Equity										
Share Capital Equity	-	-	-	-	-	-	-	-	5.4	4.5
type of asistance	7.1	5.5	11.7	9.7	9.9	8.0	6.0	5.2	6.0	4.8
e) Venture Capital	-	-	-	-	-	-	1.6	-	7.5	0.9
f) Foreign Currency Assistance										
Term Loan	-	-	-	-	-	-	-	-	7.2	0.2
Pre-shipment	-	-	-	-	-	-	-	-	1.3	0.4
Sub-total (I)	116.5	98.4	269.1	191.8	627.7	514.7	1382.0	1134.1	2806.6	1989.7
II. Indirect Assistance										
a) Refinance	2052.2	1561.5	2299.0	1634.5	2026.8	1449.9	1766.5	1390.9	1672.2	1235.5
b) Machinery Bills Rediscounting	240.0	178.6	277.9	201.1	253.9	181.2	205.6	146.3	220.5	160.1
Sub-total (II)	2292.2	1740.1	2576.9	1835.6	2280.7	1631.1	1972.1	1537.2	1892.7	1395.6
Total (I+II)	2408.7	1838.5	2846.0	2027.4	2909.4	2145.8	3354.1	2671.3	4699.3	3385.3
Growth Rate %	-	-	18	10	2	6	15	24	40	27

S = Sanctions; D - Disbursements

Source: Government of India, *Small Industries Development Bank of India, Annual Report 1994-95*, 1995, p. 33.

National Small Industries Corporation (NSIC)

The NSIC was set up in February, 1955 with the objective of promoting and developing SSIs in the country. Over the years, it has emerged as a premier institution for SSI which provides technology and marketing support. The primary function of NSIC is to help small entrepreneurs by providing both indigenous and imported machinery on hire purchase and lease basis. Other activities undertaken by NSIC include marketing of the products of SSIs on consortia basis, export marketing of small industries products, developing export–worthiness of SSIs, enlistment of SSI units for participation in Government Stores Purchase Programme, etc.

The NSIC is presently running five Prototype Production-cum-Training Centres at Okhla, New Delhi, Howrah, Madras, Rajkot and Hyderabad. The Prototype centres develop prototypes for various machinery for transfer of technology and know-how for commercial production and impart training to skilled workers and entrepreneurs in various trades. Under the Government Stores Purchase Programme, NSIC is providing institutional marketing assistance by enlisting small scale units for participation in the Government Stores Purchase Programme.

NSIC has played a leading role in improving technological capabilities of the SSS. Apart from this, NSIC has also created a strong base for export of wide variety of products. In addition to exports of products to markets in Europe, it has set up 300 turn key projects in a number of developing countries, thus creating a strong base for stepping up of exports. Thus NSIC has expertise to assist small scale units in promoting exports all over the world, particularly to developing countries.[18]

Machinery and Hire Purchase

Hire Purchase Scheme was started in 1956 with a view to promote small and ancillary units and to modernise the exsting ones by supplying both indigenous and imported machines on easy Hire Purchase terms. The machine supplied by NSIC resulted in creation of employment avenues and almost one-third of the assistance provided under the scheme is for units in backward areas and also to the special categories of entrepreneurs.

For the time being the scheme has been deemphasised and assistance under this scheme is being provided only in selected areas.

Equipment Leasing Schemes

There is now an increasing focus on the Equipment Leasing activity as the Corporation realises that this activity can help in achieving modernisation, diversification and expansion of the beneficiary units. Those units which are technically viable are given assistance under this scheme. Besides providing much needed financial support, this scheme has also become a source of technology upgradation, diversification and imrovement in the SSS enabling the sector to face competition both in domestic and international markets.

Marketing Support Programme

In the wake of the liberalisation policies adopted by the Government of India, intensive assistance is required by the small scale units to face the competition from multi-nationals and the large scale sector.

The Corporation takes up marketing of small industries products within the country (i) by forming consortia of units manufacturing same or similar products, (ii) on agency basis and (iii) by securing institutional orders. NSIC has set up market Development Centres in metro cities in the country to provide facilities for permanent show room and also retail sale, wholesale distribution, tender marketing and export.

For export of small industries products, the NSIC has adopted a 'single window' assistance approach.

Integrated Marketing Support Programme

An Integrated Marketing Support Programme was started by NSIC to avoid the problems of delayed payment by buyers against supplies made by small scale units can be mitigated. In this programme bills pertaining to supplies made by small scale units to eligible purchasers are financed by NSIC upto certain specified limits.

Raw Material Assistance Programme

The Corporation has been supplementing the availability of raw materials and components to a large number of small scale units scattered all over the country with a view to mitigate the hardships of the small scale units in the area of obtaining raw materials at economic prices and at right time. The Corporation also makes arrangements for import of raw materials.

Government's Store Purchase Programme

Government's Store Purchase Programme was launched in 1955-56 with a view to step up supplies from the SSS. The Corporation is continuously working on enlarging the number of units participating in Government Store Purchase Programme and ensuring that they supply goods of substantial value to DGS&D, public sector undertakings and Government departments. This scheme has been instrumental in bringing quality upgradation, technology advancement and diversification and also creation of a reliable source of supply to Government.

Prototype Development and Training Centres

There are five PDTCs and six sub-centres located in different parts of the country which provide diverse technical support to SSS. Three more sub-centres are shortly being set up at Cuttack, Trichur and Jammu. The centres have developed prototype of machines and equipment and provide common facilities in such areas as testing, machining, castings, electroplating etc. The Corporation has created technical infrastructure in rural and backward areas through these centres and sub-centres.

Specialised Institutions

In the preceding pages, we have discussed in detail the functions and activities of various Central level institutions which are responsible for the promotion of SSIs. Apart from these institutions, there are certain specialised institutions *viz.* Council of Scientific and Industrial Research, Department of Scientific and Industrial Research and India Investment Centre, which also look after the promotional aspect of the SSIs. Thus, it becomes necessary to discuss these specialised institutions.

Council of Scientific and Industrial Research (CSIR)

CSIR, an autonomous body, has emerged as a premier national science and technology agency with a vast network of National Laboratories, Extension and Regional Centres and Complexes spread through the length and breadth of the country. CSIR was established for the promotion, guidance and co-ordination of scientific and industrial research in India, establishment and maintenance of Laboratories for scientific studies of problems affecting industries and trades, utilisation of research results for the promotion of industries and also for the documentation, collection and dissemination of information in respect of research and other allied matters.

The Council has established "Information and Liaison Cell for Small Industries" at New Delhi. The Cell provides technical guidance and assistance in solving the problems of small industries and also to follow up of schemes taken up on behalf of small scale units by various National Laboratories.

Over these years, CSIR has made major contributions to the industrial and socio-economic development of the country besides achieving excellence in basic research and creating a strong infrastructure in terms of science and technology manpower in the country. In general, these contributions encompass three important sectors of the national fabric, viz. industrial progress, socio-economic development and generation of export potential for the country's products.[19]

Department of Scientific and Industrial Research (DSIR)

The Department of Scientific and Industrial Research (DSIR) a part of the Ministry of Science and Technology which was created through a Presidential Notification of January, 1985. The DSIR comprises of the activities fo the CSIR; Technology Promotion, Development, Utilisation and Transfer; National Information System for Science and Technology; two public enterprises *viz.* National Research Development Corporation; and Central Electronics Limited.

The major programme of the DSIR (other than CSIR) are :

i) Research and Development by Industry;

ii) Programmes Aimed at Technological Self-Reliance;
iii) Scheme to Enhance the Efficacy of Transfer of Technology;
iv) National Information System for Science and Technology; and
v) Public Enterprises.

India Investment Centre

India Investment Centre is a registered society and an autonomous body set up by the Government of India with its headquarter at New Delhi. The Centre provides valuable information regarding foreign collaboration or participation.

The main objectives of this Centre are as follows :

i) To promote wider knowledge and understanding, in the capital-exporting centres of the world, of conditions, laws, policies and procedures pertaining to investment in India and of investment opportunities in India;
ii) To advise and assist industrialists, including those engaged in medium and small industries on matters necessary to attract foreign capital and/or techniques;
iii) To advise and assist foreign businessmen on matters pertaining to investment in India, and for this purpose, if necessary, to establish branch offices abroad; etc.

The Centre has established Information Services which supply information to prospective Indian and foreign investors on various bearing on investments.

The Centre assists and advises all India entrepreneurs including those engaged in small and medium industries for substantial expansion of the existing industry or for the development of new industry.

The Centre also publishes monthly newsletter analysing the important trends in investments and recording all changes in policy, laws and regulations effecting the investment of foreign capital in India.

State Level Organisations

The primary responsibility for executive action in regard to the development of SSIs and implementation of the programme of assistance is that of the State Governments and Union Territory Administrations. The co-ordination at the State level, is in a sense, better in many, States than at the Centre because the position is more manageable with comparatively fewer organisations. Besides, the Director of Industries (or Commissioner of Industries) has been a traditional functionary even before independence, vested with considerable authority to coordinate. However, with the increasing emphasis on the development of the small industry programme, there has been a proliferation of other agencies at the State level. Prominent among the State level organisations promoting the SSIs are the Directorate of Industries, Small Industry Development Corporation, State Financial Corporation and District Industries Centres[20] which have been enumerated in the succeeding pages.

Directorate of Industries

At the State level/the Directorate of Industries is the apex body for co-ordinating and implementing various programmes. The Directorate of Industries is the executive agency for the promotion and development of the village and small industries sector. It acts under the overall guidance of SIDO and the concerned central institutions associated with various programmes of assistance. Each organisation has supporting administration and technical officers at the State headquarters. In bigger States, there are regional offices also.

The State Directorate of Industries register new units either at their headquarters or at the offices of District Industries Officers or Zonal Director of Industries. This registration number is quoted in the case of assistance like imports, machinery on Hire Purchase basis, procurement of land, industrial shed or financial assistance, etc.

Under State Aid Industries Act, the State Directorate of Industries can give loan on subsidised rate of interest. To approve this, State level committees have been formed.

State Directorate of Industries with the assistance of their field staff certify the genuineness of the claim of the industrial unit to procure either imported raw material or/and machinery and also procurement of machinery on Hire Purchase basis.

The State Directorate of Industries also keep a strict watch on the proper utilisation of import and financial assistance rendered to any unit. Besides, it sets up the Industrial Estates and the sheds or plots are being sanctioned either by the State Directorate of Industries or by their subsidiaries like State Small Industries Corporations or State Industrial Corporations either on out-right purchase or on Hire Purchase basis.

Some of the State Directorate of Industries are also assisting in export marketing through their Export Promotion Divisions. They also assist in State Government purchase programmes and preference is given to the small scale units of their respective States.

Thus we see that the functions of the State Directorate of Industries are both regulatory and developmental. Their functions have grown with the development and diversification of industries.

State Small Industries Development Corporation (SIDCs)

The SIDCs have been set up in almost all the States and Union Territories to undertake a number of commercial activities. The most important of these are responsibility of supplying scarce indigenous and imported raw materials, setting up of industrial estates and industrial areas, undertaking marketing activities including exports of small industries products, supply of machinery on Hire-Purchase basis, procurement of orders from Government departments to be sub-contracted to small industries, and, in certain circumstances, provision of financial, technical and managerial assistance to small enterprises.

Delhi State Industrial Development Corporation (DSIDC)

The DSIDC was registered under Section 617 of the Companies Act, 1956, as a Government Company on 15th February, 1971. The main objectives of the DSIDC are as follows: to aid, counsel, finance, protect and promote the interests of small industries in the Union Territory of Delhi; to undertake procurement and distribution of various raw materials; to undertake and provide marketing facilities to the SSIs in Delhi; to establish and maintain export house to promote export trade;

etc. The genesis, objectives, functions and organisational structure of DSIDC has been discussed in detail in Chapter-VI.

State Financial Corporations (SFC)

The SFCs were established with a view to finance the long-term loans to medium and small scale units and through these SFCs the State Governmental financial assistance was to be channelised. The SFCs provide financial assistance to SSIs on liberalised terms. These corporations provide both term credit as well as working capital requirements to the SSIs to acquire fixed assets like land and buildings and plant and machinery. They have also been assigned with the task of providing assistance to SSI units in backward areas. The SFCs guarantees payment for purchase of machinery from supplies within India and also guarantees loans raised by industries from commercial banks, co-operative banks, etc. Besides, the SFCs undertakes issue of shares, stocks, debentures, etc. issued by industrial concerns and acts as agent of the State or Central Government or Industrial Finance Corporation in transacting business with an industrial concern.

District Industries Centre (DIC)

DICs came into existence as a result of the recommendations of the Industrial Policy Statement of 1977. The DICs are considered as an institutional innovation to assist small industrial units of three important stages viz; pre-investment, investment and post-investment stages under a single roof.[21] DIC is a centrally sponsored scheme with the Government of India sharing the expenditure with the State Governments on a 50:50 basis. However, in the case of UTs 100 per cent expenses, on DICs, are borne by the Centre.[22]

About 430 DICs[23] have been set up covering almost all districts of the country leaving out the metropolitan cities. The DICs are envisaged as a single window interacting agency with the entrepreneur at the district level. The main thrust of this programme is on development of such industrial units in rural and semi-urban areas which would create larger employment opportunities in these areas. As the nodal agency, the DICs provide under one roof the technical guidance and financial assistance needed most by the SSS. They are the implementing arm of the Central and State Governments of the various schemes and programmes. Registration of SSIs is done at the DICs.

Management of the DICs is done by the State Governments. Since 1993-94 the scheme has been transferred to States and they will also provide funds for running DICs. The central scheme of Prime Minister's Rojgar Yojana benefitting the educated unemployed youth will also be administered by them. The performance of DICs is shown in Table 4.6 The DICs play a very significant role. The role is more developmental and promotional than regulatory. DICs should act as a data bank, an information bank and a dissemination centre, for giving prompt up-to-date and reliable information to anybody trying to set up a small scale unit.

Table 4.6
Performance of District Industries Centres - All India
(No. of Units Registered, Financial and Technical Assistance and Employment Generated)

Item	Total Achievement (April - March) 1986-87	1987-88	1988-89	1989-90	1990-91	1991-92	1992-93
No. of DICs sanctioned	419	422	422	422	422	422	422
No. of DICs reporting	418	422	422	422	422	422	422
New registration done (No. in lakhs)	3.74	3.85	3.12	2.73	3.30	3.36	3.42
New Units Established (No. in lakhs)							
i) Artisans	3.16	3.28	3.01	3.01	3.01	3.01	3.01
ii) SSI	1.06	1.12	1.20	1.22	1.23	1.24	1.25
Total	4.22	4.30	4.21	4.23	4.24	4.25	4.26
Credit Assistance provided by financial institutions through DICs (Rs. crores)	890.80	1371.50	1325.69	1714.67	1700	1700	1700
Units given technical and other assistance (Nos.)	30810	64500	228647	150246	153850	157540	-

Source : RBI, *Report on Currency and Finance*, March 1992-93, p. 63.

It has to organise market information, guide entrepreneurs in marketing their products and services under marketing assistance programmes, assess possibilities of ancillary development, export promotion and suggest to the entrepreneurs appropriate marketing strategy.

Another area in which the DICs can play an effective role is with regard to interlinkages with different institutions such as electricity department, department of water works, municipality, panchayat, town planning, commercial banks, etc. The DICs should function in close coordination with all agencies related to industrial development at the district level.

Besides these, the DICs also play regulatory role. The regulatory functions include – registration of SSI units; activities connected with policy implementation; administrative work including settlement of disputes; implementation and monitoring of programmes of both Central and State Government, processing of cases regarding supply of machinery on hire purchase, etc.

Another area is promotional work which include preparation of project reports; district action plans; entrepreneurship development; surveys; consultancy and escort services.

The tremendous progress in the establishment of DICs can be attributed to the funding policy of the Central Government. The original pattern of central financial assistance was 100 percent. From 1979-80 onwards a new pattern of central assistance was introduced under which the Central and State Governments are to share the expenditure on 50:50 basis. In the case of Union Territories 100 per cent assistance is to be provided by Central Government. Thus the liberal financial assistance provided by the Central Government is responsible for the rapid progress made in establishing DICs by the State Government.[24]

Industry Associations

Apart from the organisations/institutions at the Central and State level which promote SSIs, there are industry associations which provide SSI with a common platform to voice their needs and to initiate co-operative efforts in promoting SSIs. In recent years, the Government policies have stressed the increasing role of the industry associations and the NGOs in setting up common facilities and other co-operative ventures in areas of technology, marketing and other support services. Some of the major national associations are: Federation of Association of Small Industries of India (FASII); Indian Council of Small Industries; Indian Federation of Tiny Enterprises; World Association of Small and Medium Enterprises; All India Manufacturers Organisation; Federation of Indian Chamber of Commerce and Industry (FICCI) and Confederation of Indian Industry.

These associations provide facilities for exchange of information on small industry and co-operate with industrial business, educational and research institutions and other organisations in collection and exchange of information pertaining to small industry. These associations undertake professional, technical and management consulting service, studies, survey and research projects. Finally, these associations organise common service facilities for its members.

Conclusion

The above review has shown that a comprehensive organisational network both at the Centre and the State level has been evolved over the years to support and sustain the promotion and development of SSIs in the country. These represented the institutional arm of the Central as well as the State Governments, but it is interesting to note that each of them was structured differently to suit the specific objectives for which it was set up. The SIDO was established as a government department located in the Ministry of Industry headed by an officer designated as Development Commissioner (SSI), whose main function was to advise the Ministry on policies for the SSS and also to monitor the implementation programmes throughout the country. The NSIC was set up as a Government company under the Companies Act because its objectives were regarded as quasi-commercial: for instance, two of its major programmes were (and continue to be) to supply machines to small entrepreneurs on a hire-purchase basis and also to assist the small units to get a bigger share of the government procurement programme. The NISIET on the other hand, was set up as a registered society, meant for the training of entrepreneurs as well as officials connected with the development programme. The Directorate of Industries is the executive agency for the promotion and development of village and small industries sector. The SFCs provide financial assistance to SSIs on liberalised terms. DIC is a centrally sponsored scheme which provide under one roof the technical guidance and financial assistance needed most by the SSS. Thus we see that these institutions are in one way or the other mainly responsible for the promotion of the SSIs in the country.

In view of the vast growth of SSIs that has taken place through the years, the existing network of government institutions cannot hope to serve well the needs of the all the vast number of small industrial units throughout the country. Development of close linkages between these agencies is important for the success of the small industry programme. It is better to provide overall support to small scale enterprises rather than selecting particular sectors or units. A mutual programme of co-ordination and support for speedy promotion of small and cottage industries should be evolved. There should be proper co-ordination of work and activities of different institutions so that overlapping may be avoided. Finally, decentralisation of Central Government institutions also becomes necessary.

Endnotes

1. Vepa, Ram K., *Small Industry Development Programme,* Indian Institute of Public Administration, New Delhi, 1983, p.14.
2. *Report of the Expert Committee on Small Enterprises* (Chairman: Abid Hussain), New Delhi, January 27, 1997, p.46.
3. Government of India, *Small Scale Industries in India: Opportunities in the Small Sector,* Development Commissioner (SSIs), Department of SSI and ARI, Ministry of Industry, New Delhi, 1994, Preface.
4. Vepa, Ram K., *op.cit.,* p.14.
5. Paliwal, R.C., *Small Industries - A Reference Book,* Small Business Publications, Delhi, 1977, p.10.
6. Rangachar, S.S., "Organisational Support for *Small Industry Development*", in V.S.P. Rao and D. Nagaiya (eds.), Small Industry Development in India, Discovery Publishing House, New Delhi, 1991, p.70.
7. Government of India, *Report on Functions and Activities SIDO (1992-*

93), Development Commissioner (SSIs), Department of SSI and ARI, Ministry of Industry, New Delhi, 1994, p.7.
8. *Ibid.*, p.6.
9. Government of India, *Small Scale Industries: Incentives and Facilities for Development*, Development Commissioner (SSIs), Department of SSI and ARI, Ministry of Industry, New Delhi, 1994, p.12.
10. Vepa, R.K., op.cit., p.17.
11. *Ibid.*
12. Sankaranarayan, S., *Industrial Finance in Tamil Nadu and Pondicherry for Small Scale Industries*, K.S. Entrepreneurs Guidance Services, Madras, 1989, pp. 124-126.
13. Small Scale Industries in India: Opportunities in the Small Sector, *op.cit.*, p.67.
14. Government of India, *Annual Report 1992-93*, Ministry of Industry, New Delhi, 1993, p.42.
15. Government of India, *Annual Report 1994-95*, Khadi and Village Industries Commission, Bombay, 1995, p.4.
16. Government of India, *Annual Report 1979-80*, National Productivity Council, New Delhi, 1981, p.8.
17. Government of India, *Annual Report 1991-92*, Small Industry Development Bank of India, Bombay, 1992, p.17.
18. Government of India, *National Small Industries Corporation 40th Annual Report 1994-95*, New Delhi, 1995, p.13.
19. Government of India, *Annual Report 93/94*, Department of Scientific and Industrial Research, Ministry of Science and Technology, New Delhi, 1994, p.7.
20. Vepa, Ram K., *Modern Small Industry in India* (*Problems and Prospects*), Sage Publications, New Delhi, 1988, p.54.
21. Rao, T. Venkateshwara, *Development of Small Scale Industries Role of DICs*, Anmol Publications, New Delhi, 1995, p.1.
22. Report on Functions and Activities, SIDO (1992-93), *op.cit.*, p.16.
23. Report of the Expert Committee on Small Enterprises, *op.cit.*, p.69.
24. Rao, T. Venkateshwara, *op.cit.*, p.14.

5

Industrial Profile of Delhi

The Union Territory of Delhi is a narrow strip of the Indo-Gangetic Plain, lying between 28° 25 and 28° 53 north latitudes and 76° 50 and 77° 22 east longitude. It is bounded on the north, west and south by Haryana, on the east by Uttar Pradesh with river Yamuna flowing on its eastern border in a north-south direction. The area of Delhi is 1,485 square kilometers, its greatest length and breadth being 51.90 kilometers and 48.48 kilometers respectively.

Historical Development

Historical Delhi has been well known as the home of Master Craftsmen for their aesthetic quality of work. Yet unlike the most other metropolitan cities of India it never was considered an industrial town. Delhi has been attracting skilled craftsmen who found the court and the attending nobility a ready market for articles manufactured by them. Delhi has a rich heritage of skilled craftsmen. The various rulers with their high aesthetic tastes patronised the industries dealing with articles of luxury and decoration. It is said that Mohammed Tughlaq during his reign had employed as many as 500 expert weavers at Delhi for the manufacture of silk and brocades for the ladies of the court and for presentation to others.[1] Delhi was one of the principal seats of the manufacture of ladies slippers, embroidered shoes were prepared with the use of gold and silver wire. In olden times, Delhi gained its importance in arts, crafts and industries like jewellery, embroidery, silver vases and bowls and tea sets, ornamental jewel boxes made of brass, silk and silk embroidery, ivory carvings, handloom textiles, copper and brass utensils.

The present industrial growth can be traced to the latter half of the 19th century when three iron foundaries and engineering works were established in Delhi. The Delhi's textile industry's foundation was laid by the installation of two cotton weaving and spinning mills. The first ice factory and the first flour mill

Table 5.1
Population and Number of Workers Engaged in Industries in Delhi State: 1921-1951

Year	*Population*	*No. of Persons*	*Percentage of total working in Industries force*	*Estimated No. workers in registered factories*
1921	4,88,452	43,577	21.5	8,000
1931	6,36,245	54,036	20.1	11,000
1941	9,17,939	81,448	23.2	25,000
1951	17,44,072	1,16,585	18.2	42,635

Source : Gupta, R.K., "A Network of Industries in Delhi: Capital on the Path of Industrial Progress", in S. P. Verma and S. C. Vajpay (eds.), *Landmarks in Delhi Administration*, Gyan Publications, New Delhi, 1998, p. 271.

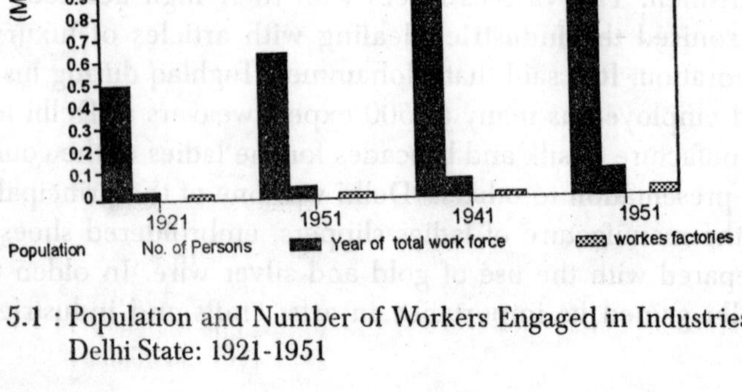

Chart 5.1 : Population and Number of Workers Engaged in Industries in Delhi State: 1921-1951

were set up in 1907 and 1917 respectively. The first match factory was set up in 1931, the first oil mill in 1932 and the acid factory in 1934.[2] The two world wars greatly helped the expansion of industries in Delhi. The partition of the country gave further impetus to the industries. The number of registered factories increased from 111 in 1939 to 227 in 1945 with a corresponding increase in the number of workers from 17,400 to 37,000 respectively.[3] Table 5.1 and Chart 5.1 indicates the true picture of the progress in the last four decades.

Delhi - An Important Centre of Small Scale Industry

Delhi has emerged as an important centre of modern Small Scale Industries (SSIs) in spite of a number of constraints on resources such as water, power etc. The statistics in the table 5.2 and chart 5.2 given below indicate the industrial progress in Delhi over the year 1951-96. (These estimates are approximation based on surveys conducted by Industries Department and DPCC. An exercise is under way to work out firm and reliable data). With an estimated capital investment of about Rs. 2524 crores, production of Rs. 6310 crores and employing about 11.35 lakh persons, Delhi has at present over 126,218 industries.[4] Except about a hundred or so, most of these industries are in the SSS. A wide spectrum of products are being manufactured by the industrial units in Delhi. An Industries census was carried out in the year 1988. The following table gives the product-wise profile

Table 5.2

Growth of Industries in Delhi

Year	*No. of Units*	*Investment (Rs. in crores)*	*Production (Rs. in crores)*	*Employment*
1951	8160	18.13	35.35	69266
1961	17000	60.00	121.00	13800
1965	19038	81.00	176.00	159731
1968	23496	129.00	280.00	192711
1978	40000	600	1100.00	350000
1988	76559	2089	3426.00	514238
1996	126218	2524	6310.00	1135962

Source : *Industrial Profile Delhi* 1997, Office of the Commissioner of Industries, Government of N.C.T. Delhi, Delhi, 1997.

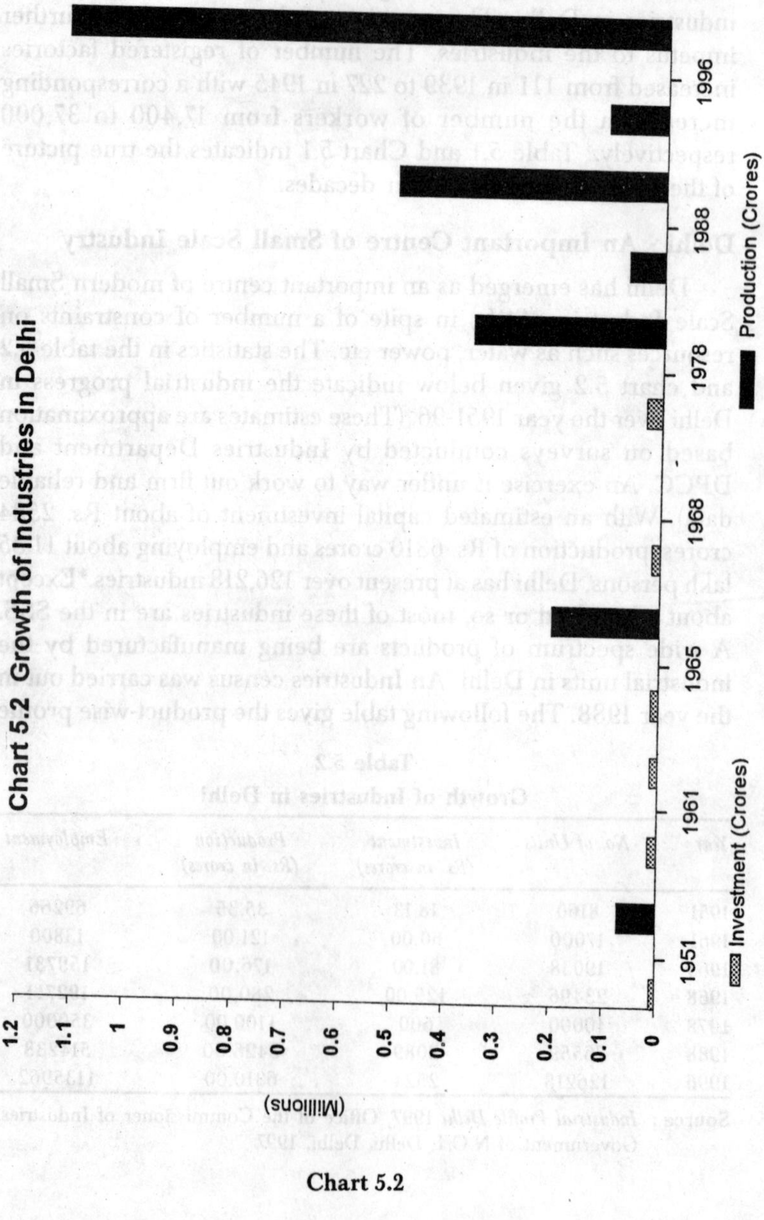
Chart 5.2 Growth of Industries in Delhi
1.2
1.1
1
0.9
0.8
0.7
0.6
0.5
0.4
0.3
0.2
0.1
0
(Millions)
1951
1961
1965
1968
1978
1988
1996
Investment (Crores)
Production (Crores)

Chart 5.2

of Industrial units in Delhi. It can be seen that the major end products of industrial units in Delhi are fabrication of garments, electrical appliances, consumer electronics, printing and publishing units, plastic goods, metal and machinery parts and food processing units.

Industrial development especially in the SSS started in Delhi in 1950s with the setting up of an Industrial Estate at Okhla. The Estate was designed spaciously in line with Delhi's growth as a garden city. Entrepreneurs were hand-picked from the areas of consumer electronics, electricals, metal fabrication, power equipment etc. Perhaps seeing the success of the Estate, the first

Table 5.3
Product-wise Profile of Industrial Units in Delhi

Sl. No.	*Product-wise Industries*	*Number*
1.	Food Products	3827
2.	Beverage, Tobacco and Tobacco Products	64
3.	Cotton Textiles	406
4.	Wool, Silk, Synthetic Products	2006
5.	Jute, Hemp and Jute Products	33
6.	Textile Products (including wearing apparel other than footwear)	15166
7.	Wood and Wood Products, Furniture and Fixtures	2633
8.	Paper and Paper Products, Printing, Publishing and Allied Industries	5662
9.	Leather and Leather Products	1495
10.	Rubber, Plastics, Petroleum, Coal Products	4599
11.	Chemicals and Allied Products	2025
12.	Non-metallic mineral Products	1387
13.	Basic metal and alloy industries	3114
14.	Metal Products except machinery and transport	5780
15.	Machinery, machine tools, machine parts electrical	7280
16.	Electrical machinery, apparatus, appliances (including electronics)	4032
17.	Transport Equipment	2844
18.	Other manufacturing industries	3014
19.	Miscellaneous and servicing industries	1292
20.	Repair services	10782
21.	Others	962
	Total	**76559**

Source: *Industrial Profile Delhi* 1997, Office of the Government of Industries, Government of N.C.T. of Delhi, Delhi 1997, pp. 1-2.

Master Plan provided for major industrialisation of Delhi, limiting, however, to the SSS because Delhi did not want to repeat the mistakes of Calcutta and Bombay.

During 1970's there was a phenomenal growth of industries in the SSS with the DDA coming up with Industrial Estates for light engineering, textiles, steel rerolling, food processing, chemical and pharmaceutical industries, forging, foundries etc. across the board. As a result, the number of small units, increased from about 17,000 in 1961 to 46,000 in 1981.[5] Delhi became a major centre for consumer electronics, household electrical appliances, garments, leather and a host of other SSIs, so much so that a mid-1985 national survey of small industries showed that Delhi was the recipient of the second highest level of industrial raw materials in the country, after Maharashtra.[6] This was possible due to the infrastructural facilities, skilled manpower and constant and cheap electricity available in Delhi.

Inspite of these developments, there were few developments which acted in the reverse direction and led to the wrong type of industries that did not suit the genius of Delhi. One of them was that the DDA went for auction of industrial plots in order to mop up revenues. As a result, the plots went to the highest bidders, even if they did not have a worthwhile project and since many of them were not entrepreneurs, they took the land for future speculations.

Secondly, the concept of flatted factories, which was meant for tiny units, created further congestion, as the employment created per unit was higher than that of the larger small scale units with higher investment in plant and machinery.

Another development was onset of electronics and its increasing application in all industries across the board. This obliterated the difference between large and small, as investment criteria became superfluous, and automation became the order of the day.

The organisations dealing with industrial land allotment policy in Delhi viz., the DDA, the urban planners and the Urban Development Ministry, were unaware of these developments because they never dealt with industrial policy and its developments, nationally or globally. Industrial land was looked as only another facet of land management, meant for profit-making for the DDA. Fortunately the Delhi Administration was not oblivious to these developments.

Master Plan for Delhi 1962

The Master Plan for Delhi 1962 was formulated with a view to check haphazard and unplanned growth of Delhi after the partition. It was the first comprehensive document for planned development of the city formulated under the Delhi Development Act, 1957 and was promulgated on September 1, 1962.

Industries Before Master Plan for Delhi (MPD)-1962 in Delhi

The industrial scenario before MPD- 1962 indicate that the working force engaged in industrial occupation was not more than 25 per cent of the total work force.[7] So far as planned industrial districts in Delhi was concerned, there were only two industrial districts– (i) along Najafgarh Road,-which was developed by erstwhile Delhi Improvement Trust, having both extensive type of manufacturing like DCM Chemicals and intensive industries, like Hindustan Goods Factory, and (ii) small scale industrial estate near Okhla, developed by the Government of India. The rest of the industries were scattered all over the city.

The Industrial scenario in Delhi prior to the formulation of MPD-1962 can be summarised as follows[8]

The total area under industrial use was about 258 hectare out of a total 15,980 hectare urban land, *i.e.* about 1.6 per cent. The total number of manufacturing and service units of various sizes were not more than 5,000 out of which 3609 units were of significant type. The average industrial plot area/unit was 710 sq.m. with average space per worker 150 sq. m. The industries were broadly classified in three groups viz.

I. Classification based on type of units

i) Area under small industries (upto 9 workers) about 34 hectare

ii) Area under medium industries (10 to 49 workers) about 44 hectare

iii) Area under large industries (more than 50 workers) about 140 hectare

II. Classification based on nuisance and non-nuisance industries

i) Area under nuisance industries 136 hectare (52%).
ii) Area under non-nuisance industries 122 hectare (47.5%).

III. Typology of nuisance industries

i) Rubber and chemical products - 25%.
ii) Clay, stone and glass products - 15%.
iii) Metal and metal products - 14.1 %.
iv) Others - 49%.

Provisions of MPD - 1962

To check the unplanned and haphazard installation of industries, for the first time, the MPD- 1962 prepared a detailed strategy which covered planning, industrial development, other related policies and demarcation of land for the installation of industries. In the MPD-1962, Delhi had prohibited certain types of industries, mainly large scale and obnoxious, from being set up in Delhi. However, this stipulation alone has not prevented the concentrated growth of the industrial sector in Delhi, mainly because of availability of excellent infrastructure facilities.[19]

The MPD- 1962 divided the whole city into eight planning divisions which were thought to be self-contained in the matter of employment, residences, recreational, shopping and other needs. The plan located land for industry, commerce, leaving play and other major types of urban land use with proper interrelation to each other for an organised development of the city. The details of various industrial areas which have been developed as a result of Planned Development of Delhi by various agencies are described in the four sections of Table 5.4.

Table 5.4 (A)
Industrial Areas Developed by DDA

Name of Scheme	*Total Areas (Acres)*	*Total No. of Plots/Units*
Okhla Industrial Area Phase-I	368.00	1097
Okhla Industrial Area Phase-II	336.00	884
Lawrence Road Industrial Area	196.00	312
Wazirpur Industrial Area	210.00	784
Wazirpur Group Industries	23.40	175
G. T. Karnal Road Industrial Area	125.00	332
Kirti Nagar Industrial Area	140.00	312
Naraina Industrial Area Phase-I	34.80	151
Naraina Industrial Area Phase-II	114.56	452
Mangolpuri Industrial Area Phase-I	212.00	223
Mangolpuri Industrial Area Phase-II	78.00	1354
Najafgarh Road Industrial Area	329.00	250
Rewari Line Mayapuri Industrial Area Phase-I	147.60	376
Rewari Line Mayapuri Industrial Area Phase -II	166.40	1337
Jhilmil Tahirpur Industrial Area	108.90	238

Table 5.4 (B)
Industrial Areas Developed by Cooperative Societies

Name of Scheme	*Total Areas (Acres)*	*Total No. of Plots/Units*
Mohan Co-operative Industrial Estate	196.16	292
Rajasthan Co-operative Industrial Area	140.00	250
and SMA Industrial Area Udyog Nagar at Rohtak Road	194.00	250

Table 5.4 (C)
Industrial Areas Developed by Directorate of Industries

Name of Scheme	*Total Area (Acres)*	*Total No. of Plots/Units*
Okhla Industrial Area Phase-3	120.00	250
Badli Industrial Area	76.00	280
Patparganj Industrial Area	100.00	500
Jhandewalan Flatted Factories	06.00	570
Flatted Factories for Leather Goods at		
(a) Wazirpur	5.00	250
(b) Bharat Nagar	5.00	120

Table 5.4 (D)
Industrial Areas Developed by DSIDC

Name of Scheme	*Total Area (Acres)*	*Total No. of Plots/Units*
I. Work Centres		
a) Jahangirpuri	2.5	88
b) Shakurpur	1.0	43
c) Wazirpur	0.73	24
d) Sangam Park	3.0	126
e) Kabir Basti	2.0	96
f) Mangolpuri	13.0	376
g) Madipur	5.0	188
h) Sultanpuri	10.5	386
i) Nangloi	6.0	222
j) Hastal	1.0	44
k) Naraina	1.3	41
l) Raghubir Nagar	1.2	45
m) Khyala	1.0	33
n) Jawalapuri	6.0	284
o) Tilak Vihar	5.0	248
p) Kalkaji	1.2	40

conti.

q) Garhi	0.6	22
r) Tigri	1.0	42
s) Madangir	0.6	27
t) Dakshinpuri	1.0	42
u) Kotla Mubarakpur	2.5	108
v) Mata Sundari Road	0.5	77
II. Industrial Sheds		
a) Okhla Phase-I	16.2	232
b) Okhla Phase-II	20.0	205
c) Jhilmil Tahirpur	2.5	32
d) Wazirpur	7.0	102
e) Lawrence Road	5.0	90
f) Rohtak Road	26.0	278
g) Mangolpuri	4.5	94
h) Kirti Nagar	6.0	216
III. Industrial Park		
Narela	600	1800

Source : Gupta, R. K., "A Network of Industries in Delhi: Capital on the Path of Industrial Progress", in S. P. Verma and S. C. Vajpay (eds.), *Landmarks in Delhi Administration*, Gyan Publications, New Delhi, 1998, pp. 274-275.

It is evident from the four parts of Table 5.4 that so far all the agencies put together have been able to provide only about 20,000 Industrial Work spaces including Industrial Plots and Flatted Factories.

Industrial areas proposed in MPD–1962 were mainly in the following category :

(i) Flatted factories, work-cum-industrial centres; (ii) light industries; and (iii) extensive industries. The flatted factories were proposed at a density of about 500 to 625 workers per hectare. Light and service industries, 100 workers per hectare and extensive industries 70 workers per hectare. With regard to location policy, the MPD–1962 outlined that small to medium size units were to be located more close to the centre of the city. Delhi was not considered desirable to locate any new units within the Central city area creating problems of waste disposal, water pollution etc. It proposed to establish large manufacturing units in Ring Towns. Keeping in view the above mentioned facts, land for industries were identified at different locations for the estimated employment generation, based on the zoning regulations provided for different types of industries.

Delhi's First Industrial Policy

Though the MPD-1962 had outlined a locational policy for industrial growth in the Union Territory of Delhi, with the rapid growth of industries over the last two decades, a fresh look was considered appropriate. It was considered desirable to give industrial growth a positive direction and an attempt was made by the Department of Industries, in consultation with other departments, agencies and local bodies, concerned with industrial matters, such as DDA, MCD, Bureau of Economics and Statistics, to prepare a policy statement, which considers future industrial growth in the Union Territory of Delhi in a compre-hensive manner. With this aim in view, the Industries Department of the Delhi Administration, for the first time, issued an Industrial Policy Statement in 1982.

The Industrial Policy Statement was to subserve Delhi's interest *i.e.* to encourage industries that are sophisticated, non-pollutant, guzzle less power, and use skilled manpower. It opposed the concept of auction of industrial land. It laid emphasis on the development of modern sophisticated SSIs, to produce a variety of quality consumer and producer goods, with special emphasis on high value added goods. It encouraged modernization, energy conservation, use of renewable sources of energy and activities allied to industries, such as marketing, services, consultancy, etc. It also laid stress on promotion of export-oriented and import substitution industries and promotion of traditional industries, *viz.*, handicrafts, handlooms, khadi and village industries and leather goods industries, where maximum benefits go to weaker sections of the society.

The basic postulates of the industrial policy for Delhi were the promotion of industries particularly, the small-scale and tiny industries, so that we may create additional jobs which may cope with the problem of unemployment among the rising population. Some of the existing industries may also expand to absorb a part of new workforce. It would, therefore, be necessary to channelise the growth of industries at an appropriate pace in desirable directions. Keeping in view the strain on infrastructure, the Government of Delhi has allowed setting-up of industries in the House-hold sector. Sixty-seven industries have been identified which can run in residential houses with upto 1 KW load, provided that the industry does not cause any pollution or congestion and can be operated within a space of 30 sq.m.[10]

Measures to Promote SSIs

In conformity with the basic postulates of the Industrial Policy, the Delhi Administration had made special attempt to develop and promote SSIs. Some of the promotional measures are:

(i) Identify the items which are reserved for manufacture in the SSS and items reserved for exclusive purchase for SSS by the Government;

(ii) Provide for adequate infrastructure in the form of industrial plots and/or built up flatted factories/ worksheds, etc., preferably functional groups;

(iii) Enable these industries to benefit from complementary and interdependence facility, the establishment of common services, introduction of modern techniques, collective purchase of raw materials and also of finished goods, joint publicity etc., to achieve external economies;

(iv) Facilitate shifting of undesirable industries from congested areas to decongested areas of the city;

(v) Provide necessary technical support through training facilities, supply of improved tools and machinery and common facility services;

(vi) Provide Government and financial institutions in a co-ordinated manner; and

(vii) Provide marketing support through trade centres, emporia, exhibitions, sale space, design development centres and marketing information centres etc.[11]

Apart from these promotional measures, there were some other programmes meant for efficient functioning of the SSIs. The small scale units were assisted in adopting latest appropriate technology, along with modern methods of management so that higher productivity may be achieved. Efforts were made to see that the modernisation process percolate down to small and tiny industries. They were encouraged to seek guidance and assistance from various institutions, concerned with productivity, modernization, standardisation and quality control. To deal with the problem of sickness of the small scale units, the Delhi Administration implemented the Central scheme of margin money. Besides, the Administration periodically examined the impact of administrative and fiscal policies and changes made therein from time to time and took necessary remedial measures so that there was no adverse impact of such policies on the development of industries which may lead to industrial sickness.

Export Promotion

Since Delhi is an important centre of small scale units, an export cell had been set up in the industry department for assisting the export-oriented units to maximise their performance. The Delhi Administration has taken certain measures for the promotion of export *viz.*,

(i) Sponsoring of SSIs, registered with Directorate of Industries as SSI units, to various export promotion councils and other concerned agencies, for registration with them, to enable them to avail of various types of incentives and assistance provided by the government;
(ii) Organising and assisting consortia of small industries for exports;
(iii) Giving adequate priority to exporting units for registration and other assistance;
(iv) Giving due weightage to exporting industries in the matters of industrial plots/ sheds/ flats/ factories and location of controlled scarce raw material; etc.[12]

The industrial policy of the Delhi Administration has taken into account the natural growth of some SSIs and also the setting up of some new medium scale industries to sustain the growth of small industries and to meet the essential needs of the local economy/population. As such, some bigger plots may be kept for such industries in the industrial areas to be developed in future.

Since 1987 the Delhi Administration has adopted a policy of encouraging only small scale industrial units and only non-polluting and non-hazardous type are encouraged in the Union Territory of Delhi. It has been decided not to develop any new industrial estates because of land constraints in Delhi. Similarly, due to the pressures posted on the power supply in Delhi, it was decided not to encourage high power consuming industrial units, and as far as possible grant SSIs registration only to those industrial units which do not require power above 65 kilowatt (80 horse power) without staggering.[13]

MPD-2001

With the fast growing number of job seekers, mostly migrants from the neighbouring States entering Delhi, with large expenses of encroached land, and with unregulated industrial growth of vast magnitude, a need was felt to make constructive adjustment and suitable modifications in the plan, keeping in view the necessity of more systematic development in the foreseeable future, thereby making the plan flexible, pragmatic and consistent with the changed scenario.[14] Accordingly, detailed background papers covering the period upto 2001 A.D. were prepared by the DDA on different aspects of planning, covering vital sectors like regional development, population, employment, physical and social infrastructure, shelters, transportation, etc.[15]

The Plan envisages that the industrial growth in Delhi should be restricted to small scale with stress on units, which require skill, less of manpower and energy and are non-nuisance and clean to largely subserve Delhi's economy. In allocating new industrial plots, which have been recommended for shifting will be given priority by the Authority by offering plots to the industrial units prior to shifting. Besides, suitable incentives would be provided to the shifting of industries and *ad hoc* licensing to industrial units shall be discontinued. It also provided that industrial area development scheme will be prepared in respect of Anand Parbat, Shahdara and Samaypur Badli areas.

No action plan was drawn up to implement any of the

provisions of MPD-2001. This left a wide gap in respect of provisions and availability of industrial land forcing industries to continue to exist in non-conforming areas.

With a view to close hazardous, obnoxious, polluting industries in non-conforming areas, the Supreme Court of India in 1996, directed the closure of these industries in Delhi in the present from. All such units/industries (about 52,000) are to be relocated to newly developed Industrial Estates/Flatted Factories Complex to be developed by the DSIDC. These units will be Hi-tech, non-polluting industries spread over several acres of land as per Master Plan of Delhi 2001.[16] For the purpose of relocating the industries functioning in residential/non-conforming areas, the Government of the NCT of Delhi has acquired 1300 acres of land for developing new Industrial Estates, besides already available land in the developed Industrial Estate at various locations. The possession of 1060 acres of land at the villages of Bawana and Holambi Kalan has been taken. Apart from this, 378 Flatted Factories have been constructed at Jhilmil industrial area under the relocation scheme.[17]

The Government of NCT Delhi has taken various other initiatives for providing alternate industrial accommodation to the affected units under the Relocation Scheme to continue their activities at the existing locations till such time as the alternate industrial accommodation with a power connection is made available to the units in newly constructed/developed Flatted Factory complexes/industrial estates. Table 5.5 highlights the possible industrial pollution control measures from different sources.

Facilities and Incentives for Promotion of SSIs

The Union Territory of Delhi has well developed infrastructure. Various facilities and assistance provided by different agencies are given below:

1. Assistance by the Government of Delhi

Directorate of Industries of the territory is primarily a service department for the development of SSIs. Rapid industrial growth in the SSS has been due to the concerted and alround assistance being rendered by the Directorate of Industries. The Directorate of Industries had 94 promotional schemes in Seventh Five Year Plan, 1985-90.[18] The various facilities and incentives given by this department are as under:

Table 5.5

Possible Industrial Pollution Control Measures from Different Sources

Source	*Pollution control strategy*
Coal/Oil fired furnace	Emissions from the furnace should be properly channelised through suction and hood arrangement followed by a stack scrubber wherever necessary.
Cupola furnace	Scrubber is a suitable equipment to control air emissions from Cupola furnace.
Induction furnace Boiler (Small)	Emissions should be properly channelized through suction and hood arrangement followed by a stack.
Steam Generation	
< 2MT/hr.	Cyclone
>2<10 MT hr.	Multiclone
> 10 < 15 MT hr.	Multiclone
15 MT hr. & above	Bag filter
	Stack height should be minimum of 11 metres from G.L.
Engineering & Stamping	To control noise pollution measures such as providing proper foundation including rubber & sand cushioning with machinery and operating the industry in closed doors.
DG sets	Acoustic enclosure with DG set or any other measure to reduce noise pollution to meet ambient noise standard at the boundary wall. H = h + 0.2* 0.414 KVA metres. Where H = Total stack height from GL. h = Building height KVA = Capacity of DG set
Dyeing	Waste water treatment by physiochemical methods accompanied by biological treatment wherever necessary.
Electroplating	Ion-exchange method which requires less space compared to the conventional ETPs.
Picking foam	Neutralisation and Physio-chemical treatment.
manufacturing	Physio-chemical treatment accompanied by biological treatment wherever necessary.
Auto service station	Oil & grease trap along with settling tank.

Source: Delhi Pollution Control Board

Registration

Before any official assistance is given to a SSI, the small scale unit has to be registered under SSI category with the Directorate. However, registration is a voluntary action and not obligatory. All working units who have valid corporation licence in the urban areas or hold Lal Dora certificate in rural areas are eligible for obtaining registration. Registration is being made both on permanent and provisional basis. While the former is meant for the units which have come into existence in conforming areas as per the Master Plan, the latter is granted where the applicants are in formative stage for setting up the industry.

Infrastructural Facilities

Infrastructural facilities are provided by the Department of Industries in the form of developed plots and flatted factories. Plots have been developed and allotted in Okhla Industrial Estate, Badli Industrial Estate, Functional Industrial Estates for Electronics at Okhla, and Functional Industrial Estates at Patparganj. Flatted sheds/factories have been constructed and allotted at Okhla, Wazirpur, Jhilmil, Tahirpur, Patparganj, Narela, Bharat Nagar, Nand Nagri, Rani Jhansi Road and Jhandewalan.

Assistance in Procuring Imported, Scarce Raw Material, Fuels and Other Inputs

The Directorate of Industries helps SSI units in procuring raw materials, fuels, and inputs like Paraffin Wax, Rubber, Coal, Furnace oil, etc. The Directorate issues essentiality certificates for issue of import licences. For import of capital goods, recommendations are made by this department to the concerned agency. It recommends units for the grant of machinery on hire-purchase basis through NSIC.

Financial Assistance

Financial assistance is being given by the Directorate of Industries, Delhi, Delhi Financial Corporation and Commercial Banks. The Directorate advances block loans to small scale units upto Rs. 10,000 at a rate of interest of 11 1/4 per cent. There is a scheme for grant of interest subsidy to engineering entrepreneurs.

NSIC at Okhla, New Delhi, also provides industrial finance by way of supply of machines on hire-purchase to SSI units in Delhi.

Assistance to Weaker Sections

The Directorate of Industries looks after the interest of the weaker sections. It gives rebate on the sale of handloom cloth through Super Bazar, Delhi State Industries Emporium and other Emporia. Flatted factories for leather goods has been constructed at Wazirpur Industrial Area for the persons belonging to Scheduled Castes/Scheduled Tribes.

Common Facility Centre

The Directorate has established a common facility centre at the Flatted Factories Complex for leather goods at Wazirpur and Rani Jhansi Road for the benefit of leather goods industries. Besides, a six months training course in footwear and leather goods manufacture is conducted at flatted factories.

Technical and Technological Support

Technical and technological support is available from the Directorate of Industries to all entrepreneurs seeking to set up new enterprises to modernise existing enterprise of diversification, etc. They can also seek assistance from SISI at Okhla. SISI also conducts different types of Entrepreneurship Development Training Programmes. There is a Testing and Development Centre at Okhla industrial area, for providing technical facilities.

A Tool Room and Training Centre set up at Wazirpur Industrial Area with Danish Collaboration is functioning since 1978. The main objectives of this Centre are: (a) to train youngmen to become tool makers and tool designers; (b) to produce high quality tools, jigs, fixtures and moulds for SSIs; (c) to extend technical consultancy services relating to tooling to SSIs; and (d) production of sophisticated injection moulded parts.[19]

One Window Information Service

The Directorate has set up a One Window Information Service at its head office at Kashmere Gate. The One Window

Information Service provides assistance for: (i) registration as a SSI; (ii) issue of municipal corporation licence; (iii) sanction of power load from DVB; (iv) financial assistance from Delhi Financial Corporation; and (iv) marketing assistance from the DSIDC.

Exports Promotion Cell

The Directorate of Industries provides special assistance for exporting the products manufactured by the SSI units in Delhi. The Cell is headed by the Joint Director Industries (Export) who is also the Nodal Officer for co-ordinating and facilitating inter-departmental solutions to the various problems of the exporting community. With a view to encourage exporting units, the Department of Industries, Government of NCT of Delhi, has introduced a scheme of State Awards for exports to small scale industrial units on the basis of their export performance during the previous year. This scheme is in operation since 1976-77. Further, an Export Advisory Committee is functioning under the Industry Minister, Government of Delhi, to identify the difficulties experienced by the exporters, so as to make an appropriate Policy Action Plan and to make suitable recommendation for improving the import/export policy. This had led to a rise in exports from Delhi.

Women Entrepreneurs Cell

For fuller utilisation of entrepreneurship amongst women, special incentives are being given to them by the Directorate of Industries. Women Entrepreneurs Cell had been set up by the Directorate of Industries to boost women entrepreneurs by giving them priority while clearing cases and also a full fledged assistance. Due weightage is given to them in the matter of allotment of land and sheds. Special schemes such as Mahila Udyami Nidhi for providing financial assistance to women entrepreneurs through Delhi Financial Corporation are available.

II. ASSISTANCE BY OTHER AGENCIES OF DELHI ADMINISTRATION

The other important agencies of the Delhi Administration promoting/assisting SSIs in Delhi are given below.

Delhi Development Authority (DDA)

The DDA auctions industrial plots in approved industrial areas from time to time. It also allots plots to the units shifting from non-conforming areas to conforming areas.

Delhi Financial Corporation(DFC)

DFC was established in 1967 under the SFCs Act, 1951 for providing term loan to small and medium scale industries in Delhi and Chandigarh. Assistance can be availed for purchase of fixed assets such as land, building, plant and machinery and working capital. The limit for grant of loan in case of companies and co-operative societies is Rs. 240.00 lakhs, while for partnership and proprietorship concerns is Rs. 90.00 lakhs. The assistance is available to new industrial units as well as to existing units for shifting, expansion, modernisation, diversification and rehabilitation of only DFC assisted sick units. It has also floated various schemes for women entrepreneurs and weaker sections of society.

The DFC has introduced the following two schemes *viz.*, (i) acquisition of ISO - 9000 series certificate by SSI units; and (ii) scheme for technology development and modernisation for SSI units. It has enhanced the ceiling of the assistance under SWS from Rs. 50 lakhs to Rs. 100 lakhs[20]. These schemes were introduced in order to promote clean and eco-friendly technology and motivate the small scale units to modernise and upgrade their technology so as to facilitate the production of quality goods with enhanced profitability and competitiveness.

The Corporation has chalked out a special programme to provide financial assistance for rehabilitation of PCV market dealers. For this purpose, DFC has drawn a special programme for giving them financial assistance for purchase of land, construction of building and working capital as per norms of the Corporation.

In view of the recent orders of the Supreme Court relating to shifting of industries from the non-conforming areas, the Corporation proposes to finance the relocation of industries to the new industrial estates developed by the Government of NCT of Delhi. This is a gigantic task and will provide an excellent opportunity to SSIs in Delhi to modernise and upgrade their technology and infrastructure.

Delhi State Industrial Development Corporation (DSIDC)

The DSIDC was set up in 1971, by the Delhi Government, under the Companies Act, 1956 in order to assist, finance and promote the interest of SSIs in Delhi. The DSIDC has always aided, counselled, assisted, financed, projected and promoted the interest of SSIs due to which, today, Delhi has carved a niche for itself as a prospering centre for SSIs with a wide variety of industrial products including high-value and high-technology goods.

The main objectives of the DSIDC are:

(i) To aid, counsel, assist, finance, protect and promote the interests of Industries in the Union Territory of Delhi.

(ii) To undertake procurement and distribution of various raw materials.

(iii) To undertake and provide marketing facilities, especially to the SSIs of Delhi.

(iv) To acquire land and develop them suitably.

(v) To effect coordination between large industries and small industries.

(vi) To promote and operate schemes for the industries of Delhi, etc.

Society for Self Employment

The Society for Self Employment has been established by the Department of Industries to provide short term training in repair of Radio and TV, fashion designing, repair and maintenance of household electrical appliances and fittings, refrigeration, and air-conditioning and plumbing. The society's main objective is to train young persons with a view to generate self employment. Training centres of the society are located at Flatted Factories Complex, Jhandewalan and Weavers Colony, Nand Nagri, Delhi. At present, training courses in all the trades are conducted at Jhandewalan and one course in fashion designing is conducted at Nand Nagri Training Centre. Training

Courses in some more trades are likely to be introduced in a phased manner.

Delhi Khadi and Village Industries Board (DKVIB)

The Government of Delhi has set up a Delhi Khadi and Village Industries Board which provides financial assistance to the entrepreneurs/artisans and co-operative societies to start units to manufacture khadi and village industry products. The Minister of Industries, Government of Delhi, is the Chairman of the Board. The Board implements two schemes *viz.* KVI Scheme and Block Loan Scheme.

Under the KVI Scheme, the DKVIB provides financial assistance to the individuals and Industrial Co-operative Societies. The funds are meant for the construction of workshed, purchase of machinery, tools and raw materials, etc. From the year 1995-96, the system of providing financial assistance is changed by the Government of India. Now the funds are provided under consortium of Banks Credit Scheme. Funds are available for setting up village industries unit and separately for marketing of exclusively leather products and also for the sale of KVI products. The Block Loan Scheme was transferred to the Board by the Industries Department, Government of NCT of Delhi, in the year 1990-91. Under this scheme, working capital loan is provided to running/existing Household industrial units established in urban and rural areas in Delhi.

Haryana Delhi Industrial Consultants Limited(HARDICON)

HARDICON provides technical and financial consultancy services to medium, small and tiny industrial units of Delhi. It is a consultancy organisation set up by All India Financial Institutions *viz.* IFCI, IDBI, ICICI in association with DFC and Nationalised Banks. It is registered with SEBI as a Merchant Banker and provides advisory services to industrial units planning to raise funds through public issue. It provides the following spectrum of industrial and technical consultancy – (i) Project identification, feasibility studies, project reports and loan syndication; (ii) Technology upgradation and technology transfer; (iii) Sick unit rehabilitation; (iv) Market survey and market consultancy; etc.

Thus, we see that SSIs in Delhi are given both the departmental as well as institutional assistance so that SSIs may flourish. The departmental and the institutional assistance is given in the field of registration of SSI unit, marketing, export, finance, infrastructural facilities, procurement of raw materials, etc. As a result of these assistance, the NCT of Delhi has emerged as one of the biggest centres of SSIs in the country.

Conclusion

Industrial development especially in the SSS started in Delhi in 1950s with the setting up of an Industrial Estate at Okhla. Seeing the success of the Estate, the first Master Plan provided for major industrialisation of Delhi in the SSS. During 1970s there was a phenomenal growth of industries in the SSS with the DDA coming up with Industrial Estate. As a result, the number of SSIs increased and Delhi became a centre for consumer electronics, household appliances, garments and a host of other SSIs. Delhi's first Industrial Policy was issued in 1982, which laid emphasis on the development of modern sophisticated SSIs, to produce a variety of quality consumer and producer goods, with special emphasis on value added goods.

Keeping in mind the basic postulates of the Industrial Policy, the Delhi Administration made special attempt to promote and develop SSIs by adopting some promotional measures like– reservation of items for the exclusive manufacture in the SSS, adequate infrastructural facilities, technical support, marketing facilities, export promotion, financial assistance etc. To provide the above mentioned facilities, the Delhi Government established certain institutions like DSIDC, DFC, DKVIB, HARD ICON etc.

The MDP 2001 envisages that the industrial growth in Delhi should be restricted to small scale with stress on units, which require skill, less of manpower and energy and are non-nuisance and clean to largely subserve Delhi's economy. However, no action plan was drawn up to implement any of the provisions of the MDP 2001.

In the era of new economic policy, where the licensing policy has been liberalised and graded participation in equity by foreign companies has been allowed and where the trade policy has been freed from the shackles of excessive controls and when rupee is fully convertible, Delhi should be allowed to take advantage by investing in futuristic industries for greater value addition and higher exports. This, by itself, would modernise Delhi's industries to international standards without causing the congestion caused by unskilled migration and pollution.

Since 1991 the Government of India has adopted policies of liberalisation in the wake of serious economic crisis. As a result of liberalisation, the direct foreign capital investment has increased. The door has been opened for MNCs due to which competition has increased. The MNCs have come up with high technology and sound capital investment and have entered into the consumer goods production which were earlier produced by the small scale industrial units. The result is that slowly and slowly MNCs started dominating and small scale industrial units started diminishing from the consumer market.

A recent survey of 98 small scale units by FICCI found that 90 percent of those surveyed perceive the entry of multinationals to be a threat. Though 60 percent of the respondents felt that allowing the MNCs to pick up equity stake had helped improve technology, 70 per-cent of the sample believe that the MNCs have been stringent in putting in the required funds. Thus, it becomes clear that the sudden push into the groove of international competition has now become a hard fought battle for survival of SSIs.[21]

Thus, the Government must adopt such a policy which is both restrictive and promotional[22]. The promotional policy means that high-tech industries must be allowed to flourish in the areas of electronics, computers, communications, telecommunications, systems, instrumentation, process control, informatics and robotics. In such a situation, the distinction between small scale and large scale loses any meaning because many of these industries would be housed in a modern building or even in a room. The restriction policy must include no licences and benefits to negative industries newly set up that do not fall within the ambit of high-tech. Similarly, units that do not modernise or contribute to pollution can be cut off from bank finance. Unfortunately, our system support these very units and any attempt to soft-pedal this and place ban on high-tech and sophisticated industries will only pull Delhi down to the level of another of the several dirty and polluted towns.[23]

As such, the role of an organisation like the DSIDC becomes crucial. Accordingly, the genesis, objectives, organisational structure and functions of the DSIDC has found place in the succeeding chapter.

Endnotes

1. *Delhi District Census Handbook: Village And Town Directory - Delhi*, Director of Census Operations, Delhi, 1993, p.62.
2. Ibid.
3. Gupta, RK., "A Network of Industries In Delhi: Capital on the Path of Industrial Progress", in S.P. Verma and S.C. Vajpay (eds.), *Landmarks in Delhi Administration*, Gyan Publishers, New Delhi, 1998, p.271.
4. Government of National Capital Territory of Delhi, Industrial Profile Delhi 1997, Office of the Commissioner of Industries, Delhi, 1997, p.l.
5. Misra, B.P., "Overview on Industrial Policy", in Omesh Saigal, et.al., *Problems and Prospects of Industrial Development in a Metropolitan City*, Mittal Publications, New Delhi, 1994, p.6.
6. Ibid.
7. Gupta, S.C. and Bansal, S.P., "Master Plan for Delhi *vis-a-vis* Industries", in Omesh Saigal, *et.al., op.cit.*, p.33.
8. *Ibid.*
9. Thakore, V.K., "Establishing Industries in DMA and NCR", in Omesh Saigal, et.al., *op.cit.*, p.74.
10. Government of National Capital Territory of Delhi, Industrial Profile Delhi 1997, *op.cit.*, p.3.
11. Vinze, Medha Dubhashi, *Women Entrepreneurs In India*, Mittal Publications, New Delhi, 1987, pp. 18-19.
12. Ibid., p. 25.
13. Mudgal, R., "Development of Industrial Complexes Jointly by Delhi and its Neighbouring States", in Omesh Saigal, et. al., *op. cit.*, p. 77.
14. Vinze, Medha Dubhashi, op. cit., p. 37.
15. *Ibid.*
16. Government of National Capital Territory of Delhi, *Industrial Profile of Delhi*, Delhi State Industrial Development Corporation, New Delhi, 1997, p. 3.

17. Government of India, *SIDBI Report on Small Scale Industries Sector 2000*, Small Industries Development Bank of India, New Delhi, 2000, p. 84.
18. *Chandra, Shanta Kohli, Development of Women Entre-preneurship in India*, Mittal Publications, New Delhi,1991, p.16.
19. Indian Investment Centre, Scope for Industries in Different States, New Delhi, 1976, p. 253.
20. Government of National Capital Territory of Delhi, Industrial Profile Delhi 1997, op. cit., p.18.
21. Nanda, Antara, "Small Sector Left in the Lurch", in *The Times of India*, New Delhi, April 15, 1998, p. 12.
22. Misra, B.P., "Overview on Industrial Policy", in Omesh Saigal, et. al., *op. cit.*, p. 10.
23. *Ibid.*, p. 11.

6

DSIDC–Genesis, Objectives, Administrative Structure and Functions

The Delhi State Industrial Development Corporation Limited (DSIDC) has played a key role in shaping the industrial growth of the Indian capital, a throbbing city of some 10 million people. Since its establishment in February 1971, the DSIDC has projected, aided, counselled, assisted, financed and promoted the interest of SSIs. Today, Delhi, once known worldwide for skilled artisans, has carved a niche for itself as a prospering centre for SSIs. In fact, Delhi has one of the largest clusters of SSIs, their number being 1,26,218 in 1996 and having mind boggling total investment of Rs. 3,444 crores.[1] Due to the large number of industries, Delhi has become the epicentre for a wide variety of industrial products including high-value and high-technology goods. The DSIDC's involvement in the industrial growth of the capital is a success story.

In this introductory background, an attempt has been made in the present chapter, to give a brief description of the genesis of the DSIDC, its objectives, functions and its administrative structure.

Genesis of DSIDC

Delhi is pre-dominantly a metropolitan urban area without much hinterland. As the National Capital it has to be maintained as a clean modern city with a healthy environment and a proper ecological balance. Delhi has emerged as an important centre of modern SSIs. A major factor leading to the predominance of SSIs in Delhi has been the non-availability of sufficient hinterland for setting up of large industries and scarcity of industrial resources like power, water, raw material etc.

Delhi being the National Capital having large and increasing population, provides a good bulk consumption and distributive market. It also provides for good export opportunities as it has a rich heritage of variety of arts and crafts. These conditions suited to evolution and development of SSIs and traditional crafts which required less space, low capital investment by following a system of day to day purchase of raw material and other inputs and quick disposal of finished goods in the local market. It provided large scale employment to entrepreneurs particularly refugees and local craftsmen and skilled, semi-skilled artisans and labourers. Since the Government was committed to rapid industrialisation of the country with a view to improve the living conditions of the common man and benefitting him by providing employment and supplying essential goods at fair prices, it made vigorous efforts to promote the small and cottage industries and crafts. To achieve this objective, the Government made suitable arrangements to provide financial, technical, infrastructural and marketing facilities through various institutions established in Delhi.

Initially, the Directorate of Industries in the Union Territory of Delhi was the sole channelising agency for all assistance provided by the Government. It still is responsible for preparing suitable plans, projects, schemes and policies and their execution either departmentally or through specialised agency.

Further, due to the rapid industrialisation of the country, the need was felt to evolve specialised agencies for detailed implementation of the general policy guidelines and specially charged with the responsibility of providing all assistance to the SSIs for their promotion. As a result, various promotional bodies were set up at Centre and the State levels. Among various other promotional bodies, State Industrial Development Corporations were set up in almost all the States and Union Territories.

Accordingly, the Delhi State Industrial Development Corporation was set up in the year 1971.

The DSIDC is a company registered under Section 617 of the Companies Act, 1956, on 15th February, 1971 initially under the name Delhi Small Industries Development Corporation Private Limited with the main objectives of promoting, developing and assisting the small scale industrial uints by providing various services. However, the name of the Company was subsequently changed in 1976, to Delhi State Industrial Development Corporation Limited with a view to bring under its fold such medium and also large industries which depend on high technology, require small space and do not cause any pollution or congestion. All the administrative powers of the DSIDC are vested in the President of India. In pursuance of the objectives of protecting and promoting the interests of the SSIs in the Union Territory of Delhi, the Company has laid down for itself the objectives of development of infrastructure, canalising the procurement and distribution of scarce raw materials, marketing assistance, technical guidance and training to young entrepreneurs, providing display and sales outlets to their finished goods, etc.

The DSIDC was initially set up with an authorised share capital of Rs. 20 lakhs which was considered inadequate and subsequently raised to Rs. 10 crores. The paid up share capital of the DSIDC increased to Rs. 21.86 crores during 1995-96.[2] During the year 1999-2000 the DSIDC achieved a business turnover of Rs. 211.34 crores as compared to a turnover of Rs. 207.86 crores during 1998-99. The profit during 1999-2000 has been Rs. 126.29 lakhs as against Rs. 34.93 lakhs during the previous year[3]. Highlights of the working of the DSIDC are given in Table 6.1. The turnover of DSIDC during the last ten years has been presented in Chart 6.1.

The President of India's nominee, the Lieutenant Governor of Delhi, is delegated with all the administrative powers. The lieutenant Governor of Delhi exercises all the powers on President's behalf in respect of DSIDC. The Lieutenant Governor, therefore, nominates the Director of the Corporation.

Table 6.1
Highlights of the Working of the DSIDC

Turnover	*1997-98*	*1998-99*	*1999-2000*
Income	20,652.95	20,785.71	21,133.78
a) Trading & Misc. Receipt/Income	21,844.80	22,559.64	22,607.61
b) Rent Industrial Estate, CWC & others	61.51	57.76	115.64
	21,906.31	22,617.40	22,718.25
Cost			
a) Operational & supporting Services	21,714.35	22,503.69	22,545.58
b) Interest (*) including 54.64 lacs interest to shed holders	(*)81.87	31.69	7.87
c) Depreciation	31.19	47.09	38.51
Total	21,827.41	22,582.47	22,591.96
Profit/Loss :			
Operational profit	78.90	34.93	126.29
Provision for tax for the year	66.59	4.00	15.00
Net profit after tax	12.31	30.93	111.29
Add (less) prior period adjustment	0.13	– (22.14)	0.59
Net profit after prior period adjustment	12.44	8.79	111.88
Less : proposed dividend	7.50	-	-
Less : Provision for income	1.16	174.10	-
tax prior year Net Profit (loss) after provision for Income Tax for prior year	3.78	(-) 165.31	111.88
Capital Structure			
Share Capital	2,186.23	2,186.23	2,186.23
Loan	935.56	807.78	834.86
Total	3,121.79	2,994.01	3,021.09

Source: Government of National Capital Region of Delhi, *Annual Report 1995-1996*, DSIDC, Delhi State Industrial Development Corporation, New Delhi, 1997, p. 8.

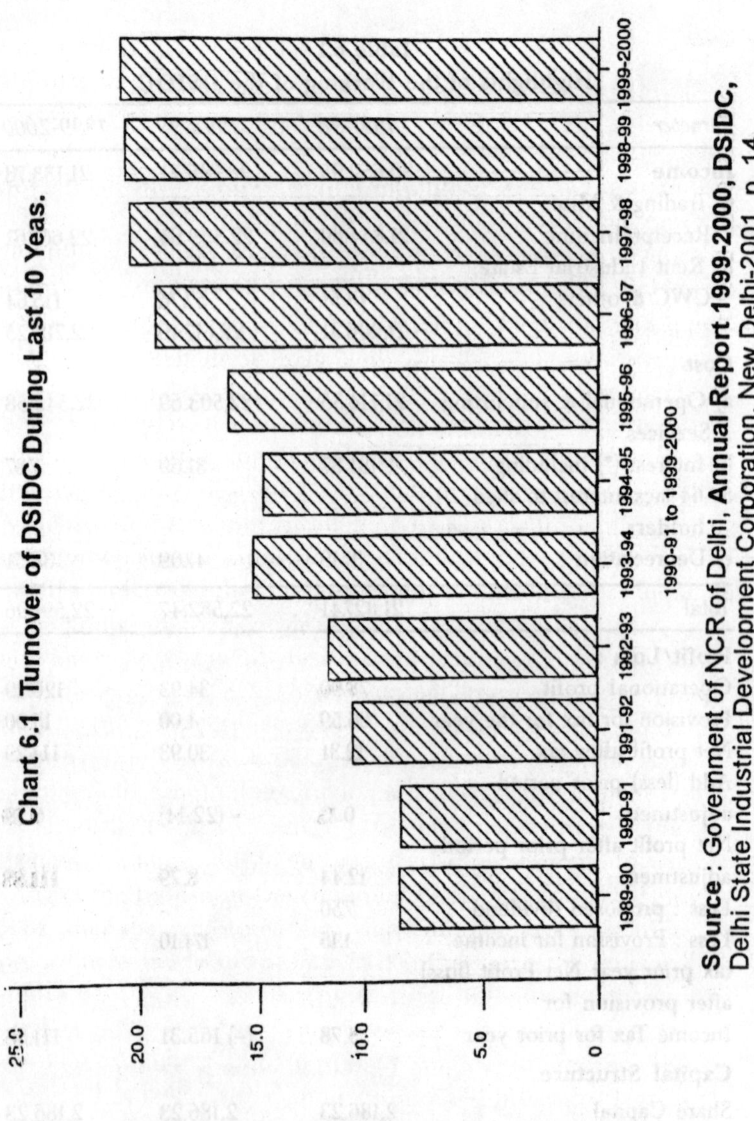

Chart 6.1 : Turnover of DSIDC During Last 10 years.

Objectives of DSIDC

The main objectives of the DSIDC, as set out in the Memorandum of Association, are–industrial development, infrastructure development, promotion of entrepreneurship, marketing assistance to small entrepreneurs, craftsmen and artisans, provide working sheds by establishing Industrial Estates and Community Work Centres (CWC) for the benefit of weaker sections of the society residing in the resettlement colonies, imparting technical and managerial trainings to the entrepreneurs. etc. The Memorandum of Association of DSIDC has laid down for itself an impressive list of eighteen main objectives, thirty-two ancillary or incidental objectives and four other objectives. Some of these objectives are given below :

(i) To aid, counsel, finance, protect and promote the interests of SSIs in the Union Territory of Delhi, whether owned or run by Government, statutory body, company, firm or individuals and to provide them with capital, credit means, resources and technical and managerial assistance for the prosecution of their work and business, to enable them to develop and improve their work methods of manufacture, management and marketing and their technique of production.

(ii) To undertake procurement and distribution of various raw materials, whether imported or indigenous allocated by Government of India to the Department of Industries, Delhi Administration, Delhi, or through canalising agencies like Mettal and Minerals Trading Corporation, State Trading Corporation etc.

(iii) To undertake and provide marketing facilities to the SSIs of Delhi.

(iv) To operate and promote scheme in collaboration with Delhi Administration for the dispersal of the SSIs in a manner conducive to the balanced regional development of the various parts of Delhi.

(v) To establish and maintain trade centres to serve as a clearing house for dissemination of information regarding SSIs.

(vi) To effect co-ordination between large industries and small industries by suitable methods, enabling small industries to manufacture satisfactorily such parts, accessories, ancillaries and components and other articles as may be required by large industries.

(vii) To establish and maintain export house to promote export trade for the benefit of SSIs.

(viii) To promote and operate schemes in collaboration with Delhi Administration for the dispersal of SSIs in a manner conducive to the balanced regional development of the various parts of Delhi.

(xi) To procure capital for or to provide machinery, equipment and other facilities to any company, person and association for the purpose of carrying into effect any objects connected with small industrial development of Delhi.[4]

Thus, we see that the DSIDC has a long list of objectives which it has to fulfil. The DSIDC took up multifarious activities in order to achieve the above mentioned objectives.

Important Activities of DSIDC

In just 26 years, the DSIDC has emerged as the lifeline of SSIs and created an environment which has transformed the city into an industrially advanced centre, becoming a role model for similar corporations in the country. Delhi's SSIs produce goods which have greatly contributed to exports. The city has come to be known for quality products in the fields of garments, electronics, machine tools, engineering items, surgical instruments, etc.

The DSIDC has undertaken a number of important activities in order to achieve the aims and objectives as laid down in the Memorandum of Association of DSIDC. Some of these activities are–Half a million Jobs Programme; Package assistance scheme; community work centres; Narela Industrial Complex; marketing assistance; mini master plan for rural areas; technical consultancy; export; exhibition; etc.

In the initial years the main activity of the DSIDC was -curement and distribution of ferrous and non-ferrous raw materials. After that commenced the marketing activities and exports promotion. Over a period of time new activities such as imports, mining activity and marketing of India Made Foreign Liquor were added to the list of activities of the DSIDC. Thus, the activity profile of DSIDC has kept on changing substantially. The activities of the DSIDC will be discussed in detail in the later part of the chapter.

Organisational Structure of DSIDC

The DSIDC was established by the Delhi Administration. As such, the DSIDC is subject to its policies and controls. The Lieutenant Governor of Delhi, who is the President's nominee, is delegated with all the administrative powers. The other Departments exercising various controls-administrative and financial, are Department of Industry, Directorate of Industries and Department of Finance, Delhi Administration.

Board of Directors

The Lieutenant Governor of Delhi constitutes the Board of Directors by nominating members from various concerned Departments and other organisations. The Board of Directors is constituted so that the aims and objectives laid down in the Articles of Association could be successfully achieved and the various industrial policies of Delhi Administration could be implemented through the DSIDC.

All the Directors are appointed by the President of India. The number of Directors of the Company cannot be more than 9 and less than 2. The number of Directors can be increased only by a General Body Meeting of the Board. The Board of Directors of the DSIDC consists of a Chairman who is a non-offical, Managing Director, two MLA's of the Government of NCT, Delhi, Commissioner Industries, Director of Small Industries Service Institute, Secretary, Finance, Government of NCT, Delhi, Chief Managing Director, Delhi Financial Corporation and Joint Secretary, Ministry of Industry, Government of India. There is no fixed criterion for constituting the Board of Directors. The Directors hold office at the pleasure of their appointing authorities *i.e.* the President or until their office become vacant in terms of the provisions of Section 283 of the Act whichever is earlier and they are not liable to retirement by rotation.[5]

For a long time the Chief Secretary of Delhi used to be the Chairman of the Board. But at present the Chairman is a political appointee. For some time the post of Chairman and the Managing Director was coupled in one person. But the Government once again reverted back to the old pattern *i.e.* the posts of Chairman and the Managing Director was vested in two different persons. In 1984, for the first time, the post of Chairman was made full time. At present, except the Managing Director of the Company, there are no other full time Directors.

The main functions of the Board are to lay down broad outlines of policy, fix targets and watch the results from time to time and monitor the performance and progress of the company. Besides, it also reviews the performance of different Divisions and the activities are so geared that the optimum results are achieved. Any important issues, lacuna in procedures etc. are also discussed and necessary steps are taken to solve them.

Managing Director

The Managing Director of the Corporation is the Chief Executive of the Company. The appointment and choice of the incumbent is limited as the appointing authority is the Delhi Administration and the Cadre Controlling Authority (for Union Territories Cadre) is the Ministry of Home Affairs. The tenure of officers is regulated by the Ministry of Home Affairs and it may so happen that the officer of appropriate seniority and experience may be available for the post of Managing Director of the Corporation but for a short while as he may be due for posting outside Delhi and because of this, the average tenure of the Managing Director has been very low. As a result, Managing Directors keep on changing frequently and in some cases two Managing Directors are changed in a single year.

General Managers

General Managers constitute the second line of management. The General Managers are incharge of various groups of activities which are grouped in divisions. In the beginning there used to be five General Managers and all of them were drawn from Indian Administrative Service. Later on their number was reduced to three and at present there is only one General Manager who is drawn from Delhi, Andaman Nicobar Islands Civil Service. Even for the General Managers there is no fixed tenure.

Divisional Managers

Below the General Manager, there are Divisional Managers. They are ten in number. They are the heads of the various Divisions. There are Deputy Managers and Assistant Managers to assist the Divisional Managers. Their number is not fixed. Down below are Supervisors and Assistants Grade I, Grade II and Grade III. Besides, there are Stenographers and Typists to assist the higher officials.

Finance Officers

Parallel to the General Manager, there is a Financial Adviser who advises the DSIDC on all financial matters. He works as the Controller of Finances. To assist the Financial Adviser, there are five Chief Accounts Officer, Section Officers, Commercial Accounts Officer and Assistant Accounts Officer. The main work of all these officers is to assist the Financial Adviser on all financial matters.

Chief Engineer

There is also one Chief Engineer who looks after the construction of the DSIDC. His post is parallel to the post of the General Manager. Whatever construction takes place by the DSIDC *i.e.* construction of industrial sheds, is to be looked after by the Chief Engineer. His main function is to carry out and monitor the construction work of the DSIDC.

Company Secretary

There is one Company Secretary to look after all the legal matters of the DSIDC. Whenever he speaks in his official capacity, he speaks on the behalf of the entire Company. Thus, he occupies an important place in the DSIDC.

Public Relation Manager

Above all, there is one Public Relation Manager/Officer in the DSIDC. He does all the public dealing and he too, occupies an important place in the DSIDC.

Divisions

After discussing the organisational structure of DSIDC in the preceding pages, we will now have a look at the various Divisions of the DSIDC.

The activities of the DSIDC are grouped into various Divisions. Previously, the Division was headed by a General Manager. But now they are headed by Divisional Managers since there is only one General Manager. The entire organisation has thus been divided into ten Divisions. They are -

(i) Commercial Division;
(ii) Personnel Division;
(iii) Works Division;
(iv) Sale of India Made Foreign Liquor;
(v) Marketing Division;
(vi) Raw Materials Division;
(vii) Accounts/ Finance Division;
(viii) Export Division;
(ix) Relocation Division; and
(x) Vigilance Division.

Thus, we see that the organisational structure of the DSIDC has been changing every now and then depending upon the convenience of the Board and availability of officers in the second level of management. Similarly, we see a change in the classification of Division according to the needs. Previously, there were five Divisions but their number has been doubled keeping in view the various activities of the DSIDC. From organisational structure, we now shift over to the functions of the DSIDC.

Functions of DSIDC

The DSIDC was established with the objectives "to aid, counsel, assist, finance, protect and promote the interests of small industries and small entrepreneurs and to provide them with capital credit, *i.e.*, resources and technical and managerial assistance for the prosecution of this work and business to enable them to develop and improve their methods of manufacture, management, marketing and their techniques of production".[6] Since its inception, the DSIDC has been striving to fulfil these objectives. It has motivated the small manufacturers to produce quality products with a wide acceptability in various markets at home and abroad. It procures and distributes a variety of raw materials among the entrepreneurs and craftsmen. It assumes various marketing functions on behalf of the SSIs and it has also entered the export market and helped the small scale products to compete in the world market. It has also provided working place in the Community Work Centres to the people belonging to the economically backward section of the society. Besides, it also provides valuable services in the field of Industrial Consultancy to small entreprenevrs.

Thus, on the basis of above background, we can classify the functions of the DSIDC into following three categories: (i) Promotional and Developmental functions; (ii) Commercial functions and (iii) Internal Management. These functions has been briefly discussed in the succeeding pages.

Promotional and Development Programme

DSIDC took up number of promotional and development programmes, some of which are discussed below.

Entrepreneur Development Programme

In the early seventies, the Government embarked upon the implementation of a number of schemes to increase and generate employment potential for the educated unemployed persons. Accordingly, DSIDC came forward to supplement the efforts of the Delhi Administration creating necessary environment, apparatus and infrastructure aiming at providing maximum employment opportunities through the small enterprises.

Half a Million Jobs Programme

Funds from Delhi Administration and financial institutions were given to DSIDC under Half a Million Jobs Programme.

Under this scheme, the main function of the DSIDC was to procure land, develop and construct low cost industrial sheds, besides selection of entrepreneurs and allotment of these sheds to the deserving entrepreneurs. Under the above scheme, the DSIDC has during 1974-1977 constructed 840 industrial sheds spread across eight well laid out complexes.[7] Most of them were located in the sprawling industrial areas of Okhla, which is home to many of the small-scale industries units. Other areas which have benefitted from the DSIDC's assistance to small scale units are Jhilmil Tahirpur, Lawrence Road, Rohtak Road and Wazirpur. These sheds were initially given on rental basis and subsequently offered on hire-purchase basis. Since the experience with regard to constructing sheds and renting it was not good, the DSIDC introduced concept of self finalising scheme and under this scheme, the DSIDC made 316 allotment.

The industrial sheds were alloted to those entrepreneurs who had undergone the Entrepreneur Development Training Programme. Under this programme, theoretical as well as practical training was given to the entrepreneurs so that they could acquire knowledge, information and skill necessary to start SSIs. The total period of training was three months *i.e.* one month for theory and two months for practical. Once the entrepreneurs completed the training they were given all assistance to set up units of their choice.

Narela Industrial Complex

The DSIDC has developed Narela Industrial Complex involving development of 250 hectares of land with about 1800 plots of various sizes.[8] Under this scheme complete infrastructural support was given to entrepreneurs and it reduces congestion in the capital as it is an environment friendly estate. This complex has been designed on modern lines and provides the entrepreneurs with commercial space, shopping complex, parking lot, common effluent treatment plants, recycling of waste water, space for warehouses, Delhi Transport Corporation depot, telephone exchange and hospital. The basic idea behind this is to generate gainful employment opportunities to maximum number of people, to accelerate industrial productivity at a greater speed and to act as a beneficial catalyst for a socio-economic transformation. The construction of facility centres providing shops and commercial spaces have already been completed and about 50,000 trees have been planted in the complex. An area of 10 acres covered under the Central park is proposed to be developed as Central Plaza. Of the remaining land available in the estate, 110 acres are being utilised for relocation of industries.

Community Work Centres

During 1975-76, the scheme for the setting up of Community Work Centres in the resettlement colonies was developed by the Delhi Development Authority, for resettling the pavment dwellers in the city area. This work was started with the objective of providing self-employment opportunities in the vicinity of their residences. Most of the residents of these colonies comprise of the weaker sections of the society having the experience of some craft or other, like, handloom weaving, handicraft, knitting and embroidery, carpentary, blacksmithy, leather crafts etc. After their settlement in the said newly developed colonies, these people experienced a lot of difficulties in finding alternative job opportunities. As such, it was considered essential under the 20-Point Programme of the Government of India to help this section of society by way of providing working space in the community work centres with a package of assistance i.e. financial assistance, technical know-how and marketing.

In 1976-77 the DSIDC took up the work and over the years, the DSIDC has provided some 4,000 work spaces to the economically poor sections of the society around their place of residence. The Community Work Centres were constructed under the Grants-in-aid scheme. The entrepreneurs are selected by a Committee consisting of the officers of the DSIDC and directorate of Industries, Delhi Administration. While selecting the entrepreneurs, it is ensured that adequate representatives of the Schedule Caste/Schedule Tribe category, who are the main ingredients under the Special Component Plan of the Government of India, gets the work space. As per the version of the officials, the DSIDC is working satisfactorily on this aspect and has helped many craftsmen to bring subsistence to their homes.

In order to meet the growing need of providing self-employment opportunities to the weaker sections of the society, DSIDC constructed 29 Community Work Centres and other 25 community work centres have been transferred by the Delhi Government. These are located in various parts of resettlement and J. J. colonies all over the NCT of Delhi in which one room workspace is allotted to the individuals belonging to the weaker sections of society to enable them to set up tiny units for self employment and also to provide employment to his/her family members. There are 54 Community Work Centres in which about 4,000 workspaces are available.

Industrial Development Programme

This unit was created under the Industries Division (started in 1983) primarily to help the existing industrial units to undertake the expansion, diversification and modernisation programme for those units which are at the verge of sickness. The main purpose of this programme was to prevent industrial sickness. This unit also looks after the rehabilitation of those sick units which can be revived by marginal requirements of finance, technology and proper choice of items, etc.

Quality Control Marketing

Testing laboratories are a crucial must for industries once the products begin to roll out. As such, the DSIDC maintains two laboratories at Okhla and Wazirpur for testing electrical, mechanical and metallurgical items produced by SSIs of Delhi. As per the version of the DSIDC officials these well-equipped laboratories are manned by highly technical and qualified personnel. The samples for testing are collected from the door steps of the small scale units at no extra cost. The costs of testing here are unbelievably low.

Package Assistance Scheme

It was one of the most outstanding initiated and implemented by the DSIDC towards entrepreneural development programme. Under this scheme, the educated unemployed entrepreneurs particularly engineering graduates, diploma holders, non-resident Indians willing to set up small scale units in Delhi are selected and given training in carefully selected trades. They are provided industrial sheds and supplied necessary machinery and equipment, capital and raw material. Besides, they are assisted in marketing their products through emporia and trade centres. The entrepreneurs were selected after due testing of their capabilities and aptitudes. The persons so selected had to undergo the Entrepreneural Development Training Programme especially designed to instil in them skills of industrial management such as marketing, advertisement, maintenance of accounts and account books, planning and control, work study and legal aspects of small industries. During the training period the entrepreneurs were required to prepare detailed individual project reports. Once the entrepreneurs complete the training, the DSIDC gives them industrial shed ready with all infrastructural facilities and provision of essential raw material and equipment. During setting up the units, they are given technical guidance. Marketing of the products produced in these units is done either by the DSIDC through its own agencies or they guide the entrepreneurs about the marketability of the products.

Mini Master Plan for Rural Areas

Under the mini master plan for development of rural Delhi, the DSIDC was allotted construction work for multi purpose community centre. The centres provide for institutional areas, commercial areas, residential infrastructure and pleasure facilities.

Consultancy Services

Besides providing plots and sheds to the entrepreneurs, the DSIDC also provides consultancy services. For this, a Technical Consultancy Organisation (TCO) has been established since 1987. The TCO recognises the need for guidance in setting up industries–a crucial input that can often make a vital difference between the success or failure of a new venture. It helps the entrepreneurs in identifying projects, undertaking techno-economic appraisal of projects and market research and survey. It prepares techno-economic feasibility reports and offers technical guidance for upgradation of technology, diversification and expansion of existing units.

A compendium of information and guidance entitled as "DSIDC Industrial Portfolio" has been compiled and published by the Industries Division for the guidance of the entrepreneurs as well as running industrial units. The Division is also providing counsel for preparation of the project profiles to the entrepreneurs who approach for help. The Division has also prepared a Directory of existing industrial units in Delhi giving details of items, production capacity, name and address of the manufacturing unit etc.

Besides, the DSIDC has a one-stop information shop known as the Centre for Industry information. This provides information support to industries and entrepreneurs on process and product technology, emerging technologies, raw material inputs and market opportunities.

Apart from the above mentioned functions in the promotional and development programmes category, there are some other functions in this category like providing machinery on hire-purchase basis, margin money for working capital, promotion of indigenous technology, setting up joint sector projects, etc.

Commercial Functions

The commercial functions of the DSIDC are discussed below.

Sale of India Made Foreign Liquor

In 1979-80, the sale of India Made Foreign Liquor was handed over to the DSIDC with the objective of making quality liquor available to the customers and prevent the sale of spurious liquor by the private vendors. This activity being a profitable one, was taken over by the DSIDC so that its weakening financial position could be strengthened. DSIDC was the first public sector organisation to take up the activity of trading in India Made

Foreign Liquor in Delhi. The rates of liquor are fixed by Delhi Administration. At present DSIDC runs over 78 retail outlets in Delhi to sell Indian Liquor.[9] This is done primarily to generate revenue to support the Corporation's development activities. Today, this activity is generating much of the company's profits to enable it to supplement inputs for industrial development. During 1999-2000 turnover of this activity was to the tune of Rs. 20,834.07 lakhs as against Rs. 20,545.01 lakhs during 1998-1999.

During the last ten years, the DSIDC has been instrumental in arranging overseas assignments to trained manpower, like Doctors, Engineers, Para-medical personnels etc.

Procurement and Distribution of Raw Material

A variety of raw materials is procured and distributed among the entrepreneurs and craftsmen by the DSIDC. The Corporation has been dealing with the both ferrous–iron and steel, and non-ferrous raw materials like coal, Poly Vinyl Chloride resin and powder, chemicals, zinc etc. The items are both imported and indigenous and are procured from Steel Authority of India, Tata Iron and Steel Company and State Trading Corporation. The raw materials are stored in the main depot and sub-depots located in Okhla Industrial Estate and distributed from there. The distribution is done on the basis of the individual entrepreneurs capacity reports, his past off-take records, his present requirement and availability of stocks. The procurement and distribution of raw materials is one of the major commercial activities of the DSIDC.

Marketing Assistance to the Small Scale Units

Marketing is a very vital aspect for the growth of SSIs. The DSIDC has been performing various marketing functions on behalf of the SSIs since 1973, recognising it as a major problem faced by the small units. The company has a scheme of providing marketing assistance to the industry by registering the interested units as Business Associates. Under this scheme, they undertake contract marketing on behalf of the industrial units with various government departments and agencies.

The products which are retailed in the local and domestic

markets, are provided support facilities for tendering by the DSIDC. It obtains information, files tenders, submits quotations, deposits earnest money and provides necessary security. It also endeavours to secure price preference to small scale industrial units from the buying organisations. In many cases the security money is waived. It secures bulk orders from government departments.

DSIDC's performance, with regard to marketing, in the past has been very well and the Corporation is making vigorous efforts to raise the marketing activity by enlisting more small scale suppliers, exploring other areas of supply, other items of requirement and approaching large and medium industries for obtaining supply order for ancillary items. The items which have been marketed in big quantity are–group cables, rubber hosepipe and garden equipments, steel furniture and school furniture, handloom curtains and floorings, etc. In addition, the DSIDC has also been executing large orders for printing of books, etc. DSIDC's efforts are giving a boost to the small scale entrepreneurs in regard to marketing and also eliminating the middle men.

Delhi State Emporium and Trade Centre

The name of the Delhi State Emporium is 'BHARATI' which is located on Baba Kharak Singh Marg and has been running since 1973. Besides the traditional handlooms and handicrafts, it displays latest in furniture, pottery, leather goods, jewellery and other such products manufactured by the small scale units. The items which are brought by the manufacturer on a consignment basis are displayed for sale. The sale proceeds of the sold items are handed over to the small scale entrepreneurs after deducting 25 per-cent service and handling charges, which are included in the cost of the items at the time of fixation of the price. The turnover of the emporium was to the tune of Rs. 149.74 lakhs during 1999-2000 as against the turnover of Rs. 143.06 lakhs during the year 1998-99.

The Trade Centre is also located in the Emporium Building itself. It serves as a centre for dissemination of information regarding products of SSIs and to book orders from prospective indigenous and foreign customers. Those suppliers who are willing, display their products and also depute their sales representatives to book the orders.

A permanent pavilion at the Pragati Maidan has been constructed by the DSIDC where the Trade Fair Authority of India holds industrial fairs on national and international levels. It acts as a show window to the industry of Delhi both during international fairs and by way of special exhibitions organised periodically. Exhibitions are also organised in different parts of Delhi to enable the small entrepreneurs to exhibit and sell their products. The interested customers choose the items of their liking and place supply orders. Handloom weavers are given an opportunity to sell their products at different places in the country by the DSIDC's participation in exhibitions nationwide. DSIDC has been organising 'Delhi Trade Fair' as an 'annual fair' since 1996.

During the past few years Exhibition Division has been participating in exhibitions abroad to provide international marketing exposure to small artisans, handicraftsmen, small scale industrial units, etc.

Export Promotion

Delhi has a very good export potential. Being the National Capital, it is frequented by a large number of overseas tourists and other visitors. Therefore, the DSIDC has taken greater interest in export of the local small scale products. With the help of Trade Centre, the promotion of overseas marketing is done. The DSIDC negotiates export deals with the foreign visitors as per their requirements and selection of items and with others on the basis of the requirements collected by the Foreign Marketing Intelligence Agencies. Various exporters have been listed in the Export Directories and Marketing Division of DSIDC's register of the Business Associates giving details of the products manufactured by them. The orders procured by DSIDC are passed on to the suitable and willing suppliers for execution. The items which are marketed/exported by the DSIDC include light engineering goods like bicycles and components, electrical appliances, electronic goods, textiles, hosiery, woollens, readymade garments, leather goods, sports goods, handloom material, handicrafts and jewellery, etc.

Deposit Works

The Delhi Government and other Government agencies, from time to time, assign various deposit works which are undertaken by the DSIDC. The DSIDC has emerged as an important constructive arm of the administration. The DSIDC has executed series of projects under the mini master plan of Rural Development of Delhi Government It has already completed a number of important projects. The other ongoing project include up-gradation of various DTC Depots, Udyog Sadan building at Patparganj, Labour Welfare Centre at Hari Nagar, Cultural Centre for the Sahitya Kala Parishad at Janak Puri, etc. Work of 70 unauthorised colonies have also been entrusted to the corporation for development works on behalf of the Urban Development Department of Delhi Government and the same are ongoing.

Other Facilities Provided by DSIDC

(a) DSIDC through its TCO helps the entrepreneurs to identify the project, preface project reports, prepare feasibility reports and gives technical advice to the entrepreneurs/prospective entrepreneurs.

(b) DSIDC through its laboratories helps the entrepreneurs to control their quality of products by testing their products at very nominal rates.

(c) DSIDC also provides facilities for holding seminars, conferences, meetings etc. by the small entrepreneurs who cannot afford this facility in their own establishments.

Thus, we see that DSIDC performs a number of commercial functions. The marketing promotion activity of the DSIDC is more of a promotional activity rather than commercial. Since the nature of activity is commercial, it has been discussed under the heading commercial functions.

The Internal Management

After discussing the promotional and development functions and commercial functions, we now switch over to the Internal Management function. Under this heading we have discussed three activities viz. (i) the personnel management, (ii) financial management, and (iii) management information system.

The Personnel Management

The basic requirement for efficient working of any organisation is to select the right people for right type of jobs. They should be trained in such a way that they take care of their work with full devotion and dedication and with a sense of belonging. They should be given responsibility supplemented by due authority *i.e.* powers should be delegated to them. The employees should be encouraged for their participation in decision making by considering their suggestions. If their suggestions are accepted, they should be appreciated for their opinions and if their suggestions are rejected, adequate reasons should be given for rejection.

In so far as the DSIDC is concerned, most of these aspects have been given inadequate attention. According of the officials of the DSIDC no personnel policy has been laid out. As a result, the personnel functions, such as recruitments, trainings, promotions and performance appraisals etc. are being dealt in an *ad-hoc* manner. Recruitment rules are there but they have not been amended in conformity with the changing job requirements. Even though Staff Selection Committees/Departmental Promotion Committees exist many people are appointed on recommendations ignoring the proper selection procedure.

Since there is no sound personnel policy, the strength of the staff of the DSIDC keeps on increasing. The work–load has reduced substantially and as such the huge work–force has become a surplus manpower with little productive work. Due to this a good number of employees, particularly at the lower and middle levels, feels stuck up and thinks as if some sort of halt has come in their career. The persons are shifted from one Division to another and asked to deal with entirely different work. As a result, development of expertise and professionalism in a particular sphere, gets adversely affected. This has also resulted in lack of cadre formation and ultimately in adverse promotion prospects and above all lack of accountability for lapses.

Financial Management

In any company, the second major support activity after manpower is the finances. A major function of financial management is efficient deployment of funds. It should be done in such a way that it regenerates itself.

The DSIDC is not a manufacturing undertaking. As such, large profits cannot be expected from its working. But its financial policy should be so designed that it may generate enough resources for its sustenance. Since the Corporation has expanded its activities, it could not consolidate them and sudden expansion resulted in heavy losses during the years 1976-77 and 1977-78. There are Bank loans overdue and the Corporations funds are locked up in various recoveries on account of certain past commercial deals. Recently, the Comptroller and Auditor General of India has detected serious lapses in the functioning of the DSIDC.

The statutory auditors in their special reports have found that fixed asset registers have not been properly maintained and quantitative details have not been properly accounted. There is no reconciliation in respect of bank loans taken earlier by the Corporation and the periodical system of trial balance is not operative. The auditors further found that the delegation of financial powers are generally not adhered to. The Corporation has no system of monitoring timely recovery of outstanding dues.[10]

The report submitted by the senior audit officer in the month of January 1998, has listed 13 cases of irregularities. Among them the most objectionable is the fact that the final accounts of the balance-sheets for the year 1996-97 signed by a person as the finance adviser was misleading thus raising the question of authencity of the final accounts. The person concerned is actually not the finance advisor.[11] Thus, it is evident that the DSIDC is passing through a bad financial phase.

Management Information System

For a management to be effective, it is a must that there should be proper information system. The activities of the DSIDC are spread over a large number of spheres with diverse operations. As such, it is not possible for the Head Office to know and control the day-to-day operational matters. Thus, it becomes necessary that a system should work to keep track of the activities of each Division for the purpose of taking necessary decisions for achieving the overall objectives of the company. The Management Information System in the DSIDC is in the form of a reporting system which demands feeding most of the data from various Divisions and units to the Head Office. The purpose of the reporting system has not been clearly defined and most functionaries get these reports for knowing as to what is happening in different Divisions. The information from various Divisions is not received in time especially in matters of accounts. Even the information about different categories of staff, their composition SC/ST and others has not been made available. In past many things have gone wrong because timely information was not furnished to top management and mid term corrections could not be applied. Thus, we see that the DSIDC has a proper Management Information System but the desired benefits are not being achieved.

Conclusion

The DSIDC has been stimulating industrial growth in Delhi ever since its inception in February 1971. It has aided, counselled, assisted, financed, projected and promoted the interests of SSIs located in the metropolitan city of Delhi.

With an aim of providing greater employment opportunities to the people of the capital, DSIDC has undertaken and successfully completed developmental activities like construction of industrial sheds in various industrial complexes, setting up of community work centres in resettlement and J.J. Colonies and construction of industrial sheds on self financing basis. In pursuance of the objectives of protecting and promoting the interests of the SSIs in the Union Territory of Delhi, the Company has laid down for itself the objectives of development of infrastructure, canalising the procurement and distribution of scarce raw materials, marketing assistance, technical guidance and training to young entrepreneurs, providing display and sales outlets to their finished goods, etc.

With regard to objectives, it can be said that the Memorandum of Association of the DSIDC had laid down for itself an impressive list of eighteen main objectives, thirty-two ancillary or incidental objectives and four other objectives. The most important among the above list of objectives is to aid, counsel, finance, protect and promote the interests of SSIs in the Union Territory of Delhi, whether owned or run by Government, statutory body, company, firm or individuals and to provide them with capital, credit means, resources and technical and managerial assistance from the prosecution of their work and business, to enable them to develop and improve their work methods of manufacture, management and marketing and their technique of production.

The DSIDC has undertaken a number of important activities in order to achieve the aims and objectives as laid down in the Memoran-dum of Association of the DSIDC. Some of these activities are–half a million jobs programme, procurement and distribution of raw materials, package assistance scheme, marketing assistance, technical consultancy, export promotion, etc. Over the years, new activities such as imports, mining activity and marketing of India Made Foreign Liquor were taken over by the DSIDC.

So far as the organisational structure of the DSIDC is concerned, we see that the Lieutenant Governor of Delhi, who is the President's nominee, has been delegated with all the administrative powers. There is a Board of Directors constituted by the Lieutenant Governor of Delhi. All the Directors of the Board are appointed by the President of India. There is also a Chairman, who is a political appointee. The Managing Director is the Chief Executive of the **DSIDC.** General Manager constitute the second line of management. Below the General Manager, there are ten Divisional Managers who are assisted by Deputy Managers and Assistant Managers.

The various functions of the DSIDC are (i) promotional and

developmental functions including entrepreneural development programme, community work centres, consultancy services, etc., (ii) commercial functions which includes Sale of India Made Foreign Liquor, marketing, export, procuring and distributing raw materials, etc. and (iii) finally, internal management which includes personnel management, financial management and management information system.

The DSIDC is proposing to provide support to entrepreneurs for IT related services for E-Commerce, for E-Governance, marketing estate for computers hardware and software development and other IT related infrastructure, to keep pace with the changing needs of the industrial sector. DSIDC has also set up its own Cyber Cafe at H.Q. Building at Connaught Circus New Delhi and allowing the entrepreneurs to set up their own cyber cafe under its Franchise Scheme.

From the foregoing discussion, it is evident that in the phenomenal growth of small scale units in Delhi, the DSIDC, since its inception, has played a significant role, though not easily quantifiable. DSIDC had a purpose which it did strive to fulfil though the economics involved in the process has not been encouraging. Failures are only a stepping stone to success and the DSIDC will have to strive harder in future, to live up to the expectation of all concerned.

Endnotes

1. Government of National Capital Region of Delhi, *Industrial Profile of Delhi,* Delhi State Industrial Development Corporation, New Delhi, 1997, p.2.
2. Government of National Capital Region of Delhi, *Annual Report 1995-96 DSIDC,* Delhi State Industrial Development Corporation, New Delhi, 1997, p. 8.
3. Government of NCR of Delhi, *Annual Report 1999-2000 DSIDC,* Delhi State Industrial Development Corporation, New Delhi, 2001, p. 13.
4. *Memorandum of Association and Articles of Association of Delhi State Industrial Development Corporation Limited,* New Delhi, 1976, pp. 1-6.
5. Ibid. p. 14

6. Government of National Capital Region of Delhi, Industrial Profile of Delhi, *op.cit.*, p. 1.
7. Government of National Capital Region of Delhi, Annual Report 1995-96, DSIDC, *op. cit.*, p. 10.
8. DSIDC - *A Changing Profile (Pamphlet)*, Delhi State Industrial Development Corporation New Delhi.
9. Annual Report 1999-2000 DSIDC, *op.cit.*, p. 17.
10. Das, Arun Kumar, "CAG Pulls up DSIDC for Gross Irregularities", in *The Times of India (Delhi Times)*, New Delhi, April 9, 1998, p. 1.
11. Ibid.

7

Perception of The Entrepreneurs Regarding The Functioning of the DSIDC

In the present chapter, an attempt has been made to evaluate the perception and awareness of the entreprenuers with regard to the functioning of the DSIDC. We have also tried to assess the entrepreneurs' response towards the different facilities being provided by the DSIDC. Besides, we have also examined the views of the entrepreneurs on the changes being introduced in the arena of Small Scale Industries (SSIs).

Selection of Entrepreneurs

The entrepreneurs were chosen on the basis of random sampling. As regards the sample size, we chose 120 entrepreneurs from different trades like–steel rolling, toy making, furniture works, leather works, garments, etc. The entrepreneurs belonged to three different industrial areas of Delhi *viz.* Okhla Industrial Area, Wazirpur Industrial Area and Anand Parbat Industrial Area. Out of the 120 entrepreneurs, 60 entrepreneurs belonged to Okhla Industrial Area, 40 to Wazirpur Industrial Area and 20 to Anand Parbat Industrial Area. (Chart 7.1).

Educational Background

After knowing the detailed background of the respondents, the first information which we collected from them were basically of general nature relating to their educational qualification, experience, training etc. It was found that around seventy-five per cent of the respondents were graduate and out of this around forty per cent had technical degree. Only twenty-five per cent of the respondents had education upto secondary level or college level. So far as training is concerned, nearly thirty-two per cent of the respondents had got training in the field of entrepreneurial development. Out of the thirty-two per cent respondents, nearly twenty-two per cent were having Industrial Training Institute degree and the remaining ten per cent were having diploma from various polytechnics. With regard to experience, we found that nearly fifty-eight per cent of the respondents had experience

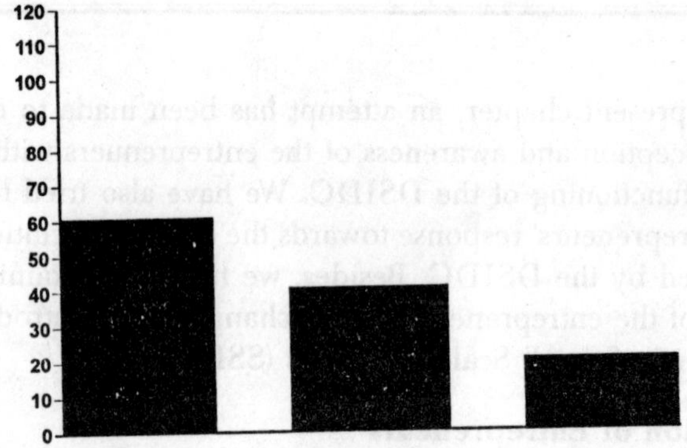

Chart 7.1

before setting up the unit. When we asked them why they started the unit, they gave a number of reasons. Some of them said that since they did not get any job, they had to start their own unit. While others stated that it was their family work *i.e.*the unit was started by their fathers/brothers etc., and they had to continue the unit. There were some others who opined that by setting up the unit, they could get self-employment and there was better prospect in this work. Finally, there was one another group which was of the view that since they had past experience and knowledge in the field of entrepreneurial development, as they were working with some other group; that's why they thought of starting their own unit instead of working for others. In short, the main reasons for starting the unit were–past experience, better prospect, self-employment and family work/business.

Problems of Registration

After getting the general information, we switched to certain queries which were related to SSIs and the DSIDC. First among this was whether their unit was registered as SSIs unit. In response to our query nearly 77.5 per cent of the entrepreneurs gave a positive reply. Only 22.5 per cent of the entrepreneurs gave a negative reply (Table 7.1). When we asked them whether they faced any problems while getting their units registered, nearly 42 per cent of the respondents replied in affirmative. We further asked them to specify the problems which they faced while getting their units registered. Most of them complained of procedural delay, unnecessary harassment, complicated registration procedure and in some cases bribery. The problem of registration is rarely faced by those entrepreneurs, who have personal contact.

Table 7.1
Whether the unit was registered as Small Scale Industries Unit?

	N	*Percentage*
Yes	93	77.5%
No	27	22.5%
Total	120	100

Government's Policy Toward SSIs

On being asked whether they were aware about the policy of the Government towards the SSIs, it was heartening to note that approximately 85.8 per cent of the respondents gave a positive reply (Table 7.2). We further asked them to give their opinion about the SSI policy of Government of India. Most of the respondents put a question mark on the Government of India's policy towards the SSIs. They were of the view that the policy is good on paper rather than in practice. They viewed that the policies were meant for the big entrepreneurs. They have welcomed the announcement made by the Prime Minister, Shri Atal Behari Vajpayee, to reduce the investment limit for SSIs from present Rs. 3 crores to 1 crore. They said that this will really benefit the small entrepreneurs. At present the big industrial houses possess four or five small units in different names and enjoy the benefits of SSIs. Whereas, the actual small entrepreneurs are the sufferers.

Table 7.2
Awareness about the policy of the Government towards Small Scale Industries

	N	*Percentage*
Yes	103	85.8%
No	17	14.2%
Total	120	100

Institutions Promoting SSIs

With regard to the knowledge about the institutions/ organisations promoting the SSIs, almost 77.5 per cent respondents said that they had the knowledge of these institutions (Table 7.3). We further asked them to specify the various institutions promoting SSIs. The entrepreneurs mentioned the names of following organisations/institutions–Delhi State Industrial Development Corporation, Delhi Financial Corporation, Directorate of Industries, National Small Industries Corporation, Small Industry Service Institute and National Institute of Entrepreneurship and Small Business Development. However, they made only a passing reference of these organisations and most of them showed their ignorance about the details of functioning of these organisations. On being asked, which out of these organisations, were the best ones so far as their performance was concerned, they did not provide the details of their activities, except the reply that both the SISI and Directorate of Industries are performing well in their stipulated areas of activity.

Table 7.3

Knowledge about Institutions/Organisations promoting Small Scale Industries

	N	*Percentage*
Yes	93	77.5
No	27	22.5%
Total	120	100

Activities of the DSIDC

After assessing their perception towards the various organisations promoting SSIs, we turned our attention towards the various activities of the DSIDC and wanted to know from our respondents as to whether they were aware of the various activities of the DSIDC. It was good to note that nearly 75.8 per cent of the respondents were aware of the various activities of the DSIDC (Table 7.4). In response to our query about the activities of the DSIDC, they replied that the main activities of the DSIDC are the following–procurement and distribution of raw material; construction of industrial estates; infrastructure facilities; marketing facilities; export promotion; etc.

Table 7.4

Knowledge about the varicus activities of the DSIDC

	N	*Percentage*
Yes	91	75.8
No	29	24.2%
Total	120	100

Financial Position

Loan and credit facilities are vital to the development of industries in a developing country like ours where per capita income is very low in comparison to other developed countries. As such, our next query from the sample respondents was whether they received any financial assistance in the form of loan/subsidy from the financial institutions/banks at the time of setting up the unit. And if financial assistance was available, which agencies provided them the loans and whether they faced any difficulty in obtaining the loans. In their reply they reported that although on paper loans and credit facilities were available to the entrepreneurs, but in practice too many difficulties came in their way. Nearly 36.7 per cent respondents have obtained the loans (Table 7.5). Most of them replied that they took loans from DFC and SISI and some others said that they took loans from nationalised banks. They pointed out that the DFC and SISI provided loan on reasonable rates but some approach was required. If the entrepreneur had some link with the authorities of such organisations, they could get the financial assistance quite easily and within no time. With regard to problems faced in obtaining the loan, they mentioned-that there were number of problems. Some of them were– the problem of guarantor; unnecessary harassment and delay, lots of paper work i.e. the procedure of sanctioning loan was very cumbersome and difficult one; in some of the cases the respondents had to pay money to the officials to get their loan sanctioned. They further pointed out that those entrepreneurs who have no links suffer badly and after spending some money and moving from pillar to post they get their project cleared and money released after a long time.

Table 7.5

Whether received any financial assistance in the form of loan/subsidy from financial institutions/banks at the time of setting up the unit?

	N	*Percentage*
Yes	44	36.7%
No	76	63.3
Total	120	100

Problem Related to Raw Materials

Another important and essential aspect of industrial development is the availability of raw materials on controlled rate prices and also in sufficient quantity. As such we wanted to know from our respondents where did they get the raw materials for the project. In response to this, nearly 66.7 per cent (Table 7.6 and Chart 7.2) of the respondents said that they get the raw materials from the local market. Another set of entrepreneurs nearly 25.0 per cent said that they get the raw materials from outside the State but within the country. Only a small percentage of entrepreneurs (8.3) were getting raw materials from outside the country. With regard to the difficulty faced in procuring the raw materials, it was heartening to note that nearly 73.3 per cent (Table 7.7) of respondents did not face any difficulty in procuring the raw materials. Only a small percentage (26.7) of the entrepreneurs faced problems in procuring the raw materials. Some of the problems faced by them were– (i) there is wide variation in the rates; (ii) in certain cases, there was monopoly business of raw materials and the entrepreneurs had to pay very high price for the raw material. Consequently the production cost of their finished goods was very high; (iii) not getting the raw materials in time; (iv) non-availability of the raw material in sufficient quantity; (v) quality is not upto the desired standard; (vi) advance payment is called upon; etc. Those who did not face any problem in getting the raw material were those who had good personal contacts in the market, because of which they got the raw materials easily and in time.

Table 7.6

From where do you get raw materials for the project?

	N	*Percentage*
Yes	80	66.7%
Outside the State but within the country	30	25.0%
Outside the country	10	8.3%
Total	120	100

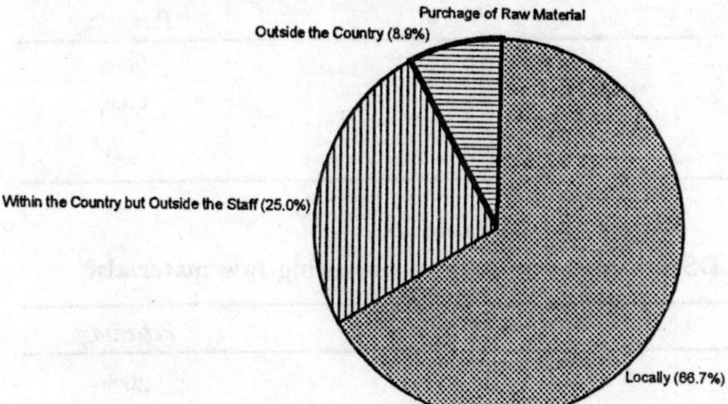

Chart 7.2

Table 7.7
Did you find difficulty in procuring raw material?

	N	*Percentage*
Yes	32	26.7%
No	88	73.3%
Total	120	100

Our immediate query was whether Government provided any help in importing the raw materials? It was disheartening to note that few sample respondents replied to this query in positive terms (Table 7.8). Those who (20 per cent) replied in positive said that Government was helping them in importing the raw materials by way of issuing essentiality certificates for issue of import licences. We further asked them whether the DSIDC was giving any help in procuring raw materials. Once again it was noticed that very few respondents replied to this query positively (Table 7.9). Only 20 per cent of the respondents said that the DSIDC was helping them in procuring raw materials. On being asked in what form, they replied that the DSIDC was providing some excise concessions and providing raw materials at concessional rates/controlled rate prices. Those who gave a negative response (nearly 80 per cent) said that the DSIDC was helping only those entrepreneurs who were known to them.

Table 7.8
Does Government help in importing raw materials?

	N	*Percentage*
Yes	24	20%
No	96	80%
Total	120	100

Table 7.9
Does DSIDC give any help in procuring raw materials?

	N	*Percentage*
Yes	24	20%
No	96	80%
Total	120	100

Problem of Market Exploration

Marketing is vital for the growth of the industrial units. No industry, small or big, can hope to succeed unless it is able to market its goods in the right manner to catch the eye of the consumer spread throughout a country. We put forward our first question, where they market their products? The response was that nearly 62.5 per cent of the respondents were marketing their products in the local market; 25.8 per cent outside the State but within the country; and very few (11.7 per cent) were marketing outside the country (Table 7.10 and Chart 7.3). Our next query with regard to marketing was whether they faced any difficulty in marketing their products. In response to this query, it was disheartening to note that approximately 74.2 per cent of the respondents were facing difficulty with regard to marketing and only 25.8 per cent of the respondents were having no marketing problems (Table 7.11). We further asked them to mention the various difficulties they face with regard to marketing. The problems faced by them were–

- (i) due to long distances, there is communication gap;
- (ii) middle men also create lots of problems *i.e.* they do all mischief by keeping the entrepreneurs in dark about the exact rate of the goods;
- (iii) heavy rate of transportation is there;
- (iv) since the tax rate is higher, so most of the entrepreneurs follow the third option *i.e.* bypassing the tax laws;
- (v) credit problem–credit period is 45 days;
- (vi) long gestation period; etc.

Our final query with regard to marketing was whether the DSIDC provides any marketing assistance. And if yes, in what form. Once again we got a similar reply as compared to raw materials. In response to our query, around 77.5 per cent of the respondents replied negatively and only 22.5 per cent of the respondents gave a positive reply (Table 7.12). They further pointed out that the DSIDC helps the entrepreneurs in marketing by securing bulk orders from government departments and marketing their products through trade centres and the Delhi Emporium.

Table 7.10

Where do you market your product?

	N	*Percentage*
Locally	75	62.5.
Outside the State but within the country	31	25.8%
Outside the country	14	11.7%
Total	120	100

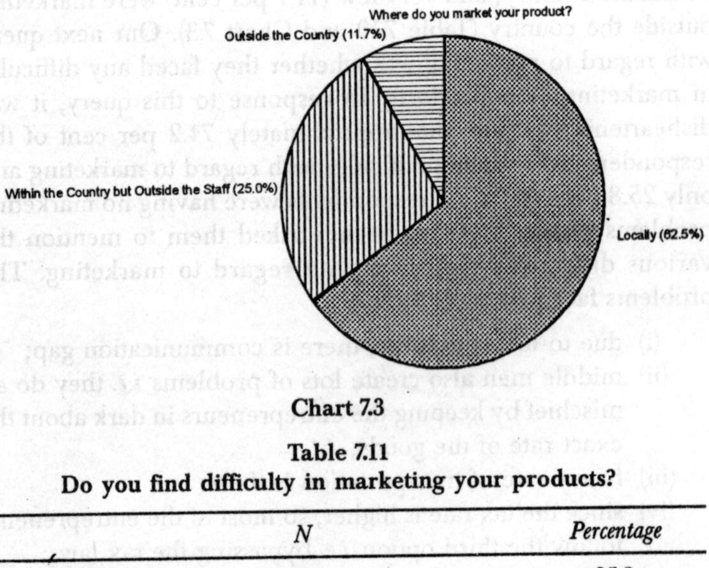

Chart 7.3

Table 7.11

Do you find difficulty in marketing your products?

	N	*Percentage*
Yes	31	25.8
No	89	74.2%
Total	120	100

Table 7.12

Does DSIDC provide any marketing assistance?

	N	*Percentage*
Yes	27	22.5%
No	93	77.5%
Total	120	100

Exporting Goods

Closely connected to marketing is exports. So we wanted to know from the sample respondents whether they were facing any problem with regard to exporting and whether the DSIDC was providing any export facilities. In response to our first query i.e. whether the respondents were facing any problem with regard to exporting, nearly 11.7 per cent (Table 7.13) of the respondents replied positively. The remaining respondents i.e. 88.3 per cent did not respond to our query because they were not exporting their products. When we asked them to mention the problems they face while exporting, they replied that due to political upheaval (like disintegration of USSR and communist block, etc.) their money gets blocked. Generally, the benefits available to entrepreneurs as exporters enjoyed by big entrepreneurs rather than small entrepreneurs. Another problem which they face is that suppose they get an order today and the goods are supplied after four-five months, and if in between the price escalates, then we have to supply our products at the old price. With regard to the DSIDC providing any help in exporting their products, nearly 9.2 per cent (Table 7.14) of the respondents gave a positive

Table 7.13

Do you face any problem while exporting?

	N	*Percentage*
Yes	14	11.7%
No	106	88.3%
Total	120	100

Table 7.14

Does DSIDC provide any help in exporting your products?

	N	*Percentage*
Yes	11	9.2%
No	109	90.8%
Total	120	100

reply. They further said that the facilities provided by the DSIDC in regard to export are that they display those items which have export potential in the emporiums and various exhibitions within and outside the country in trade-fairs where the customers from other countries place supply orders for their requirements.

Purchase of Machinery

On being asked whether they had purchased their machinery on hire-purchase, 68.3 per cent of the sample respondents responded negatively (Table 7.15). The reason behind this was that the entrepreneurs had sufficient money to purchase the machinery. Secondly, most of the entrepreneurs were not aware of this facility. Thirdly, the entrepreneurs were not sure as to whether the hired machinery is good or not. Finally, because of high rate of interest. The remaining respondents *i.e.* 31.7 per cent gave a positive reply. They were of the view that they purchased the machinery on hire-purchase because they did not have sufficient money. Secondly, the payment system is easy *i.e.* the entrepreneurs do not have to pay all the money at one time. They could buy the high priced machinery by depositing a small amount initially and later on one can make the full payment. We further asked them which institution helped them in getting the machinery on hire-purchase. They responded that NSIC had helped them in getting the machinery on hire-purchase. With regard to problems faced in getting the machinery on hire purchase, they responded that they did not face much problem except for providing guarantors.

Table 7.15
Did you purchase your machinery on hire-purchase?

	N	*Percentage*
Yes	38	31.7
No	82	68.3
Total	120	100

Functioning of Technical Consultancy Organisation

The DSIDC's Technical Consultancy Organisation drew our immediate attention. On being asked whether they were aware about the DSIDC's Technical Consultancy Organisation, 37.5 per cent of the respondents responded positively, 30.0 per cent negatively and remaining 32.5 per cent did not respond to our query (Table 7.16 and Chart 7.4). On being asked what did they think about its functioning? They responded that they were not much satisfied about its functioning. They further said that the Technical Consultancy Organisation guides the entrepreneurs in identifying projects, undertaking techno-economic appraisal of projects and market research and survey. On being asked whether they received any help from the DSIDC's Technical Consultancy Organisation, only 15 per cent of the respondents responded positively, 52.5 per cent negatively and 32.5 per cent respondents did not respond to our query (Table 7.17). They further pointed out that the help received from Technical Consultancy Organisation was in the form of guidance in setting up new industries, in identifying the projects and technical guidance for upgradation of technology and expansion of existing units.

Table 7.16
Knowledge about DSIDC's Technical Consultancy Organisation

	N	*Percentage*
Yes	45	37.5%
No	36	30.0
No response	39	32.5%
Total	120	100

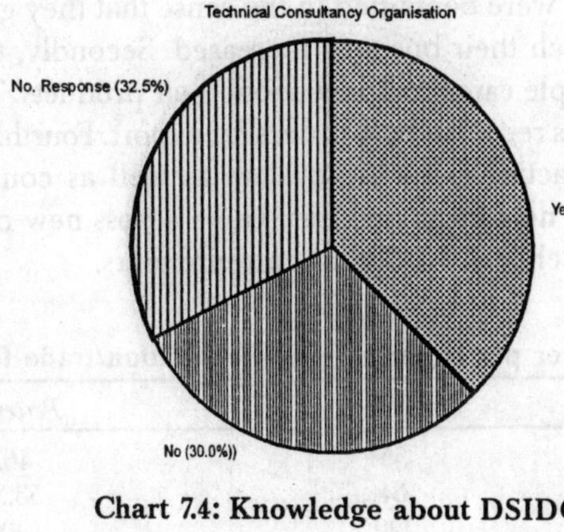

Chart 7.4: Knowledge about DSIDC's

Table 7.17
Did you receive any help from DSIDC's Technical Consultancy Organisation?

	N	Percentage
Yes	18	15%
No	63	52.5
No response	39	32.5%
Total	120	100

Participation in Exhibition/Trade Fair

On being asked whether they ever participated in any exhibition/trade fair, nearly 46.7 per cent respondents gave a positive reply and the remaining respondents *i.e.* 53.3 per cent gave negative reply (Table 7.18). The exhibitions in which they participated were Techmart, Packaging, IITF, Handloom Expo, Dastkar, Delhi Trade Fair, etc. These exhibitions are sponsored by Ministry of Textiles, Government of India, India Trade Promotion Organisation, Blind Relief Association, Government of NCT, Delhi, Commissioner of Food and Handicraft, DSIDC, etc. When we asked them in what form they participated in these exhibitions, most of them replied that they had put up their own stall. While some others said that they just visited the stalls to see what all new products have come in the market. We further asked them whether they benefitted from this exhibition, they replied that they were benefitted in the sense that they got more orders and as such their business increased. Secondly, they got publicity *i.e.* people came to know about their products. Thirdly, the entrepreneurs received bulk orders for export. Fourthly, there was direct interaction with the traders as well as consumers. Finally, they got new ideas and they came across new products which were launched by different entrepreneurs.

Table 7.18
Have you ever participated in any exhibition/trade fair?

	N	*Percentage*
Yes	56	46.7
No	64	53.3%
Total	120	100

Functioning of the DSIDC

When asked whether they were satisfied with the functioning of the DSIDC, it was disheartening to note that only 17.5 per cent of the respondents gave a positive reply and the remaining 82.5 per cent responded negatively (Table 7.19). Those who gave a positive reply, we asked them how they were satisfied with the functioning of the DSIDC. They said that the DSIDC was promoting the interests of the SSIs in the National Capital Region of Delhi. They are helping us in procuring and distributing the raw materials. They are developing industrial sheds for us and are also providing marketing facilities to the SSIs of Delhi. On the other hand, those who responded negatively, said that they were not satisfied with the functioning of the DSIDC because again personal whims played a pivotal role. They further complained that industrial sheds are not given to the interested entrepreneurs. Finally, the official files are rarely disposed off on due time and if the entrepreneurs visit the officials, they are hardly entertained even though they had the appointment.

Table 7.19
Are you satisfied with the functioning of the DSIDC?

	N	*Percentage*
Yes	21	17.5
No	99	82.5%
Total	120	100

We further asked them, what role does the DSIDC play in promotion of SSIs. In response to this, respondents said that it plays a role of catalyst in promotion of SSIs. Connected to this, we asked them whether in their opinion, the DSIDC is performing its role appropriately in response to the needs of the SSIs. In response to this query there were two opinions. The first set of sample respondents viewed that the DSIDC is performing its role appropriately in response to the needs of the SSIs. The contribution of the DSIDC towards the already established and functioning SSI units is very good. But in case of newly started units, its contribution is negligible. On the other hand, the second set of respondents had a negative opinion about the role being performed by the DSIDC. They answered that the policy of DSIDC has not been able to keep pace with the present growth of the SSIs. Another related query was that in which way, in the opinion of the sample respondents, the role of the DSIDC needs to be modified. In response to this query, the respondents made a number of suggestions: Firstly, the Government should come up with new schemes and sanction it to the different institutions and these institutions should participate in it. Secondly, the respondents emphasised that there should be a channel through which you can go and talk to the officials of the DSIDC. Thirdly, the role needs to be modified by providing better financial assistance and this assistance should be provided on the basis of the project submitted by the entrepreneur and the need of collateral security should be minimised. Fourthly, the role should be modified and it should be based on modern management techniques so that it could counter the challenges created by the MNCs. Finally, every small scale industrial unit should be visited by the officials of the DSIDC so that they are able to know the exact problems faced by the small entrepreneurs.

Entrepreneurs Satisfaction with DSIDC's Organisational Structure

From role modification, we turned to the organisational structure of the DSIDC. On being asked whether they are satisfied with the organisational structure of the DSIDC, nearly 6.7 per cent of the respondents gave a positive reply, 16.7 per cent responded negatively and 76.6 per cent of the sample respondents did not respond to our query as they were not aware of the organisational structure of the DSIDC (Table 7.20). When we asked to provide reasons for their above response, the respondents whose response were positive said that since they were not directly concerned with the organisational structure of the DSIDC, they thought that the present organisational structure is satisfactory. On the other hand, the other group of respondents (*i.e.* negative response group) were of the view that at present the organisational structure of the DSIDC is not satisfactory because vast manpower is involved in it. Their further suggestions were that since the small entrepreneurs are not the part of the DSIDC, so we are not satisfied with the structure of the DSIDC. Finally, in their view the organisational structure is rather traditional which gives rise to inspector raj and delay in decision-making. Our next query from them was whether they would like to give some suggestions with regard to the organisational structure of the DSIDC. The respondents suggested that first of all, there is no use of such a vast manpower, so the staff of DSIDC should be reduced to half. Secondly, the organisational structure of the DSIDC should have representation from the SSI association. Thirdly, voluntary retirement should be promoted so that there will be accommodation of the small scale entrepreneurs. One of the entrepreneurs who was harassed by the officials even viewed that the DSIDC should be wound up.

Table 7.20
Are you satisfied with the organisational structure of the DSIDC?

	N	*Percentage*
Yes	8	6.7%
No	20	16.7%
No response	92	76.6%
Total	120	100

Rendering Suggestions About DSIDC's Functioning

After getting their response on the organisational structure of the DSIDC, we asked them to give some suggestions for improvement in the functioning of the DSIDC. The respondents had a number of suggestions to make. Some of them are mentioned below. Firstly, they suggested that a Committee should be appointed by the Government to look into the problems, faced by the small scale entrepreneurs. Secondly, they emphasised that whenever any new scheme is launched by the Government or the DSIDC, no agent shall be involved. Before launching any new scheme, the DSIDC should talk to the association of the small scale entrepreneurs so that only those schemes are introduced which are going to help large number of small entrepreneurs. They further suggested that there should be monitoring agency to look after all the new schemes launched by the DSIDC and to ensure that the schemes are implemented properly. Thirdly, only those entrepreneurs who have political connection and are influential gets the help from the DSIDC. The respondents were of the view that this should be stopped and the DSIDC should come forward and help the needy entrepreneurs. They also wanted a proper channel through which the small entrepreneurs could meet the officials of the DSIDC. They complained that the DSIDC officials are not ready to meet the small entrepreneurs. Fourthly, with regard to finance, they said that they have a number of problems. As such, they suggested that the loan criteria should be simplified and the credit facilities should be given without guarantors like the Citi Bank does. They further suggested that whenever they required finance, the DSIDC should recommend their name so that the entrepreneurs get the finance without any difficulty. But it is remarkable here that they were over zealous in their financial assistance from the DSIDC. Fifthly, they suggested that the DSIDC should change its role from being a Government organisation. In other words, their entire outlook should be changed *i.e.*from bureaucratic to professionalised people who will advice and assist the small entrepreneurs and will also encourage them to carry on their business properly. Finally, since they were having a number of problems like water, electricity, transport, etc., they suggested that the DSIDC should take up the matter with the Government to solve the problems faced by the small entrepreneurs.

Environmental Awareness

Besides the above queries, the other aspect *i.e.* environment need to be asked here. On being asked whether the DSIDC provide any assistance in making the SSIs environment friendly, nearly 15 per cent of the respondents gave a positive reply, 55 per cent of them responded negatively and 30 per cent of them did not respond to our query (Table 7.21). We further asked them in what way is the DSIDC making the SSIs environment friendly, the respondents said that they have developed industrial plots at Narela Industrial Complex which is an environment friendly estate. We also asked them whether in their opinion the DSIDC has an obligation to make the new environment friendly technology available to the SSIs. Around 70 per cent of the respondents observed that the DSIDC has an obligation to make the new environment friendly technology available to the SSIs (Table 7.22). For achieving co-ordination between the DSIDC and the small scale entrepreneurs, the respondents were of the view that a coordination committee consisting of members of both the groups, *i.e.*, the DSIDC officials and the small scale entrepreneurs, be constituted so that the functioning of the DSIDC could be reviewed at regular intervals of time and the entrepreneurs are able to discuss their problem with the DSIDC officials.

Table 7.21
Does DSIDC provide any assistance in making the Small Scale Industries Environment friendly?

	N	*Percentage*
Yes	18	15%
No	66	55%
No response	36	30%
Total	120	100

Table 7.22
Do you think that the DSIDC has an obligation to make the new environment friendly technology available to the Small Scale Industries?

	N	*Percentage*
Yes	84	70%
No	36	30%
Total	120	100

Our next query from the sample respondents was that according to their perception, what should be the aim of the DSIDC. The respondents perception was that the DSIDC should act as a multi-purpose single window corporation whose main aim is to help the small scale entrepreneurs. They also wanted that the DSIDC should encourage the unemployed educated youths to set up their own small scale unit. Besides, they also wanted that the DSIDC should become more professionalised rather than bureaucratic.

Our final query from the respondents was what should be the role of the DSIDC in the context of present industrial development. In response to our query they replied that the DSIDC should work as a catalyst to advance the process of industrialisation so that SSIs can compete with the international market and can meet the challenges created by the present global industrial development. They proposed that the DSIDC should act as a right hand of the small entrepreneurs which should provide better finance, marketing, export, infrastructural facilities etc. It should motivate the employees of the sick industrial units to start their own business by providing them technical know how. Finally, they should keep a data bank of all the employees of sick industrial units, give them training at nominal cost and help them by providing employment in the small scale industrial units.

Conclusion

The above discussion is a clear indication of the fact that the small scale entrepreneurs are well aware of the policy of the Government towards the SSIs. They are also aware of the various activities of DSIDC and the functioning of DSIDC. However, very few of them are satisfied with the functioning of the DSIDC. They are of the view that DSIDC is helping only those entrepreneurs who have personal contacts and are influential. This is not completely true. What we observed during our survey was that the DSIDC is helping the small scale entrepreneurs but not upto their expectation. As such they are not satisfied with its functioning. They were of the view that the DSIDC should change its role *i.e.* at present it is bureaucratic in nature which is evident from delay in decision making. It should become more professional. It should work in such a way that the small scale entrepreneurs are really benefitted from them. They further suggested that the DSIDC should allot sheds to the genuine entrepreneurs and not to those who are not serious about entrepreneurship. What has been practised is that previously sheds were alloted to the entrepreneurs and they in turn used to sell it to some other entrepreneurs. This caused a problem in the sense that all the payments were being done in the name of old entrepreneur because all the papers were in his name. As such, the entrepreneurs wanted that once they purchase the sheds, all the papers should be transferred in their name so that they do not face unnecessary problems. They also wanted that the registration procedure should be simplified and once the entrepreneurs are registered as SSI unit, they should automatically get registered with the other organisations in Delhi. Similarly, they wanted that the loan procedure should be simplified. With the paper work they are even asked for guarantors. All these causes delay in getting the loan sanctioned. In spite of all the above problems, the entrepreneurs did appreciate the DSIDC for developing environment friendly estates at Narela Industrial Complex. They viewed that the contribution of the DSIDC towards the already settled and functioning SSI units is very good. But in case of new units, their contribution is negligible. Besides, they also appreciated the DSIDC for helping them in procuring raw materials by providing excise concession and providing the raw materials at concessional rates.

Thus, we see that there are two contradictory views on the functioning of the DSIDC. One group of respondents are satisfied with the functioning of the DSIDC, while the others and not. Both the contradictory groups have some times shared the same view, for *e.g.*, both groups of respondents wanted that DSIDC should change its role especially in promoting more entrepreneurs in the field of SSIs. The findings thus go to prove the initial hypotheses of the present research. We began with the hypotheses that a perfect inter-organisational co-ordination may provide greater scope for the promotion of SSIs; the helping and co-operative attitude of DSIDC may encourage the new entrepreneurs to enter into the small-scale industrial sector; and the accessibility of raw material, and better marketing facilities of finished goods will provide greater scope for higher production and will help accelerate the growth of SSIs.

All these hypotheses have proved to be correct after the empirical investigation and field survey. There seems to be a consensus among the respondents *i.e.* the entrepreneurs, that the role of DSIDC and the various allied organisations in the field of SSIs is crucial for promotion of the SSIs. A more integrated approach based on a better co-ordination among the various such organisations can prove to be congenial for the healthy growth of SSIs.

8

Perception of The Officials of The DSIDC With Regard to Its Role in Promotion of Small Scale Industries

In the preceeding chapter, we had evaluated the perception and awareness of the small scale entrepreneurs with regard to the functioning of the DSIDC. In order to substantiate their perception, it becomes necessary to evaluate the perceptions of the DSIDC officials as well so that we can get a clear picture of the role being played by the DSIDC. Accordingly, an attempt has been made in the present chapter to evaluate the perception of the DSIDC officials with regard to its role in promotion of SSIs. Besides, we have provided the due suggestions of the DSIDC officials as to how the DSIDC can improve its functioning.

Selection of Officials

The officials were chosen on the basis of random sampling. As regards the sample size, we chose 25 officials of the DSIDC for interview purpose. A care was taken to cover the officials from all the hierarchies *i.e.* General Manager, Divisional Managers, Deputy Managers and Assistant Managers. Besides, the Company Secretary and the Public Relation Officer were also interviewed to have a composite view of the problem.

Awareness About Government's Policy

Our first query was with regard to their awareness about the policy of the Government towards the SSIs. It was heartening to note that all the 25 officials (100 per cent) were aware of the Government's policy towards the SSIs (Table 8.1). They viewed that since beginning, Government's policy was directed towards promotion of SSIs. To this end, the Government has reserved certain items which can be produced in the SSS. The Government has established certain institutions for promotion of SSIs and these institutions are helping the small scale entrepreneurs in many ways like providing raw materials, marketing facilities, infrastructural facilities, training programmes, financial assistance etc. Consequent to the unveiling of the new economic policies, a separate set of policy measures were introduced for the promotion and strengthening of SSIs in 1991. This new policy statement was a clear re-affirmation of the commitment of the Government towards the importance of this sector in economic growth objectives. On the whole, the officials were satisfied with the policy of the Government towards SSIs. All the officials have welcomed the announcement made by the present Prime Minister, Shri Atal Behari Vajpayee, that the investment limit for SSIs will be reduced to Rs.1 crore from the present Rs. 3 crores. They emphasised that this will really help the small entrepreneurs because at present the big entrepreneurs or those entrepreneurs who have a cluster of small industries, are enjoying the benefits of the SSIs and the small entrepreneurs are the sufferers.

Table 8.1

Awareness about the policy of the Government towards Small Scale Industries

	N	*Percentage*
Yes	25	100%
No	0	0%
Total	25	100

Institutions Promoting SSIs

Secondly, on the question whether they had the knowledge

about the organisations/institutions promoting SSIs, it was once again heartening to note that 100 per cent (Table 8.2) of the officials had the knowledge about these institutions. On being asked to specify the various institutions promoting SSIs, they mentioned the names of Directorate of Industries, SIDO, SISI, NSIC, SIDBI, DSIDC, NIESBUD, NISIET, DFC, DIC, etc. They said that the Office of the Development Commissioner (SSIs) was created at the Central level with branches in all States to guide and promote the programmes for small industry development. It also led to the creation of a large number of autonomous institutions and corporate bodies which were assigned specific functions. Finally, they said that the above mentioned organisations render various services to the SSIs like consultancy in technical and managerial aspects; training; marketing and marketing assistance; export promotion; machinery on hire-purchase; raw material assistance; credit facilities; etc.

Table 8.2
Knowledge about Institutions/Organisations Promoting Small Scale Industries

	N	*Percentage*
Yes	25	100%
No	0	0%
Total	25	100

Activities of the DSIDC

It was encouraging to note that all the 25 officials were having knowledge about the various activities of the DSIDC (Table 8.3). According to the officials, the activities of the DSIDC are– (i) the DSIDC provides assistance to SSI units of Delhi in marketing their products; (ii) it provides self employment opportunities to the under privileged sections of the society; (iii) it procures and distributes raw materials; (iv) provides technical assistance *i.e.* it helps the entrepreneurs in identifying projects, undertaking techno-economic appraisal of projects and market research and survey; (v) constructs industrial sheds; (vi) undertakes the export of products of small industries in Delhi; (vii) organises exhibitions in different parts of Delhi to enable the small entrepreneurs to exhibit and sell their products; etc.

Table 8.3
Knowledge about the various activities of the DSIDC

	N	*Percentage*
Yes	25	100%
No	0	0%
Total	25	100

Import of Raw Materials

We further enquired whether the Government helps in importing the raw materials. Once again we got cent per cent reply (Table 8.4). When we asked them in what way does the Government helps in importing the raw materials, they replied that by way of issuing essentiality certificates for issue of import licences. We further asked them whether the DSIDC was giving any help in procuring raw materials. Here again we received 100 per cent (Table 8.5) positive reply. On being asked in what form, the officials replied that the DSIDC was providing some excise concessions and providing raw materials at concessional rates. This was done to enable the SSIs to compete on favourable terms with their counterparts in the large and medium sector.

Table 8.4
Does Government help in importing the raw material?

	N	*Percentage*
Yes	25	100
No	0	0%
Total	25	100

Table 8.5
Does DSIDC give any help in procuring the raw materials?

	N	*Percentage*
Yes	25	100%
No	0	0%
Total	25	100

Marketing Assistance

Closely connected to the above query was whether the DSIDC provide any marketing assistance. It was encouraging to note that 100 per cent of the officials responded positively (Table 8.6). They further pointed out that the DSIDC helps the entrepreneurs in marketing by securing bulk orders from Government departments and marketing their products through trade centres and the Delhi Emporium. Besides, the Marketing Division enrols small scale units as its business associates and publicises their products and also collects information from intending purchasers, files tenders, submits quotations and conducts negotiations with the producers.

Table 8.6
Does DSIDC provide any marketing assistance?

	N	*Percentage*
Yes	25	100
No	0	0%
Total	25	100

Exporting Facility

Another related aspect was exports. As such we wanted to know from the officials whether the DSIDC provide any exporting facility. In response to this query, all the respondents (Table 8.7) gave a positive reply. They said that the DSIDC helps in export by way of displaying those items which have export potential in the Emporium and various Exhibitions within the country and outside in the trade fairs where the customers from other countries place supply orders for their requirements. Apart from this, the Export Division introduces foreign buyers in the local market.

Table 8.7
Does DSIDC provide any exporting facility?

	N	*Percentage*
Yes	25	100%
No	0	0%
Total	25	100

Functioning of the Technical Consultancy Organisation

On being asked whether they have heard about the Technical Consultancy Organisation of the DSIDC, all the respondents had knowledge about the Technical Consultancy Organisation (Table 8.8). On being asked about its functioning, they said that the Technical Consultancy Organisation guides the entrepreneurs in identifying projects, undertaking techno-economic appraisal of projects and market research and survey. We further asked them whether they were satisfied with the functioning of the Technical Consultancy Organisation (TCO). Almost 76 per cent of the officials showed their satisfaction while 24 per cent of the officials showed their dissatisfaction (Table 8.9). Those who were not satisfied were of the opinion that the TCO is not performing its job properly. Previously, whenever any entrepreneur needed any help while setting up his/her unit, the TCO would help them. But nowadays the entrepreneurs are well aware of each and every thing and as such they do not require TCO's assistance. In other words, the TCO is not performing its role appropriately.

Table 8.8
Knowledge about DSIDC's Technical Consultancy Organisation

	N	*Percentage*
Yes	25	100%
No	0	0%
Total	25	100

Table 8.9
Are you satisfied with the functioning of the Technical Consultancy Organisation?

	N	*Percentage*
Yes	19	76%
No	6	24%
Total	25	100

Participation in Exhibition/Trade Fair

On enquiring whether they have ever participated in any exhibition/trade fair. In response to this, all the officials gave a positive reply (Table 8.10). The officials said that they participate in the IITF every year. They also participate in exhibitions held abroad. At IITF they put up their own stall. All these exhibitions have benefitted both the DSIDC and the entrepreneurs because they got bulk orders and they came to know about the new products which were launched in the market. The DSIDC has a permanent pavilion at the Exhibition grounds i.e. Pragati Maidan, New Delhi, which acts as a show window to the industry of Delhi both during international fairs and by way of special exhibitions organised periodically.

Table 8.10

Have you ever participated in any exhibition/trade fair?

	N	*Percentage*
Yes	25	100%
No	0	0%
Total	25	100

Functioning of the DSIDC

From exhibitions we switched to the functioning of the DSIDC. As such, we wanted to know from the officials whether they were satisfied with the functioning of the DSIDC. In response to our query, nearly 72 per cent of the officials gave a positive reply and the remaining 28 per cent officials replied negatively (Table 8.11). The officials who gave a positive reply said that we are functioning satisfactorily and we are working for the cause of the small entrepreneurs in real sense. We are providing them numerous facilities like raw materials, marketing, exports, technical help, construction of environment friendly industrial sheds, etc. Besides, we also organise exhibitions in different parts of Delhi to enable the small entrepreneurs to exhibit and sell their products. The officials further pointed out that they give opportunity to the handloom weavers to sell their products at different places in the country. However, there were some other officers who were not satisfied with the functioning of the DSIDC. The reason behind their dissatisfaction was that the DSIDC was established with the objective to aid, counsel, assist, finance, protect and promote the interests of small industries in Delhi. In other words, it's main objective was promotion of SSIs in Delhi. But over the years it has diverted itself from its objective and has started selling liquor. This way they are making money. The officials further viewed that DSIDC is good for nothing. It can just sell liquor.

Table 8.11

Are you satisfied with the functioning of the DSIDC?

	N	*Percentage*
Yes	18	72%
No	7	28
Total	25	100

Organisational Structure of the DSIDC

On being asked whether they were satisfied with the organisational structure of the DSIDC, it was disheartening to note that 80 per cent of the officials were not satisfied with the structure of the DSIDC (Table 8.12). Only 20 per cent of the respondents were satisfied with the structure of the DSIDC. According to them, except political interference, the structure of the DSIDC is alright. Those who were dissatisfied with the organisational structure emphasised that the structure is not appropriate. Secondly, there is no fixed tenure for the Managing Director and the General Manager.

Table 8.12

Are you satisfied with the organisational structure of the DSIDC?

	N	*Percentage*
Yes	5	20%
No	20	80%
Total	25	100

The officials had a number of suggestions to make with regard to the organisational structure of the DSIDC. Firstly, there is no need of two posts of the Chairman and the Managing Director because whenever there are two persons, they may differ on certain issues and hence the work may get delayed. Thus, they suggested that both the posts should be vested in one person *i.e.* there should be a Chief Managing Director who will look after both the posts. This provision was there for some time but the system was discontinued because the Chief Managing Director did not bow to the demands of the politician. Secondly, initially there were five General Managers but later on their number was reduced to three and at present there is only one General Manager who is the head of all the Divisions. Besides, previously the General Managers were drawn from IAS but now they are drawn from Delhi, Andaman Nicobar Islands Civil Service. They viewed that there is no harm in having a General Manager drawn from Delhi, Andaman Nicobar Islands Civil Service but there is a total degradation in the working procedure of top level management. They suggested that the policy of having five or three General Managers was good in the sense that the work was equally divided among them. But now the workload is on one person. As such, the previous system should be continued. Thirdly, in the Board of Directors, there are two political appointees *i.e.* two M.L.A's. who always interfere in the matters of the Corporation. The officials suggested that in place of the political appointees, some professionals from Tata, Bajaj, Reliance, etc. should be drawn and inducted in the Board of Directors. In this way there will be less political interference and we will be benefitted from the knowledge of the professionals. Fourthly, at present there is no fixed tenure for Managing Director and the General Manager. By the time they learn about the organisation *i.e.* the functioning of the DSIDC, they are transferred to some other organisation. As such, they suggested that the tenure for these officers should be fixed *i.e.* a minimum period of five years for the Managing Director and three years for the General Manager . If their tenure is fixed, they can concentrate on their work and the DSIDC can really benefit from this. Finally, at present, there are Divisional Managers below the General Manager, who are the heads of various Divisions which means that in between General Manager and the Divisional Managers there should be the post of Chief Managers so that better communication and better co-ordination could be achieved.

Suggestions for Improvement in the Functioning of the DSIDC

Once the officials gave us the suggestions regarding the organisational structure of the DSIDC, we asked them to give some other suggestions for improvement in the functioning of the DSIDC. To this they replied that the DSIDC can function more efficiently if there is a provision for inter-departmental promotion. They viewed that there must be time bound promotion schemes to motivate the employees of the DSIDC so that they could work hard and fulfil the objectives of the DSIDC *i.e.* it should work for promotion of SSIs in Delhi. They further proposed that the DSIDC should provide accommodation facilities to its staff at par with the Central Government. In other words, they should get all the facilities which are provided by the Central Government. Thirdly, they said that selling liquor is not an activity of the DSIDC. No SSIDC is selling liquor. As such, they suggested that DSIDC should either stop selling liquor or should devote very little time to this activity. Fourthly, the DSIDC should encourage the setting up of those industries which do not add to the problems of congestion and pollution. In other words, the DSIDC should encourage the growth of environment friendly industries. Fifthly, the DSIDC should devote its energies towards bringing about innovations in the technology in the SSIs which has become obselete and is affecting the quality and quantity and ultimately the competitiveness in the international market. Sixthly, they further proposed that the DSIDC should expand its retail outlet network on the pattern of Super Bazar to achieve the goals and targets of marketing activity. Finally, the DSIDC should provide guidance and assistance to the prospective entrepreneurs in the selection of the projects, keeping in view their resource constraints, qualifications, family backgrounds, etc.

Environmental Aspect

After getting their suggestions for improvement in the functioning of the DSIDC, we turned to some queries which were related to environment. Accordingly, we wanted to know from the officials, whether the DSIDC provide any assistance in making the SSIs environment friendly. In response to our query all the 25 officials gave a positive reply (Table 8.13). They were of the opinion that the DSIDC is providing assistance in making the SSIs environment friendly by way of developing industrial sheds in the environment friendly areas. It has developed around 1,800 industrial plots in an environment friendly estate spread over nearly 250 hectares at Narela Industrial Complex. About 200 entrepreneurs have almost completed the construction of their factories in the plots and some of them have also become operational. It has been conditioned that the industrial units coming up here would have to be pollution free. We further asked them whether the DSIDC has an obligation to make the new environment friendly technology available to the SSIs. Once again all the officials responded positively (Table 8.14). They acknowledged that after the latest verdict of the Supreme Court with regard to shifting of polluting units from the non-conforming areas, it has become obligatory for the DSIDC to make the new environment friendly technology available to the SSIs. Accordingly, the DSIDC has started working towards this end. The Delhi Administration has acquired 1050 acres of land in Bawana for the development of industrial plots. The DSIDC has been entrusted with the work of developing the area and build a modern Industrial Complex at Bawana with all modern amenities like adequate electricity and water supply, sewage etc.

Table 8.13
Does the DSIDC provide any assistance in making the Small Scale Industries environment friendly?

	N	*Percentage*
Yes	25	100%
No	0	0%
Total	25	100

Co-ordination Between DSIDC and the Small Entrepreneurs

When asked how a co-ordination between the DSIDC and the small scale entrepreneurs can be achieved, they replied that there is proper co-ordination between the two. However, they stressed that in order to make environment friendly techniques available to the entrepreneurs, they should provide the required amount for the setting up of the Common Treatment Plant.

Table 8.14
Do you think that the DSIDC has an obligation to make the new environment friendly technology available to the Small Scale Industries?

	N	*Percentage*
Yes	25	100%
No	0	0%
Total	25	100

Role of the DSIDC

Now we come to our final query *i.e.* what should be the role of the DSIDC in the context of present industrial development. They suggested that the DSIDC should function in such a way that the SSIs can compete with the international market and can meet the challenges created by the present global industrial development. They should review its role in completely new perspective and come out as pioneer agency for industrial planning for Delhi. It should devote its time, energy and expertise to plan industrial future of Delhi, on the lines of the Delhi Development Authority for the Housing Plan. Finally, they should identify industries which are pollution free, does not cause congestion and are environment friendly, and encourage them to be developed in the environment friendly estate.

Conclusion

It is clear from the above analysis that the officials of the DSIDC are well aware of the policies of the Government with regard to the SSIs. They are even satisfied with the policies of the Government. They suggested that in future also the Government should make only those policies which are going to help the small entrepreneurs in the real sense. The previous Government had raised the investment limit of the SSS. The argument given was to take care of inflation. The limits were hiked from time to time in keeping with inflation, devaluation of rupee, etc. The price index between May, 1990 and May, 1997 has increased by only 88 per cent, the justification for raising the investment limit by 400 per cent seems to be unsustainable. Mere raising of limits will seldom impart viability and strength to the SSS, particularly, when 95 per cent of the units are not getting more than 3 per cent of their credit. In view of this aspect, the present Government's announcement to lower the investment limit to Rs. one crore from the present Rs. three crores, has been welcomed by the officials. They envisaged that this will really benefit the small entrepreneurs because there will be entry of more new small scale entrepreneurs. Similarly, they were satisfied with the functioning of the DSIDC provided some suggestions are incorporated for their better functioning. Their main grievance was against the new activity of the DSIDC *i.e.* selling of liquor. They were of the opinion that since no SSIDC is selling liquor and since this activity is taking away most of time, the DSIDC should stop this activity. Their another grievance was with regard to the organisational structure of the DSIDC. Most of them were not satisfied with the organisational structure of the DSIDC and wanted that some changes should be introduced. They were vehemently against the political appointees. Instead some professionals from big companies should be inducted in the Board of Directors. They also suggested that the post of Chairman and Managing Director should be combined in one person and he should be called the Chief Managing Director. They had also certain grievances with regard to the TCO. They emphasised that the TCO used to help the entrepreneurs in initial years but at present the TCO is not providing much help.

Thus, we see that the officials have certain grievances from the DSIDC but on the whole they are satisfied with the functioning of the DSIDC. They said that if the above mentioned suggestions are taken into account, the DSIDC will really have a bright future as the SSIs will be able to cope up with the problem posed by the globalisation of international market.

Interestingly enough the initial hypotheses were corroborated by the officials too. The study began with the hypothesis that a perfect inter-organisational co-ordination may provide greater scope for the promotion of SSIs. The findings from the response of the officials proved the hypotheses. It was, according to them, the most essentially required reform for a better.structure and functional operation of the DSIDC and the various allied organisations. Another hypotheses was the need of a helping and co-operative attitude of DSIDC to encourage the new entrepreneurs to enter into the SSI sector. The officials agreed to this need in theory, however, they admitted that they were not always able to extend the required help and co-operation due to the bureaucratic structure of the organisation and the various hierarchies involved in it. From the response of the officials, our hypotheses that the accessibility of the raw material and better marketing facilities of finished goods will provide greater scope for higher production and will help accelerate the growth of SSIs, also proved to be correct.

Thus, the field survey and analysis of the data collected have proved all our initial hypotheses to be correct. Largely the respondents *i.e.* the officials of the DSIDC agreed that the role of the DSIDC and the various allied organisations is crucial for the promotion of the SSIs. They also felt that a more integrated approach based on a better co-ordination among the various allied organisations can prove to be conducive for the growth of SSIs. However, the officials added that a better co-ordination among the officials and entrepreneurs can facilitate the promotion of SSIs.

9

Conclusion

Giving a final glance to the entire research, the present chapter deals with the findings and its assessment in different perspectives with certain recommendations as we wish to put forward here for the better functioning of the DSIDC. The chapter has been divided into two parts. In the first part, the findings of the study has been summarised. In the second part recommendations have been provided.

The study began with the following hypotheses: in the broader framework of the State activities, the development of SSIs is not only essential for the overall well being of the society but also to sustain the basic requirements of the society; SSIs serve as a conduit to the overall industrial development of the country; perfect inter-organisational co-ordination, may provide greater scope for the promotion of SSIs; the helping and cooperative attitude of the DSIDC may encourage the entrepreneurs to enter into the small-scale industrial sector and the accessibility of raw material and better marketing facilities of finished goods, will provide greater scope for higher production and will help accelerate the growth of SSIs.

The first two hypotheses were general in nature and related to the role and functions of SSIs in the overall economy of the State. On the basis of the study and analysis of the literature available on the subject it was found that the initial observation was correct. With as variegated demography and as large agricultural and rural population, the economy can not sustain without the proper cultivation and promotion of the SSIs. The study also revealed that the State being the largest employer and manager of industries, its role in the promotion of SSIs remains the most crucial. The response of the sample interviewed by the researcher seems to emphasise the essentiality of the role of the State in this regard.

The empirical investigation, field survey and analysis of data collected have proved the rest of the hypotheses correct. The initial hypotheses were corroborated both by the small scale entrepreneurs as well as the officials. There seems to be a consensus among the respondents *i.e.* the entrepreneurs as well as the officials that the role of the DSIDC and the various allied organisations in the field of SSIs, is crucial for the promotion of SSIs. Both categories of respondents felt that a more integrated approach based on a better co-ordination among the various such organisations can prove to be congenial for the healthy growth of SSIs. The officials also added that a better co-ordination among the officials and entrepreneurs can facilitate the promotion of SSIs. Thus a new hypothesis to the already existing ones can be added after the study *i.e.* besides the coordination among the DSIDC and allied organisations, a better coordination among the officials and entrepreneurs is also crucial for promotion and healthy growth of the SSIs.

Findings

Industry in India, during the British rule, was like a neglected child because the policy of the British Government was not to encourage industries in India. As such, industries suffered for want of State encouragement and help. It was in the year 1937 that the State intervention in respect of Small Scale Industries (SSIs) began in India by way of giving impetus, protection and encouragement for development of small industries and village and cottage industries, by making available a number of facilities.

The immediate attention of the new Government after independence, was committed to the promotion and encouragement of village and SSIs which is evident from the various IPRs and statements. The role of cottage and SSIs had been widely acknowledged in the IPR, 1948 which mentions its importance in the national economy. In respect to certain type of essential consumer goods like food, cloth and agricultural implements, these industries are particularly suited for better utilisation of local resources and for the achievement of local self sufficiency. In the successive resolutions a prime place was assigned to the village and the SSS in the industrial development of the country.

We witness a major seachange in the Government's attitude especially after 1991. The shift was in the direction to unveiling off the new economic policies. For the first time, a separate set of policy measures were introduced for the promotion and strengthening of SSIs in August, 1991. This new policy statement was a clear re-affirmation of the commitment of the Government towards the importance of this sector in achieving the objectives of economic growth.

The key planks of India's policy for the development of small industry have been reservations, fiscal concessions by way of lower excise duties, extension of business services by the Government and preferential procurement by the Government. Excise duty concessions have been given to the SSIs to enable them to compete on favourable terms with their counterparts in the large and medium sector. At present, we do not find any exclusive scheme of direct tax concessions for SSIs. If more than 10 persons are employed then new small scale units can avail income tax rebate by way of deduction equal to 25 per cent of their profits for a period of 10 years. A large number of products are earmarked for exclusive manufacture by the SSIs. The Government also provides purchase and price preference for the SSIs. Besides, the Government has had a focussed credit policy, national equity fund scheme and single window scheme for SSIs.

Promotion and growth of the SSIs sector has always been a concern to the Indian Industrial Policy. Accordingly, a number of institutions/organisations have been set up at the Central and State levels for promotion of SSIs. These institutions are engaged in the areas of credit lending, technology support services, infrastructural services and a host of marketing and support related services. At the top of the administrative hierarchy is the

Department of SSIs in the Government of India. It sets out the policy framework for promotion and development of SSIs; monitors and evaluates the growth and performance of the sector; and implements appropriate policies, programmes and schemes. The other institutions are SIDO, SISI, NSIC, NIESBUD, SIDBI, KVIC, NISIET, Directorate of Industries, SIDC, SFC, Industry Associations, etc. Besides these, there are certain specialised institutions *viz.* CSIR, DSIR and India Investment Centre, which look after the promotional aspect of the SSIs.

A detailed analysis of their working and functions brings to light that there is more or less same type of functioning in some of the institutions. For example NISIET and NIESBUD are providing training of Entrepreneurship Development Programmes. Similarly, SSIDCs and NSIC are providing raw materials and hire purchase machinery etc. Performance wise SIDBI, SSIDCs and SISIs are working satisfactorily. While other institutions like NSIC have lost their credibility and soundness with regard to certain functions. During the recent years, some of its functions like raw material assistance, hire-purchase of machinery, is slowly diminishing. The main reason behind this is lack of proper co-ordination and direction between these institutions. The DIC which acts as single window agency to co-ordinate all the activities for the promotion of SSI units, is not able to achieve its objective.

In view of the vast growth of SSIs that has taken place through the years, the existing network of Government institutions cannot hope to serve well the needs of all the vast number of small industrial units throughout the country. Development of close linkages between these agencies is important for the success of the small industry programme. It is better to provide overall support to small scale enterprises rather than selecting particular sectors or units.

So far as growth of SSIs in Delhi is concerned, the survey data clearly reflects that Delhi has emerged as an important centre of modern. SSIs despite a number of odds prevailing in the way of accumulation of resources such as water, power etc. Keeping in view the basic postulates of the Industrial Policy of Delhi, the Delhi Administration made special attempt to promote and develop SSIs by adopting some promotional measures like–reservation of items for the exclusive manufacture in the SSS, adequate infrastructural facilities, technical support, marketing facilities, export promotion, financial assistance etc. To provide the above mentioned facilities, the Delhi Administration has established certain institutions like DFC, Delhi Development Authority, DSIDC, DKVIB, HARDICON etc. From the survey it was clear that there is overlapping of functions between Delhi Development Authority, DSIDC and Directorate of Industries. It was found that the Directorate of Industries is performing many such functions which are under the purview of the DSIDC. Similarly, the Delhi Development Authority is also engaged in developing and allotting industrial areas and plots and there is no clear cut demarcation between Delhi Development Authority and the DSIDC. So this resemblance is a clear cut overlapping of functions.

The MPD 2001 envisages that the industrial growth in Delhi should be restricted to small scale with stress on units, which require skill, less of manpower and energy and are non-nuisance and clean to largely subserve Delhi's economy. However, no action plan has been drawn up to implement any of the provisions of the MPD 2001.

The DSIDC was established in February 1971 with the objective to aid, counsel, assist, finance, protect and promote the interests of SSIs in Delhi. We see that there are too many objectives in the Memorandum of Association of the DSIDC. There is no definite and clear statement of the social costs prepared to be borne by the Government for the development of industries. There is a dichotomy in the role of the DSIDC *i.e.* whether it is a development service oriented organisation or a commercial enterprise of the Government.

The survey reveals that the DSIDC has drifted from its original activities of marketing, procuring raw material, export promotion, etc. and has taken up a new activity *viz*, selling of India Made Foreign Liquor. This activity was taken up primarily to generate revenues to support the corporation's development activities. But from the survey it becomes clear that the time of the DSIDC is wasted in this activity. As a result, the important activities are being neglected.

The survey further reveals that in the initial years intensive programme of Entrepreneurs Development was taken up by the DSIDC, under which the entrepreneurs were given technical as well as managerial training, industrial sheds were constructed and allotted and all relevant assistance was extended to trained entrepreneurs under the Package Assistance Programme to enable them to set up their own units. Sale and distribution of mass consumption goods, assistance in marketing their products in the country and abroad, quality marking service, etc. were taken up on large scale.

However, during the late seventies and early eighties, the activities of the DSIDC started declining in almost every sphere. The rate of progress in marketing activity and total turnover declined and the DSIDC incurred heavy losses. The reason behind this was that huge stocks of various items including exportable items were accumulated and subsequently they were disposed off at very low prices *i.e.* prices much below their cost. As a result of this the quality deteriorated, value of stock reduced and the burden of interest on the commercial borrowings increased. Another major factor contributing to financial problems was the non-payment of rent of sheds, water and power charges by the entrepreneurs to whom the sheds had been allotted on rental basis. Besides, the sudden change of Government in 1977 also came as a set-back.

An indepth study of working procedures of the DSIDC during late seventies and early eighties reveals that there was no proper system of procuring and stocking the raw material. Accounts of procurement and distribution were not maintained properly. Regular stock verifications were not conducted.

With regards to marketing it was found that the poor quality manufacturers approached DSIDC for sale of their products. The bills and payments were not processed in time as a result of which payment to suppliers was delayed. Mass consumption goods were purchased without any market survey and goods so procured were at times of poor quality with no marketability.

Similar was the case of industrial sheds. Recovery of investment on sheds was poor on account of non-finalisation of the policy on rental or hire-purchase basis. Accounts of the rent paid were not maintained properly. And above all, the selection of entrepreneurs for allotment of sheds was made in haste without going into the details of their backgrounds. Some of the sheds were allotted to those entrepreneurs who were not really interested in entrepreneurship. A few years later they sold the sheds to some other entrepreneurs.

However, after mid-eighties there was some change in the functioning of the DSIDC. The Corporation started taking remedial steps to check the declining trend of industrial activity. For the first time a full time Chairman was appointed keeping in view the continued poor financial performance of the company. A permanent pavilion at Pragati Maidan was constructed to exhibit the products of small entrepreneurs of Delhi. An environment friendly estate has been constructed at Narela Industrial Complex. An independent Industries Division has been created to develop technical consultancy, quality certification, setting up of joint ventures etc.

Though these changes were introduced in the DSIDC, yet one area which requires thorough restructuring is the personnel policy of the DSIDC. From the survey it becomes clear that there is absence of proper personnel policy. The officials are not given any promotional benefits. They are shifted from one Division to another and are asked to deal with entirely different work. As a result, development of expertise and professionalism in a particular sphere, has been adversely affected. Nobody is intended to borrow the burden of accountability for lapses. Besides, the tenure of Managing Director and General Manager is not fixed. By the time they know about the organisation and its functioning they are transferred to some other organisation. No long term planning can be done without a long term possession of a department by the high rank authority.

With regards to industrial sheds, the study reveals that the industrial sheds are not properly constructed. These sheds are totally against the Factory Act. According to the Factory Act, there should be a front and a back opening. The DSIDC has constructed the sheds in violation of the Factory Act. There is no mechanism for fire safety.

Among the problem being faced by SSI units, the survey revealed inadequacy of infrastructural facilities such as power shortage, poor roads, water problem, transport problem, communication problem and absence of basic amenities including canteen. The entrepreneurs suffer badly due to the lack of these facilities. The intensity of these problems varied from one industrial area to other. In Wazirpur industrial area, one tastes acid in their drinking water which is contaminated. In Okhla Industrial Area, the shortage of water led them to pay Rs. one hundred on each alternate day. In Anand Parbat industrial area, the units being small and mostly situated in the residential areas, the situation is a bit better. On the other hand we find some other sort of problems for example extremely polluted air due to a number of rubber factories.

Similarly, in all the three industrial areas in which the survey was conducted the entrepreneurs are suffering seriously due to want of electricity. Most of the industries in Delhi are being run on electricity and the position of electric supply in Delhi especially during summers is very poor. As a result, the desired quantity of finished goods is not produced. During the course of field study some irregularities in regard to power supply was observed. There was misuse of electricity and we also observed electricity theft *i.e.* most of the entrepreneurs were not paying any amount towards electricity charges. No meter was installed in their premises. Employee from the electricity department visited the industrial areas for installation of meters. But they were paid some amount to fix the meter in such a way that it shows very little amount of electricity consumed and in this way benefitted both the entrepreneurs and the employees of the electricity department. Thus a nexus is witnessed here. As such, the entrepreneurs have to pay very little towards electricity charges and in this way an embezzlement of the Government revenue. Due to this, there are a number of other entrepreneurs who suffer badly.

The Central Government has levied excise duties, besides the various taxes imposed by the State Governments. These taxes vary from State to State. In some States, there is no sales tax at all, in some others it is 4 per cent and still some others it varies from 7 to 8 per cent. The survey revealed that the sales tax/ service tax is very high in Delhi *i.e.* 7 per cent. If this tax is a bit lower one would avoid bypassing the tax law using the illegitimate means. As such, the Government is losing heavy sales tax/service tax.

We further observed that the entrepreneurs are not aware of the various schemes launched by the DSIDC and the concessions and incentives offered by State/Central Government to SSI unit. For example, most of the entrepreneurs were not aware of the DSIDC's Technical Consultancy Organisation and its functions. Similarly, some of the entrepreneurs were not aware of the Hire-Purchase Scheme of the NSIC.

So far as raw material is concerned, we found that there is wide price variation *i.e.* the entrepreneurs are not getting the raw materials at the listed price which appear in newspaper. Moreover, the raw materials supplied by Government is sometimes of inferior quality. The entrepreneurs even do not get the raw material in desired quantity and most of the units make additional purchases from open market at high rates. As their requirements are small they never enjoy the benefit of concession that goes with the larger purchase. There is no separate place for storage of raw material in the Industrial Estates. It was observed that due to paucity of space and smaller production, there is scanty purchase of raw materials which is not very economical. The small entrepreneurs also faced the problem of undue delay and procedural complications in import licence for raw material.

Besides, we also found that the entrepreneurs are having marketing problem. No doubt the DSIDC has come forward to help the SSS in the field of marketing SSI products, but very few of them have benefitted by the measures taken by the DSIDC. The major problem is lack of information and proper guidance. Those entrepreneurs who have good connection were able to market their product without any stark problem. But there were some other entrepreneurs who were really suffering due to this. They get cheated by the middle men, who are making lots of money by keeping the entrepreneurs in dark about the exact rate.

From the survey it was found that small industries in most of the cases do not depend on any agency for marketing of their products which are mainly sold directly to consumers. Most of the SSIs are oriented to local market. Majority of the units do not make use of modern marketing techniques due to its non-availability at general. The entrepreneurs do not use the accounting procedure and market information system to analyse, implement and monitor the operations to get the feedback information. Many entrepreneurs reported that 'provision of credit' to buyers and 'low prices' were mainly used to market their products, as there is stiff competition within the SSS and from large scale sector as well. The existing marketing support does not meet the requirements of small entrepreneurs.

In every industrial estate, there are small entrepreneurs associations to look after the problems of small entrepreneurs. The survey revealed that these associations are doing nothing for the cause of the SSI units. Rather they are making money by providing facility to their intimate.

The field survey clearly reveals that the small entrepreneurs face procedural bottlenecks while dealing with Government's rules and regulations. An industrial unit has to obtain more than dozen clearances or permit from the concerned departments depending on the line of product before starting the production. Some of the important licences are from Health Department, Municipal Department, Electricity Board, Pollution Control Board, Commercial Tax Department, Factories Department etc. These procedures are cumbersome, and time consuming and tiring. The survey highlighted undue delay experienced by many sample units in getting the above approvals, which in turn delayed the commencement of production. The entrepreneurs face procedural technicalities and time consuming procedures at every stage such as registration, procurement of licence for raw material, supply of power, sanctioning of loan etc. Though a number of recommendations have been made for simplification of procedures from time to time; yet there is no significant change.

Of late, though the registration procedure was simplified to some extent, yet a number of formalities has to be completed. Inspite of the simplification in the registration procedure, the entrepreneurs are still having problems with regard to registration. It was very discouraging to note that many entrepreneurs do not prefer to register their units because of the cumbersome and time consuming procedure.

The survey further revealed that once the units are registered as SSI units, these units must be registered with other organisations like SISI, NSIC, DFC etc. in order to avail the benefits provided by these organisations time to time. The process of registration in these institutions are as it used to be for enrollingas SSI which again leads to the wastage of time and energy.

It is clear from the survey data that the procedural problems and technicalities also exist while availing loans from banks and financial institutions. Many entrepreneurs complained that banks and financial institutions have adopted cumbersome procedures and heavy paper work in advancing a loan. Apart from these problems faced by the small entrepreneurs the amount of loan sanctioned is very less which grossly affects cost of production. The high cost of production leads to loss of profit of the units. With commercial banks becoming more reluctant and security oriented towards SSS, the financial position of the SSS are very meagre.

The survey data reveals that loan gets sanctioned in no time but disbursement of the loan takes a great deal of time. Besides, scrutinising and processing of applications by bankers causes undue delay and hardship in sanctioning of loans.

Banks and other commercial institutions insists for fund flow statement, working capital requirement, balance sheets, profit and loss account etc., for 5-7 years even before the commencement of business. Since the new entrepreneur does not know what to do, he seeks the help of a Chartered Accountant, who prepares an imaginary statement which have no relevance to the unit. Such an attitude of the banks and entrepreneurs should be immediately changed.

Another difficulty voiced by the small entrepreneurs during survey is the collateral security insisted upon by banks. As suggested by the entrepreneurs, collateral security of third party guarantee should not be insisted upon for a limit upto Rs. 5,00,000.

The DSIDC has established a Technical Consultancy Organisation to provide guidance in setting up units, identifying projects, project feasibility, technology, market research and survey etc. It was found during the survey that the services of TCO was not upto the standard and it provided only general information and that too to those small entrepreneurs who had some personal contact in the DSIDC.

Suggestion

In the present section some suggestions, based on the findings of the study and our exhaustive field experience, have been highlighted to further strengthen the functioning of the DSIDC which would be helpful in overcoming the problems faced by the small entrepreneurs. These suggestions, it is hoped, would strengthen and promote SSIs as well as foster entrepreneurship. Though our suggestions are confined to the micro situation of Delhi, yet we feel that these suggestions have their relevance for other State of the country.

The State plays a very important role in industrial development of the country in general and SSIs in particular. To this end, certain items are reserved for manufacture in the SSS. The Abid Hussain Committee recommended abolition of reservation of items for exclusive manufacture in the SSS and the Government should provide instead, concessional funds in terms of equity support and interest, for upgrading technologies in those SSI units affected by de-reservation. The Committee was of the opinion that a large number of reserved products are either not manufactured at all by SSI or their sales turnover is insignificant. Secondly, the policy of reservation is inconsistent with ongoing trade policy reforms which allows free import of a large number of products covered by reservation.

The Government chose to continue the reservation policy but in a slight different manner. In place of total abolition, the Government opted for product de-reservation in a phased manner. Accordingly, in April 1997 and February 1999, 15 and 9 items respectively were de-reserved. As a result of de-reservation, instead of 836 items, now the SSS can manufacture only 812 items.

This important issue was also considered by the study group on the development of Small Scale Enterprises. The group was set up by the Planning Commission in 1999 under the chairmanship of Dr. S. P. Gupta. The Committee was of the opinion that the reservation of items, as a policy for the development of the SSS, should continue on the ground that the reserved components of the SSI sector are making significant contribution to employment, output and exports.

In order to meet out the various requirements of this expanding SSS, both Central as well as State Governments provide adequate institutional assistance to it. A detailed analysis of their working and functions brings to light that there is much duplication of work. As such it is suggested that the role and functions of these institutions should be clearly defined so that no two institutions will provide the same assistance. Further, in order to prevent duplication of effort and achieve a more focussed specialised approach wherever feasible, it is suggested that the number of support agencies, should be rationalised and their working should be reviewed so that we achieve more inter institutional co-ordination and integration of the difficult schemes and programmes being run by each. In order to make these institutions really effective, they need to be restructured and their functions modified so that necessary information, assistance, and other infrastructure are made available to the SSS. Development of close linkages between these agencies is important for the success of the small industry development programme. It is better to provide overall support to small scale enterprises rather than selecting particular sectors or units. A mutual programme of co-ordination and support for speedy promotion of small and cottage industries should be evolved. There should be proper co-ordination of work and activities of different institutions so that overlapping may be avoided. Finally, decentralisation of Central Government institutions also become necessary. Hence, it is suggested that SIDO should deal only with important functions like policy formulation, preparation of Five Year Plans, inter-state co-ordination and export etc., and transfer rest of its functions to State Government.

Some of the institutions that need restructuring are NSIC,

DIC and SSIDCs. As marketing function forms an important criterion for SSS, NSIC should deal mainly with marketing activity at local, national and international level and other activities like raw material supply and Government purchase assistance could be looked after by SSIDCs. The DICs should be strengthened by delegating appropriate powers to their officers by the respective State Governments. NISIET and NIESBUD are performing almost similar functions. As such it is suggested that both these organisations should be given different and specific role to perform so that overlapping of functions do not occur.

So far as the institutional assistance in Delhi is concerned, here also we find the resemblance of functions among the DSIDC, Directorate of Industries and DDA. Thus, to sort out this problem it is suggested that the functions of all these three institutions should be clearly spelt out and they should share information amongst themselves to let each other and the beneficiary group know what services are available.

Following the verdict of the Supreme Court, the Government of NCT of Delhi is working in the direction of shifting the polluting units from non-conforming areas. But it is to be acknowledged here that political whims make the Government reluctant in this process. Accordingly, it is suggested that the Government should follow the hard yardsticks and should encourage only those industries in Delhi which do not add to the problems of congestion and pollution and which are environment friendly. It is further suggested that SIDC's should be declared as a 'Nodal Agency' to undertake pollution prevention and environmental improvement efforts.

To solve the problem of space, it is recommended that the industrial policy of Delhi be suitably modified to accommodate the sophisticated, high-tech, household, handicraft, cottage, village and service industries. These small industries be allowed to grow but in a phased manner. So far as the scarcity of land is concerned, the industrial space be created or increased in the following manner– (i) the unused space in the existing industrial estates or the space which has been encroached upon by the people in unauthorised manner may be vacated and planned development of that space be made to accommodate more small industries; (ii) the land lying vacant at the various Community Work Centres of the DSIDC may be utilised by constructing flatted work centres to accommodate tiny units; (iii) underground industrial complexes (on the lines of Palika Bazar) may be developed by the Government to cater to the needs of the small industries which are sophisticated, high-tech and non-pollutant type; and (iv) the space under the flyovers in the various parts of the NCR may be a potential area for establishment of small, tiny, handicrafts, cottage, sophisticated, high-tech and service industries and we may utilise that space for the development and growth of the small units.

The Government makes various policies for the promotion of SSIs but very few of them are benefitted from these. In most of the cases the entrepreneurs are not aware of these policies. As such, it is suggested that whenever the Government has to make any new policy with regard to SSIs, they should first call a meeting of the DSIDC officials, officials from Directorate of Industries and members of small scale entrepreneurs association. Only after detailed discussion with the above officials and entrepreneurs, the Government should formulate the new policies. This way only those policies will be made which are really going to help the small entrepreneurs. Besides, an all out effort should be made by the Government to create an environment of mutual trust between the Government and the entrepreneurs so that small industries may survive and grow in the changing scenario of economic and industrial development in the world over.

We see that there are too many objectives in the Memorandum of Association of the DSIDC. Thus, it is suggested that the objectives should be clearly defined and their number should be reduced so that the DSIDC should work towards achieving the objectives in an effective manner.

The DSIDC has taken up a new activity of selling India Made Foreign Liquor which is consuming more time than the other activities and most of the officials are busy in exploring this particular activity. So our suggestion here is that the DSIDC should also manage enough time to look after the other important activities, which are getting neglected.

The DSIDC should once again take up the Entrepreneur Development Programme which was involved in providing technical and managerial training to the entrepreneurs. This programme, helped the small entrepreneurs in the past. As such it is vehemently recommended that this programme should be revived.

With regard to industrial sheds, in view of the Factory Act, we found a clear violation of this Act. This Act proposed for two gates one from front side and other in the back side for safety purposes and a mechanism for fire safety should also be developed. But no body followed this guideline. Even the Government built sheds have only one gate. So it is a kind of violation of Factory Act. Hence it is suggested that the Government should make it mandatory that every entrepreneur should have fire extinguisher in their sheds and two gates. These sheds should be allotted to needy entrepreneurs and not to those who are less interested in entrepreneurship. This can be done through vigorous scrutiny of their application forms. The provision of infrastructural facilities like proper roads, water facility, transport facility, proper electricity etc., have to be an integral part of SSI development. It is suggested that infrastructural facilities available in Industrial Estate should be reviewed by DSIDC and all attempts should be made to further strengthen them.

Acute shortage of power has been acknowledged in the industrial estates. So it is suggested that all efforts should be made to solve power shortage problem. Government should take up more power projects. Identification of new sources of energy generation should be encouraged. Though in order to reduce the intensity of this problem, the Government has been providing subsidy for installation of generator sets, the interest on loans for Diesel Generator sets are high. Hence, reduction in interest is demanded so that small entrepreneurs may easily purchase it. Transformers and boosters/stabilizers, should be installed in those areas which are having low voltage problem. Meters should be installed in all the industrial sheds by the Government agents to stop theft of electricity. Government agent should visit the industrial estates after every three months to check whether the entrepreneurs are paying the bill or not and whether the meter is functioning properly. Further, the Government should take immediate steps to minimise the difficulty of getting power connection.

To solve the problem of raw materials, it is suggested that the Government should see that the entrepreneurs gets the raw materials at the listed price and Government should make all the efforts to keep the prices of raw materials as reasonable as possible. The Government should rationalize tax/tariff structures on raw materials to make cost of production mere competitive than imported finished products in the same line. If regular checks are made on the utilisation of quota and heavy punitive measures are enforced on unscrupulous entrepreneurs, the malpractices adopted by them in disposing off their quota for illicit gains can be curbed. Proper care should be taken by the Government to ascertain the quality of raw material while purchasing from the manufacturers for supply to SSIs. The raw material depots of the DSIDC should anticipate the requirement of essentials scarcity and import raw material in advance and make necessary arrangement to distribute them in adequate quantity. The DSIDC should expand its raw material assistance scheme and can open a raw material bank with buffer stock of raw material in its growth centres. In order to ensure adequate supply, the quota should be fixed on the basis of previous consumption of the unit and reviewed annually. The DSIDC can supply raw material requirements at concessional rate on credit basis which would help in sorting out the inadequacy of working capital. Besides, a single agency should be developed in a particular region which would look after all raw material assistance to SSI units, instead of the small entrepreneurs running around to get necessary licences and quota allocation. Apart from this private and public sector agencies can be encouraged with some incentives to service SSI units raw material and machinery needs through bulk purchases, or help with individual orders, for specialized needs.

It may further be suggested that some sort of co-operative among the small entrepreneurs should be formed. This way the entrepreneurs will be saving their time and energy because they have to run to the Directorate of Industries for procuring quotas and licences. Instead if the present system of allocation of raw material is replaced by a system of co-operative purchasing, the raw material crisis may be overcome without any problem. The co-operative societies formed among similar types of entrepreneurs in a particular area, can pool together the requirements of members and purchase directly from the manufacturers or large wholesalers. This would enable the entrepreneurs to get the advantages of bulk purchase on the one hand and help in eliminating the fake units on the other, from indulging in making illicit gains through the sale of quota. However, such a system of co-operative purchasing of raw materials can be successful if it is based on the sincerity of the members and only when industrial units of similar type are concentrated in a particular area.

With regards to marketing, it is suggested that the DSIDC should expand its retail outlet network on the pattern of Super Bazar to achieve the goals and targets of marketing activity. The products of the SSIs must be so designed and marketed that they cater to all the modern domestic needs. The units producing the same type of products should join together and form a group marketing strategy to market their products. Besides, training in marketing attributes should be given to small entrepreneurs by the existing institutions. The private marketing enterprises which would market goods on behalf of several SSI units should be strengthened since the SSI units need to depend on professional network to sell their products rather than depend on Government buying agencies. Finally, market research and surveys should be conducted on a systematic basis not only to explore market potential, new market areas etc., but also to provide meaningful data base to expand the market for the SSI sector. A welcome step in the direction of marketing is the construction of marketing estate at Okhla, Phase-II, Pocket 'A'. The estimated cost of the project is Rs. 419.80 lakhs. The scheme was approved by BOD during its meeting held on 10/02/2000.

Even in Government purchase programme malpractices has been witnessed. Moreover no technical guidance is provided to

SSI units while supplying to Government departments. Hence it is suggested that the programme of Government purchase should be reoriented so that it is made effective.

The small industry associations should be strengthened and effort should be made to see that they are really helping the small entrepreneurs and are not only interested in making money and lobbying more for micro level gains which benefit certain members with greater clout, rather than address macro level issues and develop strategies for the overall benefit of the group in the long run. These associations should concentrate on analyzing strength and weaknesses, opportunities and threats of the particular industry, and draw up time bond Action Plans with quantified targets on the crucial issues like infrastructure development, technology upgradation, quality improvement, marketing facilities, training etc.

With regard to the cumbersome and time consuming registration procedure, it is suggested that the registration procedure should be simplified. This would go a long way in clearing up the backlog of permits. Instead of getting a number of clearances from a number of departments before starting a unit, the entrepreneurs should go for one or two clearances. This will save a lot of time and energy of the entrepreneur. For this an organisation should be created which could give all the clearances under one roof so that the entrepreneurs do not have to run from pillar to post to get licences before starting his/her unit. The creation of such separate organisation may take some time. So for the time being, it is suggested that Government should issue strict orders to various departments as not to delay the issue of licence/permit and clear the same within 15 days, except in certain exceptional industries hazardous to environment. Besides, there should be one registration i.e. once the entrepreneurs are registered as a SSI unit, they should get automatic registration with the different organisations. This way they will be saving lot of time and energy.

Loan and credit facilities are vital to the development of industries. Lack of financial resources causes sickness. Faulty appraisal of projects, delays in the release of loans and working capital, inadequate sanctions, make the SSI unit unviable even before it has a chance to develop. As such it is suggested that consultancy services should be provided by SSI specialised banks within their establishments, in a package deal that is part of the loan. This would ensure that non-viable projects are not funded, and where credit is given, that it is used in productive investments. To solve the financial problem it is further suggested that the procedure of sanctioning loans to small entrepreneurs should be simplified and the paper formalities should be reduced. Once the loans are sanctioned, it should be immediately disbursed. While sanctioning the loan, the banks should not ask for guarantors. Efforts should be made by the Government to see that the entrepreneurs get the desired amount of loan. At present the practice is that the entrepreneurs do not get the loan for the amount applied. Rather some percentage of the loan is deducted and they get very little amount and even the sanctioned amount are rarely given to the entrepreneurs in full amount. The higher banking authority procures some money for sanctioning the required amount and if they are not paid the entrepreneurs are harassed. As such, they have to arrange the extra amount from some other source. Thus, this problem has to be taken care of. Apart from this, unnecessary and old data particulars are called for, which poses the new problem to the entrepreneurs. Hence the entrepreneur gets fed up and gives up the idea of availing loan from Government financial institutions. These practices should be avoided. Yet another suggestion could be that the persons from Government financial institutions should visit the industrial estates and apprise the entrepreneurs to the various facilities/schemes given by them for setting up the new units, extension of the old units etc. This positive approach on the part of the Government financial institutions will encourage the entrepreneurs to come forward and seek their help.

The entrepreneurs are willing to pay tax only once *i.e.*on their final product and not at different rates in different States which cause variation in the rate of their products in varying States. So it is recommended that a unanimous tax rate should be evolved and it should be reduced from 7 per cent to a fair rate system.

Payment for goods supplied to the Government departments,

public sector enterprises and large firms must be made within 15 days. Otherwise provision for recovery of delayed payments with interest must be strictly enforced as the entrepreneurs have to pay interest on their borrowed funds.

Most of the entrepreneurs are unaware of the various concessions/incentives available to SSI units. Hence publicity of such schemes become essential. Besides, whenever any new scheme is launched, there should be a monitoring agency to look after the various schemes launched and this agency should work in the direction of ensuring for the proper implementation of the scheme.

The DSIDC has a permanent pavilion at the Pragati Maidan where fairs and exhibitions are organised periodically. But this is within the the reach of very few small entrepreneurs. Hence it is suggested that the DSIDC should open an exhibition cum trade centre on permanent basis in each of the Industrial Complexes. This may be jointly managed by the DSIDC and the association of the entrepreneurs of the complex. The products manufactured in that complex may be displayed there for exhibition and sale and the trade enquiries from domestic and foreign markets may be entertained properly. Joint delegations consisting of officers of DSIDC and the entrepreneurs may be sponsored for tours to the various industrial complexes in the different States and also abroad for taking stock of the latest developments of technologies and techniques relating to the production and marketing of the products of the SSIs. The expenses of such delegations may be borne jointly by the DSIDC and the associations or entrepreneurs individually.

There is a lack of well laid out personnel policy in the DSIDC. As such it is suggested that a proper personnel policy should be made by the DSIDC which should take care of personnel functions, such as recruitment, training, promotion, performance appraisal etc. A lot of changes needs to be brought in the organisational structure of the DSIDC. Firstly, in order to avoid political interference, it becomes a necessity that the two M.L.A.s, involved in its structure and functioning, who often influence its working in one way or other, should be removed from the Board of Directors of the DSIDC and they may be replaced by experts/professionals from big companies. Secondly, the post of Chairman and Managing Director should be vested in one person who will be the Chief Executive and will look after responsibilities inherent in both the offices. Thirdly, the tenure of the Managing Director, Board of Directors and the General Manager should be fixed for a minimum period of five years, so that they can be fully involved in the long-term planning and implementation of the policies. Fourthly, power should be delegated from the top to the lower level. Finally, the DSIDC should also take a considered view about the necessity of taking people on deputation. The officers who come on deputation have neither any vital responsibility nor any roots in the corporation, as such they normally do not or cannot make the required contribution. Most of these officials come from Government departments hence the working is impaired as their approach towards problems is based on Government rules and procedures. They also block the promotion avenues of the existing persons and causes resentment and indifference in them. Accordingly, a systematic review of the problem should be made and these officials should be retained only if there is no competent substitute in the organisation or till such time an existing employee becomes eligible to man the post.

With regard to technology, it is suggested that the DSIDC should devote its energies to bring technical know how to cope up with the competing market nature existing in the present face of globalisation. Technology upgradation is the need of the hour. As such, the DSIDC should strive to supply upgraded technology to the entrepreneurs so that the marketability of SSI products could increase.

To maintain a proper coordination between the small entrepreneurs and the DSIDC officials, it is suggested that a quarterly meeting of the entrepreneurs and the officials should be called so that the officials get first hand knowledge about the problems faced by the small entrepreneurs and accordingly, they could provide the assistance. Besides, the officials could apprise the entrepreneurs of the various schemes launched by the DSIDC. This will help in reducing the gap between the small entrepreneurs and the DSIDC officials.

The small entrepreneurs are not happy with the services and information rendered by Government institutions as they do not have up-to-date information and their services are not quick. Besides the Government institutions, there are several other organisations which have current information on technology, and foreign market. But there is no apex body to collect and communicate these informations. Accordingly, the SIDO should establish a central information centre which should act as a data bank for information on products, industries, technology, foreign markets etc. This information can then be passed on to industry associations, private and public sector information networks.

To solve the problem of corruption in the functioning of the DSIDC, it is suggested that the functioning of the DSIDC should be made transparent. They should become more professional rather than bureaucratic.

In the era of liberalisation, the SSS has to cope with competition from big industries. Hence the policy of exclusiveness in favour of SSI sector products are not produced by medium and large industries should be strictly adhered to. Besides, the DSIDC should function in such a way that the SSIs can compete with the international market and can meet the challenges created by the present global industrial development. The DSIDC should review its role completely in new perspective and come out as pioneer agency for industrial planning for Delhi. It should devote its time, energy and expertise to plan industrial future of Delhi.

It is further suggested that the Government should reduce the investment limit for SSIs to Rs. 1 crores from the present Rs. 3 crores. The ideal investment limit for SSI is somewhere between Rs. 75 lakhs to Rs. 1 crore. The reason behind this is that the big industrial houses possess four or five small units in different names and they are enjoying the real benefits of SSIs. Whereas the actual small entrepreneurs are the sufferers. Therefore, the investment limit should be reduced. The Prime Minister, Shri Atal Behari Vajpayee has announced a major package to bolster and protect the SSIs. As part of this, the Prime Minister stated that the investment limit in this sector will be reduced to Rs.1 crore from Rs. 3 crore. He has also ruled out further dereservation on this segment of industry, hence putting aside the Abid Hussain Committee report on SSI reforms. He further said that the Government will work out ways to ensure easy credit to the sector irrespective of the size of the loan. This announcement was made on April 29, 1998, at a Conference organised by the Laghu Udyog Bharati in New Delhi. Time will only tell whether the Government is really interested in working for the cause of SSIs, i.e. promotion of SSIs, or not.

The recent years have witnessed a dramatic expansion in the small business sector in almost all parts of the world. It is not only the developing countries that have experienced such a phenomenon but a similar experience has also been gathered by a large number of industrially developed countries. With proper understanding, realistic policy support and fiscal measures the average capacity of this sector could be raised from its present 30 per cent to 60 per cent in short period resulting additional production, additional employment, additional export and so on which ultimately contribute to our economy a sustainable targeted growth.

The most revolutionary content of this sector is its inherent contradiction to monopoly and centralised economy. It peacefully and imperceptively transforms capitalist economy towards socialist objectives. Our analysis, thus, reveals that the policy implementing agency at the centre and the States should pay more attention for the betterment of the SSIs.

The policy implementing agency i.e. the Department of SSIs in the Government of India is functioning satisfactorily. But the policy making agency is not working well to the formulation of policies such as to compete and correlate our national goals of employment generation and many age-old problems of SSIs which have become more vexed in the phase of globalisation.

The rationale behind assigning the power of implementation to the Department of SSIs, Government of India, has been that this agency will have a final say in the affairs of the SSIs and their promotion within and outside the country. Since we have a socialist republic, so we have different aims and objectives to be pursued. Our Government cannot take the risk of opening flood gates to the world business community blindly. The various

Central and State level institutions are working towards this end *i.e.*, promotion of SSIs and generating mass employment. Especially in the phase of globalisation these institutions have to play even bigger role *i.e.* a sustainable policy should be formulated and work for the revival of the sick small scale units. This would not only speed up rehabilitation of potentially viable units but also help to identify areas for policy correction, to remove the cause of sickness and reduce its incidence among units of the group. New entrepreneurs should also be invited to invest in this field and for this purpose they should be provided with credit at a subsidized rate of interest and raw materials and new technology. To meet the above mentioned needs, the importance of these government institutions has increased.

Since the policy measures adopted were protection of SSIs through a common protection programme, differential tax treatment and direct subsidy in the form of concessional credit, these institutions help/is widely sought for. The Prime Minister's Rojgar Yojana which envisages creating self employment programmes is still to be integrated with the growth process. Hence, the importance of these institutions.

Bibliography

PRIMARY SOURCES

Documents

1. Delhi District Census Handbook: *Village and Town Directory - Delhi*, Director of Census Operations, Delhi, 1993.
2. Government of India, *Annual Report 1979-80, National Productivity Council*, New Delhi, 1981.
3. Government of India, *Annual Report 1991-92, Small Industry Development Bank of India*, Bombay, 1992.
4. Government of India, *Annual Report 1992-93, Ministry* of Industry, New Delhi, 1993.
5. Government of India, *Annual Report 93/94, Department of Scientific and Industrial Research*, Ministry of Science and Technology, New Delhi, 1994.
6. Government of India, *Assistance to Small Scale Industries,* Ministry of Civil Supplies, Small Scale Industries Board, Delhi, 1975.
7. Government of India, *Draft Approach Paper to the Ninth Five Year Plan, 1997-2002,* Planning Commission, New Delhi, 1997.
8. Government of India, *Draft Fifth Plan, Vol.II,* Planning Commission, New Delhi, 1975.
9. Government of India, *Eighth Five Year Plan, Vol.II, 1992-97*, Planning Commission, New Delhi, 1992.

10. Government of India, *First Five Year Plan, 1951-56*, Planning Commission, New Delhi, 1951.
11. Government of India, *Fourth Five Year Plan, 1969-74*, Planning Commission, New Delhi, 1969.
12. Government of India, *India's Industrial Policies From 1948 to 1991*, Office of the Development Commissioner (SSIs), Department of SSIs and ARI, Ministry of Industries, New Delhi, 1997.
13. Government of India, *National Small Industries Corporation 40th Annual Report 1994-95*, New Delhi, 1995.
14. Government of India, Public Enterprise Survey, 1993-94, Vol.I, Department of Public Enterprises, Ministry of Industry, New Delhi, 1993.
15. Government of India, *Report of the Fiscal Commission*, 1949-50.
16. Government of India, *Report on Functions and Activities, SIDO (1992-93)*, Development Commissioner (SSIs); Department of SSI and ARI, Ministry of Industry, New Delhi, 1994.
17. Government of India, *Report of the Indian Industrial Commission, 1916-18.*
18. Government of India, *Report of the International Perspective Planning Team on Small Scale Industry in India*, Delhi, 1963.
19. Government of India, *Report on the Small Scale Sector*, Administrative Reforms Commission, Delhi, 1969.
20. Government of India, *Report of the Village and Small Scale Industries Committee*, Planning Commission, New Delhi, 1956.
21. Government of India, *Second Five Year Plan, 1956-61*, Planning Commission, New Delhi, 1956.
22. Government of India, *Seventh Five Year Plan, 1985-90*, Planning Commission, New Delhi, 1985.
23. Government of India, *Sixth Five Year Plan, 1980-85*, Planning Commission, New Delhi, 1980.
24. Government of India, *Small Industries Assistance Programme*

in India, New Delhi, 1979.

25. Government of India, *Small Scale Industries in India*, Development Commissioner (SSIs), New Delhi, 1968.
26. Government of India, *Small Scale Industries in India: Opportunities in the Small Sector*, Development Commissioner (SSIs), Department of SSI and ARI, Ministry of Industry, New Delhi, 1994.
27. Government of India, *Small Scale Industries: Incentives and Facilities for Development*, Development Commissioner (SSIs), Department of SSI and ARI, Ministry of Industry, New Delhi, 1994.
28. Government of India, *States Report on Small Scale Industry in India*, New Delhi, 1960.
29. Government of India, *The International Planning Team: Report on Small Scale Industries in India*, Delhi, 1954.
30. Government of India, Third Five Year Plan, 1961-66, Planning Commission, New Delhi, 1961.
31. Government of India, *Twenty-Five Years of Progress*, Ministry of Industrial Development (SSI), New Delhi, 1971.
32. Government of India, *Working Group on Small Scale Industries - Evaluation Report,* Delhi, August, 1959.
33. Government of National Capital Region of Delhi, *Annual Repбrt 1993-94 DSIDC*, Delhi State Industrial Development Corporation, New Delhi, 1995.
34. Government of National Capital Region of Delhi, *Annual Report 1994-95 DSIDC*, Delhi State Industrial Development Corporation, New Delhi, 1996.
35. Government of National Capital Region of Delhi, *Annual Report 1995-96 DSIDC*, Delhi State Industrial Development Corporation, New Delhi, 1997.
36. Government of National Capital Territory of Delhi, *Industrial Profile Delhi* 1997, Office of the Commissioner of Industries, Delhi, 1997.
37. Government of National Capital Territory of Delhi,

Industrial Profile of Delhi, Delhi State Industrial Development Corporation, New Delhi, 1997.

38. Government of Tamil Nadu, *Small Scale Industries–Second SSI Census,* Directorate of Industries and Commerce, Tamil Nadu, 1988.
39. *Report of the Committee on Finance for the Private Sector,* Reserve Bank of India, Bombay, April 1954.
40. *Report of the Expert Committee on Small Enterprises* (Chairman: Abid Hussain), New Delhi, January 1997.
41. *Seminar on Small Scale Industries in India, Vol.II, 1976,* Srimati Jawahari Devi Birla Institute of Home Science, Jadavpur University.
42. United Nations, *Consultative Group on Industries Estates and Industrial Areas,* Department of Economic and Social Affairs, Geneva, 1966 (Papers and Proceedings).
43. United Nations, *Industrial Estates in Africa,* Department of Economic and Social Affairs, New York, 1965 (No.66, II B-2).
44. United Nations, *Industrial Estates in Asia and the Far East,*Department of Economic and Social Affairs, New York, 1962(No.62, II B-5).
45. United Nations, *Industrial Estates: Policies, Plans and Progress - A Comparative Analysis of International Experience,* Department of Economic and Social Affairs, New York, 1966 (No.6, B-16).
46. United Nations, *Physical Planning of Industrial Estates,* Department of Economic and Social Affairs, New York, 1962(No.62, II B-4).
47. United Nations, *World Economic Survey,* Department of International Economic and Social Affairs, New York, 1965.

SECONDARY SOURCES

Books

1. Ahluwalia, Isher Judge, *Industrial Growth in India Stagnation Since the Mid-Sixties,* Oxford University Press, Delhi, 1985.

2. Ahuja, B.N., *Small Scale Industries in India,* Varma Brothers, New Delhi, 1981.
3. Akram, S., *Development of Small Scale Industries in Bihar: A Case Study of Bihar State Small Industries* Corporation, Capital, Delhi, 1984.
4. Alexander, P.C., *Industrial Estates in India*, Asia Publishing House, Bombay, 1963.
5. Arya, Krishan, *Structure and Functioning of Delhi State Industrial Development Corporation Ltd.*, APPPA Dissertation, Indian Institute of Public Administration, New Delhi, 1984-85 (unpublished).
6. Ashok Kumar, S., *Entrepreneurship in Small Industry,* Discovery Publishing House, New Delhi, 1990.
7. Ayar, T.N. Krishna, *Guidelines for Financing of Small Scale Industries,* Vora, Bombay, 1976.
8. Balakrishnan, G., *Financing Small Scale Industry in India, 1950-52*, Gokhale Institute of Politics and Economics, Poona, 1961.
9. Bala, Mohandass, *Ancillary Industrial Development,* Andhra University Press, Waltaire, 1982.
10. Bandyopadhyaya, K., *Industrialisation through Industrial Estates,* Bookland Pvt. Ltd., Calcutta, 1969.
11. Basu, S.K., *Place and Problems of Small Industries*, A. Mukherjee and Co., Calcutta, 1957.
12. Basu, S.K., Ghose, Alak and Roy, Subrata, *Problems and Possibilities of Ancillary Industries in a Developing Economy,* World Press, Calcutta, 1965.
13. Berna, James J., *Industrial Entrepreneurship in Madras State,* Asia Publishing House, Bombay, 1960.
14. Bhalla, A.S.(ed.), *Small and Medium Enterprises,* Intermediate Technology Publications, London, 1992.
15. Bhandari, P.M., *A Hand Book of Small Scale Industries,* Peerless Publishers, New Delhi, 1978.
16. Bhandari, R.C.S., *State and Industrial Development,* Commonwealth Publishers, New Delhi, 1998.

17. Bhanushali, S.G., *Entrepreneurship Development - An Interdisciplinary Approach*, Himalaya Publishing House, Bombay, 1976.

18. Bharti, R.K., *Industrial Estates in Developing Economies*, National Publishing House, New Delhi, 1978.

19. Bhati, G.S., *Industrial Estates–An Evaluation, A Case Study of the Programme in Rajasthan*, University of Bombay, Bombay, 1976.

20. Bhattacharya, Hrishikes, *Entrepreneur Banker and Small Scale Industry*, Deep and Deep Publications, New Delhi, 1984.

21. Bhattacharya, S.N., *Development of Small Scale and Cottage Industries*, Metropolitan Book Company, New Delhi, 1986.

22. Bhattacharya, S.N., *Entrepreneurship Development in India and the South-East Asian Countries*, Light and Life Publishers, New Delhi, 1979.

23. Birla Economic Research Foundation, *Industrial Policy in India*, Radiant Publishers, New Delhi, 1996.

24. Carr, Marilyn, *Developing Small Scale Industry in India: An Integrated Approach*, Intermediate Technology Publication, London, 1981.

25. Chandra, Shanta Kohli, *Development of Women Entrepreneurship in India*, Mittal Publications, New Delhi, 1991.

26. Chellaswami, T., "Policy Relating to Small Scale Sector", in J.N. Mongia (ed.), *India's Economic Policies, 1947-77*, Allied Publishers, New Delhi, 1980.

27. Dawar, Ram, *Institutional Finance to Small Scale Industries*, Deep and Deep Publications, New Delhi, 1986.

28. Desai, S.S.M., *Industrial Economy of India*, Himalaya Publishing House, Bombay, 1988.

29. Desai, Vasant, *Organisation and Management of Small Industries*, Himalaya Publishing House, Bombay, 1983.

30. Desai, Vasant, *Problems and Prospects of Small Scale*

Industries, Himalaya Publishing House, Bombay, 1983.

31. Deshpande, M.U., *Entrepreneurship of Small Scale Industries*, Deep and Deep Publications, New Delhi, 1982.
32. Dhar, P.N., *Small Scale Industries in Delhi*, Asia Publishing House, New Delhi, 1958.
33. Dhar, P.N., and Lydall, H.F., *The Role of Small Enterprises in Indian Economic Development*, Asia Publishing House, New Delhi, 1961.
34. Dhingra, Om Prakash, *Development and Growth of Small Industries A Case Study of Union Territory of Delhi*, MBA Project Report, Indira Gandhi National Open University, New Delhi, 1992(unpublished).
35. Dua, D.R., *Small Industries and Handicrafts*, Sarvodaya Publishers, New Delhi, 1966.
36. Dutt, Ruddar and Sundaram, K.P.M., *Industrial Economy*, S. Chand Company Ltd., New Delhi, 1992.
37. Gadgil, D.R., *Origins of the Modern Indian Business Class - An Interim Report*, International Secretariat, Institute of Pacific Relations, New York, 1959.
38. Gadgil, D.R., *The Industrial Evolution of India in Recent Times: 1860-1939*, Oxford University Press, Bombay, 1971.
39. Gaikwad, V.R., and Tripathi, R.N., Socio-Psychological Factors Influencing Industrial Entrepreneurship in Rural Areas, National Institute of Community Development, Hyderabad, 1970.
40. Gangadhara Rao, N., *Entrepreneurship and Growth of Enterprise in Industrial Estates*, Deep and Deep Publications, New Delhi, 1986.
41. Ghosh, Alak, *Indian Economy, Its Nature and Problems*, 20th Edition, The World Press Pvt. Ltd., Calcutta, 1976.
42. Ghosh, Biswanath, *The Changing Profile of India's Industrial Economy*, The World Press Private Ltd., Calcutta, 1974.
43. Ghosh, D.N., *Small Industries: Their Place in Post-war Industrialisation*, General Printers and Publishers Ltd., Calcutta, 1947.

44. Goyal, S.K., et.al., *Small Scale Sector and Big Business*, Indian Institute of Public Administration, New Delhi, 1984(Mimeo).
45. Gupta, Kali Charan, *Small Scale Industries*, Dehati Pustak Bhandar, Delhi, 1962.
46. Gupta, M.C., *Entrepreneurship in Small Scale Industries*, Anmol Publications, New Delhi, 1987.
47. Gupta, N.S. and Singh, Amarjit, *Industrial Economy of India*, Light and Life Publications, New Delhi, 1978.
48. Gupta, R.K., "A Network of Industries in Delhi: Capital on the path of Industrial Progress", in S.P. Verma and S.C. Vajpeyi (eds.), *Landmarks in Delhi Administration*, Gyan Publishers, New Delhi, 1988.
49. Gupta, S.C. and Bansal, S.P., "Master Plan for Delhi *vis-a-vis* Industries", in Omesh Saigal, *et.al.*, *Problems and Prospects of Industrial Development in a Metropolitan City*, Mittal Publications, New Delhi, 1994.
50. Hadimani, R.N., *Dynamics of Industrial Entrepreneurship*, Ashish Publishing House, New Delhi, 1985.
51. Hamid, Syed Abdul, *Management Development of Small Scale Industries*, Anmol Publications, New Delhi, 1989.
52. Hanson, A.H.(ed.), *Nationalisation: A Book of Readings*, George Allen and Unwin Ltd., London, 1963.
53. Harper, Malcolm and Soon, Tan Thiam, *Small Enterprises in Developing Countries Case Studies and Conclusions*, Intermediate Technology Publications Ltd., London, 1979.
54. Hasnat, M.A., *Role of Nationalised Banks in the Development of Small Scale Industries*, Classified Publishing Company, New Delhi, 1991.
55. Hattangdi, Anil, *Banker's Handbook on Small Scale Industries*, IBH Publishing Company, Delhi, 1973.
56. Hoselitz, Bert F.(ed.), *The Role of Small Industry in the Process of Economic Growth*, Mouton, The Hague, Paris, 1968.

57. Hundekar, S.G., Das, V.B. Mohan and Banerjee, G.D., *Challenges Before Small Scale Industries*, Horizon, Allahabad, 1998.

58. India Investment Centre, *Scope for Industries in Different States*, New Delhi, 1976.

59. Inove, Kyoko, *Industrial Development Policy of India*, Institute of Developing Economies, Tokyo, 1992.

60. Iyengar, K.S., *The Philosophy of Small Scale Industrial Management*, Today and Tomorrow's Printers and Publishers, New Delhi, 1968.

61. Jaimini, R.K., *Management of Small Scale Industries*, Prateeksha Publication, Jaipur, 1988.

62. James T. Mc Crory, *Case Studies in Latent Industrial Potential: Small Industry in a North Indian Town*, Ministry of Commerce and Industry, Government of India, Delhi, 1956.

63. Khanka, S.S., *Entrepreneurship in Small Scale Industries*, Himalaya Publishing House, Bombay, 1990.

64. Kuchhal, S.C., *The Industrial Economy of India,*Chaitanya Publishing House, Allahabad, 1970.

65. Kumar, D. Narendra, *Entrepreneurship in Small Scale Sector*, Discovery Publishing House, New Delhi, 1995.

66. Kumar, Sharad, *Industrial Organisation and Management*, Discovery Publishing House, New Delhi, 1997.

67. Lakshmana Rao, V., *Industrial Entrepreneurship in India*, Chugh Publications, Allahabad, 1986.

68. Maheshwari, R.P. and Gupta, A.N., *Business, Government and Society*, Vikas Publishing House, New Delhi, 1985.

69. Malik, R.K., *Reference Book and Directory for Small Industries*, The Institute, Delhi, 1978.

70. Mallika, A.S., *A Study of Small Scale Industries in Industrial Estates*, Ph.D. Thesis, University of Madras, Madras, 1994(unpublished).

71. Mathur, O.P., *Manual on Industrial Estate Planning*, Small Industry Extension Training Institute, Hyderabad, 1971.

72. Mathur, S.P., *Economics of Small Scale Industries*, Sundeep Prakashan, Delhi, 1979.

73. Mehan, K.K., *Small Industry Entrepreneurs Handbook*, Productivity Service International, Bombay, 1973.

74. Mehta, Anil, Organisation and Working of Industrial Estates, Deep and Deep Publications, New Delhi, 1987.

75. Memoria, C.B. and Singh, Chauhal S.D., *Cottage and Small Scale Industries*, Sahitya Bhavan, Agra, 1963.

76. Misra, B.P., "Overview on Industrial Policy", in Omesh Saigal, et.al., *Problems and Prospects of Industrial Development in a Metropolitan* City, Mittal Publications, New Delhi, 1994.

77. Mishra, S.N., and Sharma, Kushal, *Organisational Requirements of Village and Small Scale Industries*, Mittal Publications, New Delhi, 1986.

78. Mitra, Lalit Kumar, *Employment and Output in Small Enterprises of India*, Bookland Pvt. Ltd., Delhi, 1967.

79. Mohanty, Bedabati, *Economics of Small Scale Industries*, Ashish Publishing House, New Delhi, 1986.

80. Mudgal, R., "Development of Industrial Complexes Jointly by Delhi and its Neighbouring States, in Omesh Saigal, et.al., Problems and Prospects of Industrial *Development in a Metropolitan City*, Mittal Publications, New Delhi, 1994.

81. Mukherji, A.K., *Economics of Indian Industry*, S. Chand and Company Ltd., New Delhi, 1985.

82. Nafziger, E.W., *Class, Caste, and Entrepreneurship - A Study of Indian Industrialists*, An East-West Centre, The University Press of Hawaii, Honolulu, 1978.

83. Nagaiya, D., *Industrial Estates Programme - The Indian Experience*, Small Industry Extension Training Institute, Hyderabad, 1971.

84. Nagaiya, D.(Ed.), *Industrial Sickness*, Discovery Publishing House, New Delhi, 1991.

85. Nanjundan, S., et.al., *Economic Research for Small Industry*

Development: Illustrated by India's Experience, Asia Publishing House, Bombay, 1962.

86. Narendra S. Bisht, and Pamila K. Sharma, *Entrepreneurship: Expectations and Experience*, Himalaya Publishing House, Bombay, 1991.
87. Narsimha Murthy, B.E. V.V., *Entrepreneurship in Small Towns,* Mittal Publications, New Delhi, 1989.
88. Neck, Philip A. and Nelson, Robert E.(eds.), *Small Enterprise Development: Policies and Programmes*, International Labour Office, Geneva, 2nd Edition, 1987.
89. Oomen, M.A., *Small Industry in Economic Growth: A Case Study of Kerala*, S.B. Press, Trivandrum, 1972.
90. Padhy, K.S. and Behera, A.K., *Industrial Policy of India*, Discovery Publishing House, Delhi, 1988.
91. Paliwal, R.C., *Small Industries–A Reference Book*, Small Business Publications, Delhi, 1977.
92. Panikker, P.N.S., *A Handbook of Small Industries*, Industrial Efficiency Services, Madras, 1965.
93. Pareek, H.S., *Financing of Small Scale Industries in a Developing Economy*, National Publishing House, New Delhi, 1978.
94. Pattnaik, S.M., *Development Strategy for Small Industries,* Himalaya Publishing House, Bombay, 1988.
95. Pradhan, Gopinath, *Industrial Estates and State Development,* Criterion Publications, New Delhi, 1985.
96. Ramakrishna, K.T., *Finances for Small Scale Industry in India,* Asia Publishing House, Delhi, 1962.
97. Ramakrishnan, P., *New Entrepreneurship in Small Scale Industries in Delhi*, Economic and Scientific Research Foundation, New Delhi, 1975.
98. Rangachar, S.S., "Organisational Support for Small Industry Development", in V.S.P. Rao and D. Nagaiya (eds.), *Small Industry Development in India*, Discovery Publishing House, New Delhi, 1991.
99. Rao, Ch. Umamaheshwara, Small Scale Industries, Popular Prakashan, Bombay, 1965.

100. Rao, M.G. and Odeyar Hegged, M., (eds.), *Industrial Economy Trends, Problems and Prospects*, Kanishka Publishing House, Delhi, 1973.

101. Rao, P. Subba and Sundaram, M., *Economics of Entrepreneurial Development*, Kanishka Publishers, Delhi, 1993.

102. Rao, R.V., *Cottage and Small Scale Industries and Planned Economy*, Sterling Publishers, Delhi, 1967.

103. Rao, R.V., *Small Industries and the Developing Economy in India*, Concept Publishing Company, New Delhi, 1979.

104. Rao, V.S.P. and Nagaiya, D.(eds.), *Small Industry Development in India*, Discovery Publishing House, New Delhi, 1991.

105. Rao, Venkateswara T., *Development of Small Scale Industries*, Anmol Publications Pvt. Ltd., New Delhi, 1995.

106. Ray, Rajat Kanta (ed.), *Entrepreneurship and Industry in India*, 1800-1947, Oxford University Press, Delhi, 1992.

107. Reddy, T.S. and Reddy, L.V., *Sickness in Small Industries*, Himalaya Publishing House, New Delhi, 1988.

108. Saigal, Omesh, et.al., *Problems and Prospects of Industrial Development in a Metropolitan City*, Mittal Publications, New Delhi, 1994.

109. Samiuddin, et.al., *Entrepreneurial Development in India*, Mittal Publications, New Delhi, 1990.

110. Sandesara, J.C., *Efficacy of Incentives for Small Industries*, Industries Development Bank of India, Bombay, 1982.

111. Sanghvi, R.L., *Role of Industrial Estates in a Developing Economy*, Multi-tech Publishing Co., Bombay, 1979.

112. Sankaranarayan, S., *Industrial Finance in Tamil Nadu and Pondicherry for Small Scale Industries*, K.S. Entrepreneurs Guidance Services, Madras, 1989.

113. Sen, Sunil Kumar, *Studies in Industrial Policy and Development of India* (1858-1914), Progressive Publishers, Calcutta, 1964.

114. *Services for Small Scale Industry*, International Labour Office, Geneva, 1961.

115. Sharma, K.L., *Entrepreneurial Growth and Industrial Development Programmes in Punjab and Uttar Pradesh: A Comparative Study of Small Entrepreneurs,* Department of Economics and Sociology, Punjab Agricultural University, Ludhiana, 1976.

116. Sharma, K.L., *Entrepreneurial Performance in Role Perspective,* Abhinav Publications, New Delhi, 1975.

117. Sharma, P.K., *Development Banks and Entrepreneurship Promotion in India,* Mittal Publications, New Delhi, 1990.

118. Sharma, R.A., *Entrepreneurial Change in Indian Industry*, Sterling Publishers, New Delhi, 1980.

119. Sharma, S.V.S. and Akhouri, M.M.P., *Small Entrepreneurial Development*, SIET Institute, Hyderabad, 1978.

120. Sharma, S.V.S. et.al., *Developing Entrepreneurship Issues and Problems*, SIET Institute, Hyderabad, 1980.

121. Sharma, S.V.S., *Small Entrepreneurial Development in Some Asian Countries–A Comparative Study*, Light and Life Publishers, New Delhi, 1979.

122. Sharma, Tulsi Ram and Chauhan, S.D. Singh, *Indian Industries (Development, Management, Finance and Organisation)*, 2nd ed., Shiva Lal Agarwala and Co. (P) Ltd., Agra, 1965.

123. Shashi Bala, *Management of Small Scale Industries*, Deep and Deep Publications, New Delhi, 1988.

124. Shetty, M.C., *Small Scale and Household Industries in Developing* Economy, Asia Publishing House, Bombay, 1963.

125. Shirokov, G.K., *Industrialisation of India, People's* Publishing House, New Delhi, 1980.

126. Singh, Inderjit and Gupta, N.C., *Financing of Small Industries*, S. Chand and Co., New Delhi, 1977.

127. Singh, K. Ramchandra Prasad, *State and Industrialisation of Developing Countries with Special Reference to India*, Sterling Publishers, Delhi, 1969.

128. Singh, N.N., *Scientific Management of Small Scale Industries*, Lalwani Publishing House, New Delhi, 1970.

129. Singh, Pretam, (ed.), *The Role of Entrepreneurship in Economic Development*, Vora and Co. Publishers (P) Ltd., Bombay, 1966.

130. Singh, P.N., *Developing Entrepreneurship for Economic Growth*, Vikas Publishing House, New Delhi, 1986.

131. Sinha, R.P., *Some Problems of Small Scale Industries*, Jain Bros., New Delhi, 1986.

132. Sirkin, Gerald, *The Visible Hand: The Fundamentals of Economic Planning*, McGraw Hill, New York, 1968.

133. *Small Scale Industries of Mysore*, National Council of Applied Economic Research, New Delhi, 1963.

134. Society for Social and Economic Studies, *Capital for Medium and Small Industries*, Asia Publishing House, Bombay, 1959.

135. Somasekhara, N., *Efficacy of Industrial Estate in India*, Vikas Publishing House, New Delhi, 1975.

136. Staley, Eugene and Morse, *Richard, Modern Small Industry for Developing Countries*, McGraw Hill Book Company, New York, 1965.

137. Stevenson, Lois A., "Entrepreneurship of Women" in Kalbagh, C.(ed.), *Women and Development*, Discovery Publishing House, New Delhi, 1992.

138. Subramanian, R., Shiva Kumar, K. and Palanisami, M., *Entrepreneurship in Small Scale Industries in Madurai City and its Environs*, Sangam Publishers, Madras, 1975.

139. Sudharshan, Lal, *How to Prevent Industrial Sickness*, Navrang Publishers, New Delhi, 1985.

140. Suri, K.B. (ed.), *Small Scale Enterprises in Industrial Development: The Indian Experience*, Sage Publications, New Delhi, 1988.

141. Suryakant, Parikh, How to Finance Small Business Enterprises, MacMillan Company of India Ltd., Meerut, 1977.

142. Sutcliffe, R.B., *Industry and Underdevelopment*, Addison-Wesley, London, 1971.

143. Swaroop, Gopal, *Advances to Small Industries and Small Borrowers*, Sultan Chand and Sons, New Delhi, 1981.

144. Tandon, B.C., *Environment and Entrepreneur*, Chugh Publications, Allahabad, 1975.

145. Tarun, Tara Nand Singh, *Small Scale Industries, India's Economic Development,* Deep and Deep, Delhi, 1986.

146. Thakore, V.K., "Establishing Industries in DMA and NCR", in Omesh Saigal, et.al., *Problems and Prospects of Industrial* Development in a Metropolitan City, Mittal Publications, New Delhi, 1994.

147. Tulsi, S.K., *Incentives for Small Scale Industries: An Evaluation,* Kunj, Delhi, 1980.

148. Tyabji, Nasir, *The Small Industries Policy in India*, Oxford University Press, Calcutta, 1989.

149. UNESCO Research Centre, *Social Aspects of Small Industries in India: Studies in Howrah and Bombay*, UNESCO Research Centre on Social and Economic Development in Southern Asia, Delhi, 1962.

150. Vakil, C.N. (ed.), *Industrial Development of India: Policy and Problems*, Orient Longman, New Delhi, 1973.

151. Vepa, Ram K., *Modern Small Industry in India (Problems and Prospects)*, Sage Publications, New Delhi, 1988.

152. Vepa, Ram K., *Small Industry Development Programme*, Indian Institute of Public Administration, New Delhi, 1983.

153. Vepa, Ram K., *Small Industry in the Seventies*, Vikas Publications, Delhi, 1971.

154. Vepa, Ram K., *Small Industry, The Challenge of Eighties*, Vikas Publishing House, New Delhi, 1983.

155. Verma, S.P. and Vajpeyi, S.C. (eds.), *Landmarks in Delhi Administration*, Gyan Publishers, New Delhi, 1988.

156. Vinze, Medha Dubhashi, *Women Entrepreneurs in India*, Mittal Publications, New Delhi, 1987.

157. Vas, Loretta, M., *Small Scale Industries and the Challenge of Liberalisation*, Indian Institute of Public Administration, New Delhi, 2001.

158. Vyas, J.N., Small Scale Industry Handbook, N.V. Vyas Trust, Bombay, 1986.

Articles in Journals, Periodicals and Newspapers

1. Adhikari, C.S. and Singh, Narendra, "District Industries Centre, The Case for Institutional Restructuring", *Productivity*, Vol.31, No.2, July-September, 1990.

2. Agarwal, C., "Status of Small Industries in India–A Study", *Southern Economist*, Vol.27, No.11, October 1988.

3. Alexander, P.C., "Modernisation of Small Scale Industries", *Indian Worker*, Vol.23, No.17, 3 January, 1975.

4. Bala Subrahmanya, M.H., "Small Industry Reservation Policy, *Economic and Political Weekly*, Vol.30, No.45, 11 November, 1995.

5. Bala Subrahmanya, M. H., "India's Small Industry Policy in the 90s: Waning Protectionism", *Indian Economic Journal*, Vol. 47, No.2, October-December, 1999-2000.

6. Barathan, D., "Village and Small Industries Sector", *Third Concept*, Vol.10, Nos. 110-11, April-May, 1996.

7. Basavaraja, M.G., "The Budget and the Small Scale Sector", *Yojana*, Vol.39, No.7, May 1995.

8. Bhat, Khursheed A., " Performance of Promotional Institutions in the Development of SSI", *TheBusiness Review*, Vol. 6, No. 182,2000.

9. Bhatia, B.S., "New Industrial Entrepreneurs: Their Origins and Problems", *Journal of General Management*, Autumn, 1974.

10. Dalmia, S.N., "Development of Small Scale Industries", *Management Accountant*, Vol.17, No.3, March 1982.
11. Das, Arun Kumar, "CAG Pulls up DSIDC for Gross Irregularities", *The Times of India (Delhi Times)*, New Delhi, April 9, 1948.
12. Dawar, Ram, "Small Scale Sector in India: A Study of Institutionalised Hire-Purchase Finance", *Institute of Public Enterprise Journal*, Vol.8, No.2, April-June, 1985.
13. Dhar, P.N., "Some Observations on Small Scale Enterprise Development", *Man and Development*, Vol.4, No.2, June 1980.
14. Dhoopar, B.L. and Rajagopalan, R., "Training of Small Scale Entrepreneurs", *Young Alliance*, Vol.4, No.8, August 1972.
15. Focus on Small Scale Sector, *Yojana*, Vol.32, No.4, 1 March, 1988.
16. Government Suggests Central Tribunal for Ailing SSIs, *The Times of India*, July 24, 1995.
17. Guha, B.P., "Problems and Prospects of Small Scale Industries", *Journal of the Lal Bahadur National Academy of Administration*, Vol.20, No.4, Winter 1975.
18. Hanumantha Rao, K.S. and Sumithra, D.G., "Planning and the Growth of Industrial Entrepreneurship in India", *The Indian Journal of Commerce*, No.65, December 1965.
19. Himachalam, D., "Entrepreneurship in Small Scale Sector", Yojana, Vol.34, No.3, February 16-24, 1990.
20. *ICSI Herald*, Vol.IX, No.3, March 1998.
21. *ICSI Herald*, Vol.IX, No.4, April 1998.
22. *ICSI Herald*, Vol.IX, No.5, May, 1998.
23. *IIPA Newsletter*, Vol.XLII, No.1, January 1998.
24. "Industrial Sickness and Small Scale Sector", *ICSI Herald*, Vol.IX, No.5, May 1998.
25. Jain, S.K., "The Role of Small Scale Industries in Creating Employment Opportunities", *Development Policy*

and Administration Review, Vol.4, No.2, July-December, 1979.

26. Jayalakshmi, L., "Small Sector–The Panacea for Unemployment", *Yojana*, Vol.22, No.16, 1 September, 1978.
27. Joshi, Navin Chandra, "Rejuvenating Small Industrial Sector, Yojana, Vol.39, No.13, November 1995.
28. Kesary, V.G., "The Small Scale Sector", *Lok Udyog*, Vol.11, No.1, April 1977.
29. Khanka, Shobhan Singh, "Entrepreneurship in Small Scale Industries in Kumaun, Uttar Pradesh", Journal of Rural Development, Vol.8, No.4, July, 1989.
30. Khanka, S.S., "Growth vis-a-vis Sickness in Small Scale Industries in India", Productivity, Vol.35, No.3, October-December, 1994.
31. Nag, A., "Growth of Small Scale Sector: An Assessment", *Yojana*, Vol.22, No.23, 16 December 1978.
32. Nag, Sumantra, "Small Industry and the Public Sector", *State Enterprise*, Vol.2, No.4, October-December, 1983.
33. Nanda, Antara, "Small Scale Sector Left in the Lurch, *The Times of India*, New Delhi, April 15, 1998.
34. Nawab, Ali Khan, "Development of Small Scale Sector in India", *Yojana*, October 1-15, 1989.
35. Neelamegam, R. and Inigo, R. Maria, "Management of Working Capital in Small Scale Industries in India, *Abhigyan*, Autumn 1996.
36. "Package to Boost SSIs", *The Economic Times*, New Delhi, April 29, 1998.
37. Pande, Sahdeo, "A Critique of Problems of Small and Cottage Industries in India, *Khadi Gramodyog*, Vol.37, No.2, November 1990.
38. Pant, S.K., "Productivity Paradox in Small Scale Industries", Khadi *Gramodyog*, Vol.31, No.7, April 1985.
39. Paranjyothi, G.S.and Sujatha, T.M., "Entrepreneurship

Development Amongst Rural Women", Kurukshetra, Vol.XXXIX, No.6, March 1991.

40. Parmar, Renu, "SIDBI and Small Units", *Yojana*, Vol.39, No.9, July 1995.
41. Parmar, Renu S., "Preventing SSI Sickness: Some Policy Implications", *Yojana*, Vol.39, No.13, November 1995.
42. Patnaik, Umesh C., "Contribution of the DIC Programme to Small Scale Industries in India", *Journal of Rural Development*, Vol.9, No.2, March 1990.
43. Pattanayak, J.N. and Agarwal, R.K., "Transfer of Technology for Small Scale Industries in India: The Institutional Framework", *Asian Economic Review*, Vol.37, No.1, April 1995.
44. "Policy Measures for Small, Tiny and Village Units", *Yojana*, Vol.35, No.19, 31 October 1991.
45. Prasad, Bhagwan, "Small Scale Industries, Structure and Growth Trend", *Economic Times*, 25 May, 1974.
46. Prasad, C.S., "Financing Small Industries: Some Recent Changes", *Yojana*, Vol.39, No.3, 28 February, 1995.
47. Prasad, C.S., "Policy for Small Scale Industries in India", The *Indian Journal of Public Administration*, Vol.XLIII, No.3, July-September, 1997.
48. Raju, B. Yerram, "Planning for Growth: A Small Industry Perspective", *South Asian Journal of Management*, Vol.IV, No.2, April-June, 1997.
49. Raju, B. Yerram, "Small Industries: An Overview", *Yojana*, Vol.39, No.13, November 1995.
50. Raju, B. Yerram, "Small Scale Industries in India: A Policy Perspective", *ASCI Journal of Management*, Vol.25, No.2, March 1996.
51. Rao, A. Rama, "Refinancing of Village and Small Industries by NABARD", Kurukshetra, Vol.XXXVII, No.3, December 1988.
52. Rao, B.S. Venkata, "Small Scale Industry: Retrospect and Prospect", *Eastern Economist*, Vol.62, No.18, 3 May 1974.

53. Rao, Prabhakara, "Problems and Causes of Sickness of Small and Tiny Industries", *Khadigramodyog*, June, 1991.

54. Rathor, B.S., "Managerial Practices in Small Scale Industries in India", *Indian Management*, Vol.18, No.10, October 1979.

55. Reddeppa, L. and Naidu, K. Munidoraswamy, "Effect of Investment Subsidy on Development of Small Scale Industries in A Backward District: A Study of Chittoor District", *Journal of Rural Development*, Vol.11, No.2, March 1992.

56. Reddy, Mohan, and Reddy, Subbi, "Actors and Factors in Location of Small Scale Industry", *SEDME Journal*, Vol.XV, September 1988.

57. Sahai, B.M., The Small Scale Sector: Need for New Orientation, *Monthly Commentary on Indian Economic Conditions*, Vol.27, No.8, March 1986.

58. Sanal, K.C., "Liberalisation and its, Adverse Impact on Informal Sector Workers", *Man and Development*, Vol XXII, No.2, June 2000.

59. Sandesara, J.C., "Modern Small Industry, 1972 and 1987-88: Aspects of Growth and Structural Change", *Economic and Political Weekly*, Vol.28, No.6, February 1993.

60. Sandesara, J.C., "Small Scale Industrialisation–The Indian Experience", Economic and Political Weekly, March 1988.

61. Sharma, S.C. and Tomar, A.K., "Problems of Small Scale Industry in India", *Southern Economist*, Vol.XXV, No.17, 1 January 1987.

62. Shetty, M.C., "Entrepreneurship in Small Industry", *The Economic Weekly*, May 30, 1964.

63. Singhania, S. S., "Small Scale Sector and Government Policy", *Souvenir*, Indian Institute of Public Administration-Delhi Regional Branch, New Delhi, August, 1998.

64. "Small Industries: Spreading Wings", *Yojana*, Vol.39, No.13, November 1995.

65. Special Issue on the Role of Small and Medium Industries in Economic Development, *Asian Development Review*, Vol.6, No.2, 1988.

66. Sriram, K.S., "Quality in Small Scale Sector", Productivity, Vol.27, No.4, January-March, 1987.

67. "SSIs Seek VDIS to Broaden Tax Base", *The Hindustan Times*, June 1, 1998.

68. Sundaram, Satya, "Institutional Finance for Small Scale Sector", *Journal of the Indian Institute of Bankers*, Vol.55, No.2, April-June 1984.

69. Thaleyar khan, Homi, J.H., "Problems of Small Scale Industries", *Southern Economist*, Vol.32, No.11, October 1993.

70. Thanulingom, N. and Natrajan K., "Inventices help Promote Small Scale Industry", *Yojana*, Vol.33, No.4, 15 March, 1989.

71. *The Economic Times*, October 30, 1969.

72. Tyabji, Nasir, "Nature of Small Enterprise Development: Political Aims and Socio-Economic Reality", *Economic and Political Weekly*, Vol.19, Nos. 31, 32 and 33, August 1984.

73. Vepa, Ram K., "Small Industry", *Economic Times*, 21 October 1980.

74. Vepa, Ram K., "Small Industry Development: Restructuring the Institutional Frame", Economic and Political Weekly, Vol.22, No.35, 29 August, 1987.

75. Wali, Aditya, "Small Scale Units Cry for Support", *The Times of India (Delhi Times)*, November 20, 1997.

76. Wanchoo, N. N., "Growth of Entrepreneurship: Vital Role of Small Industries", *Productivity*, Vol.12, No.1, April-June, 1971.

Appendix - I

Question Schedule

Role of State in Promotion of Small Scale Industries: A Case Study of Delhi State Industrial Development Corporation

Researcher
Sweta Mishra

DEPARTMENT OF POLITICAL SCIENCE
University of Delhi
Delhi -110007

QUESTIONNAIRE

1. Name
2. Age
   (i) Present
   (ii) At the time of starting the enterprise
3. Educational Qualification(please tick the appropriate one)
   (i) Secondary Education ( )
   (ii) College Education but not Graduate ( )
   (iii) Graduate ( )
   (iv) Post Graduate ( )
   (v) Technical/Professional Degree ( )
   (vi) Any other ( )
4. Training if any (please specify).
5. Did you have any experience before setting up the unit? Yes/No

5.1 If yes, please mention the reasons for leaving the industrial unit you were working before?

6. What are the reasons for starting this unit?
7. Is your unit registered as Small Scale Industries unit? Yes/No

7.1 If yes, please specify the problems you had undergone while getting your unit registered?

8. Did you face any problem while getting your project cleared from the following:
   (i) Municipal Corporation
   (ii) Health Department
   (iii) Factoriés Department
   (iv) Commercial Tax Department
   (v) Electricity Board
   (vi) Pollution Control Board
   (vii) Any other departments, please specify.
9. Are you aware of the policy of the Government towards Small Scale Industries? Yes/No

9.1 If yes, what is your opinion about the Government of India policy?

10. Do you know that there are certain institutions/organisations which promote Small Scale Industries? Yes/No

10.1 If yes, please specify.

11. Do you have any idea about the various activities of the Delhi State Industrial Development Corporation? Yes/No

11.1 If yes, what do you think are the various activities of the Delhi State Industrial Development Corporation?

12. Did you get any financial assistance in the form of loan/ subsidy from the financial institutions/banks at the time of setting up the unit? Yes/No

12.1 If yes, have you obtained loans?

12.2 Which agencies provided you the loans?

12.3 What problems did you face in obtaining the loans? Please specify.

13. From where do you get raw materials for the project? (please tick)
    (i) Locally
    (ii) Within the State
    (iii) Outside the state but within the country
    (iv) Outside the country
    (v) Any other (please specify).

14. Do you find difficulty in procuring raw material?Yes/No

14.1 If yes, please specify the kinds of difficulties that you face in obtaining the raw materials?

15. Does the Government help you in importing raw materials? Yes/No

15.1 If yes, in what ways?

16. Does Delhi State Industrial Development Corporation give any help in procuring raw materials? Yes/No

16.1 If yes, in what form?

17. Where do you market your products?
    (i) Locally ()
    (ii) Within the State ()
    (iii) Outside the State but within the country ()
    (iv) Outside the country. ()

18. Do you find difficulty in marketing your products? Yes/ No

18.1 If yes, what difficulties do you face?

19. Does Delhi State Industrial Development Corporation

provide any marketing assistance? Yes/No

19.1 If yes, in what form?

20. Do you face any problem while exporting? Yes/No

20.1 If yes, please mention the problems.

21. Does Delhi State Industrial Development Corporation provide any help in exporting your products? Yes/No

21.1 If yes, mention the facilities.

22. Did you purchase your machinery on hire-purchase? Yes/No

22.1 Assign reasons, why?

22.2 Which institution helped you in getting the machinery on hire purchase?

22.3 What problems did you face in getting the machinery on hire purchase?

23. Have you heard about Delhi State Industrial Development Corporation's Technical Consultancy Organisation? Yes/No

23.1 If yes, what do you think about its functioning?

23.2 Did you receive any help from Delhi State Industrial Development Corporation's Technical Consultancy Organisation? Yes/No

23.3 If yes, in what form and to what extent?

24. What are the major problems you face in respect of the following:

(i) Choosing location
(ii) Procuring raw material
(iii) Marketing facilities
(iv) Personnel resources
(v) Financial assistance
(vi) Technical assistance
(vii) Any other.

25. Have you ever participated in any exhibition/trade fair? Yes/No

25.1 If yes, which fair/exhibition and sponsored by which organisation?

25.2 In what way?

25.3 To what extent did it benefit you?

26. Are you satisfied with the functioning of the Delhi State

Industrial Development Corporation? Yes/No

26.1 If yes, how?

26.2 If no, why?

27. What role do you think the Delhi State Industrial Development Corporation plays in promotion of Small Scale Industries?

28. Do you think that the Delhi State Industrial Development Corporation is performing its role appropriately in response to the needs of the Small Scale Industries?

29. In which way do you think that the role needs to be modified?

30. Are you satisfied with the organisational structure of Delhi State Industrial Development Corporation? Yes/No

30.1 Assign reasons, why?

31. Would you like to give any suggestions with regard to the organisational structure of the Delhi State Industrial Development Corporation?

32. What are your suggestions for improvement in the functioning of the Delhi State Industrial Development Corporation?

33. Does the Delhi State Industrial Development Corporation provide any assistance in making the Small Scale Industries environment friendly? Yes/No

33.1 If yes, in what way?

34. Do you think that the Delhi State Industrial Development Corporation has an obligation to make the new environment friendly technology available to the Small Scale Industries? Yes/No

34.1 If yes, how do you think that a co-ordination between the Delhi State Industrial Development Corporation and the Small Scale Entrepreneurs can be achieved?

35. What do you perceive should be the role of Delhi State Industrial Development Corporation?

35.1 What should be the new role of Delhi State Industrial Development Corporation in the context of present industrial development ?

Appendix II

Memorandum of Association
AND
Articles of Association
OF
DELHI STATE INDUSTRIAL DEVELOPMENT CORPORATION LIMITED
NEW DELHI-110001

Fresh Certificate of Incorporation Consequent on Change of Name Co. No. 5536

In the Office of the Registrar of Companies Delhi and Haryana [Under the Co. Act, 1956 (1 of 1956)]

In the matter of M/s. Delhi Small Industries Development Corporation Limited.

I hereby certify that Delhi Small Industries Development Corporation Limited, which was originally incorporated on 15th day of February, 1971 under the Companies Act, 1956 and under the name Delhi Small Industries Development Corporation Private Limited, having duly passed the necessary resolution in terms of section 21 of Companies Act, 1956 and the approval of the Central Government signified in writing having been accorded thereto in the Ministry of Law, Justice & Company Affairs (Company Law Board) Regional Director, Northern Region, Kanpur letter NO. 1920-D/3598 dated 15-5-1976 the name of the said company is this day changed to M/s. Delhi State Industrial Development Corporation Limited and this certificate is issued pursuent to section 23(1) of the said Act,

Given under my hand at New Delhi this 20th day of May, 1976. (One thousand nine hundred Seventy six).

Seal

Sd/

(Mrs. C. Kapoor) Asstt. Registrar of Cos.
Delhi and Haryana

The Companies Act, 1956

(Company Limited by Shares)

Memorandum of Association of Delhi State Industrial Development Corporation Limited

I. The name of the company was "Delhi Small Industries Development Corporation Limited". Which was subsequently changed Delhi State Industrial Development Corporation.

II. The registered office of the Company will be situated in the Union Territory of Delhi.

III. The objects for which the company is established are:

(a) The Main Objects of the Company to be pursued by the Co. on Its Incorporation

(1) To aid, counsel, assist, finance, protect and promote the interests of Small Industries in the Union Territory of Delhi, whether owned or run by Government, statutory body, company, firm or individuals and to provide them with capital, credit. means, resources and technical and managerial assistance for the prosecution of their work and business, to enable them to develop and improve their methods of manufacture, management and marketing and their technique of production.

(2) To undertake procurement and distribution of various raw materials, whether imported or indigenous allocated by the Government of India to the Department of Industries, Delhi Administration, Delhi or through M.M.T.C. and S.T.C. or any other agency for supply to

the Small Scale Industries on the prices fixed by the Corporation. Besides the Government allocations, the Corporation may arrange to procure the raw materials available in short supply in the country for distribution to the bonafide small scale actual users whether for the supply of end products in the home market or for export purposes.

(3) To operate upon import licences/releases orders issued to small scale industries and to club them together for placing indents on the foreign or indigenous suppliers and get the raw materials, components, spares imported and to arrange to deliver the material to such licence holders/release order holders on predetermined service charges to enable the small scale units of Delhi to utilise small value licences/release orders.

Explanation : The expression 'Small Scale Industry' appearing in these articles means an industry having capital investment on plant, equipment and machinery not exceeding the value of Rs. 7.5 lakhs.

However, this definition is open to amendment, revision, alteration by the Government of India and such amended, revised or altered definition shall be deemed to have been substituted for the above definition.

(4) To establish and maintain trade centre (s) to serve as a clearing house for dissemination of information regarding small scale industries and for the purpose of display or exhibit their products and to maintain liaison between the small scale industries of Delhi and the interested buyers for securing contract on their behalf and to do all such acts for execution and implementation of such contracts and orders.

(5) To establish and maintain export house (s) to promote export trade and participate in export trade for the benefit of small scale industries.

(6) To undertake and provide marketing facilities to the Small Scale Industries of Delhi.

(7) To acquire lands develop them suitably by providing communications, power supply, water supply and other

facilities at places determined by the company and make them available on such terms and conditions as may be agreed upon to any individual, firm, company, association or concern for the purpose of establishing new small scale industries or for the purpose of shifting the existing small scale industries from any congested area and to take over or establish and administer Industrial Estates in the Union Territory of Delhi.

(8) To effect co-ordination between Large Industries and Small Industries by suitable methods, enabling Small Industries to manufacture satisfactorily such parts, accessories, ancillaries and components and other articles as may be required by large industries.

(9) To promote and operate schemes of the small industries development of Delhi and for that purpose to prepare and get or cause to be prepared investigations and studies for feasibility reports, detailed project reports, market studies, statistics, and other relevant information for the establishment of any industries undertaking and to promote and establish companies, and associations for the execution of such industrial projects. To plan, formulate and execute projects, in particular for setting up industries in the lines of production which are important in the opinion of the Company for the small industries development of Delhi.

(10) To guarantee to the National Small Industries Corporation, in respect of moneys to be paid by an entrepreneur to the National Small Industries Corporation under the scheme for the hire purchase of machinery on such conditions, as may be prescribed for the purpose.

(11) Subject to section 384 of the Companies Act, to direct the management, control and supervision of and arrangement of any company, association, firm or concern by nominating directors, controllers, supervisors, advisors or otherwise, or to collaborate with any company or association or firm or concern formed for carrying on any manufacturing or other business within the objects

of the company.

(12) To promote and operate schemes in collaboration with Delhi Administration for the dispersal of the small scale industries in a manner conducive to the balanced regional development of the various parts of Delhi.

(13) To enter into arrangement with Government of India, Delhi Administration or any other Government, or States, or Local authority for the purpose of carrying out the objects of the company or furthering its interest and to obtain from such Government or authority or persons any charters, subsidies, loans, indemnities, grants, contracts, licenses, rights, concessions, privileges or immunities which the company may think it desirable to obtain and exercise or to comply with any such arrangement, rights, privileges, and concessions.

(14) To procure capital for or to provide machinery, equipment and other facilities to any company, person and association for the purpose of carrying into effect any objects connected with the small industrial development of Delhi.

(15) To seek for and secure openings for the employment of capital in Delhi and elsewhere and with a view thereto to prospect, inquire, examine, explore and text, and to despatch and employ expeditions, commissioners, experts and other agents.

(16) To carry on business of dealers, buyers, selling agents, commission agents, importers and exporters of all types of consumer goods, merchandise, brass and silver wares, textile goods, readymade garments and any other item in the Union Territory of Delhi or at any congenient place within India or outside India by itself or in collaboration with co-operetive institutions, firms of entrepeneurs developed by the Corporation.

(17) To promote and develop industries of all types including wholly public sector and Joint Sector Undertakings and to improve and develop infrastructure for promotion of

industrial Complexes in the Union Territory of Delhi.

(18) To establish and maintain Man Power Export Bureau to export Man Power to foreign countries and to do all such things which are directly or indirectly related to the above activity.

(b) Ancillary Or incidental Objects

(1) To enter into contracts with, and take up indents from the Government of India and State Governments in the Union of India and Corporation and other subsidiaries and branches and from any agency or officer thereof having the necessary powers, for fabrication, manufacture, assembly and supply of goods materials articles and equipment of every description and to arrange for the performance of such contracts and indents by sub-contracting them to, or placing orders in respect thereof with, Small Industries or others for the fabrication, manufacture, assembly or supply of such goods, materials, articles or equipment or parts thereof, servicing or processing in connection therewith or such managerial services as may be necessary for the due performance of such contracts and indents, and to have the goods, materials, articles and equipment fabricated, manufactured, assembled and supplied.

(2) To establish and maintain quality control, testing and common facility centre (s) for ensuring standard quality of industrial products and providing such facilities that may be required for the purpose and subscribe or to subsidise or become member of Training Institutions, Research Laboratories, Research Institutions and Experimental workshop for scientific technical research and experiments.

(3) To certify to the appropriate Government officers with respect to the competency, as to capacity and credit, of any small industrial concern or group of such concerns to perform any specific Government contract.

(4) To obtain from any Government, or other agency such reports concerning the giving of contracts and sub-contracts and making loans to business concerns as may be deemed necessary for carrying out the aforesaid objects.

(5) To grant or guarantee or recommend the grant of loans to Small Industries, to which sub-contracts are given or orders are issued, as aforesaid, in order to enable them, in carrying out the sub-contracts or orders, to finance plant construction, conversion or expansion, including the acquisition of land, or to finance the acquisition of equipment, facilities, machinery supplies or materials, or to supply such concerns with working capital to be used in the manufacture of articles equipment, supplies or materials under contract to Government or to this company, to provide them with such financial, technical, managerial and other assistance as may be deemed necessary for the purpose of enabling them to execute and carry out the sub-contracts and orders satisfactorily and to organise production and manufacture for meeting such contracts and sub-contracts and orders adequately and according to specification and to ensure satisfactory production by all necessary instruction, assistance, inspection and supervision.

(6) To promote and establish such Companies, Associations, Advisory Boards and other suitable bodies as may be deemed necessary in order to carry out the aforesaid objects effectively.

(7) To procure capital or financial assistance or accommodation for or provide machinery, equipment, technical and managerial assistance, information, instruction, inspection, supervision and other facilities to any company, person, or association for the purpose of carrying into effect any of the aforesaid objects.

(8) To manufacture, buy, sell, import, export, install, work and generally deal in any plant, machinery substances, tools, materials, goods or things of any description which, in the opinion of the company, may be conveniently

dealt with by the Company in connection with any of its objects.

(9) To enter into any partnership or arrangement for joint working in business, sharing of profits, pooling of any industrial undertaking, joint venture or reciprocal concession or amalgamation, with any other company, firm or person, carrying on or engaged in any manufacture or business within the objects of this Company or similar thereto.

(10) To establish, promote, subsidise and otherwise assist, any company or companies' syndicate or other concern for the purpose of setting up any small industry.

(11) Generally to purchase, take on lease or in exchange, here, or otherwise, any real and personal property and any rights or privileges which the Company may think necessary or convenient for the purpose of its business and in particular any land, buildings, easements, machinery, plant, and stock-in trade.

(12) To sell, dispose of by way of lease or on hire or otherwise transfer business property and undertakings of the Company, or any part thereof, for cash, stock or shares of any other company or for any other consideration which the company may see fit to accept for the attainment of its objects.

(13) To sell, improve, manage, develop, exchange, lease, mortgage, enfranchise, dispose of, turn to account or otherwise deal with, all or any part of the property and rights of the Company.

(14) To accept stock or shares in, or the debentures, mortgage debentures or other securities of other company in payment or part payment for and services rendered or for any sale made to or debt owning from any such company.

(15) To carry on any other trade or business (whether manufacturing or otherwise) which may seem to the Company capable of being conveniently carried on in

connection with the above calculated directly or indirectly to enhance the value of or render profitable any of the Company's property or rights.

(16) To acquire and undertake the whole or any part of the business, property, and liablities of any person or company carrying on any business which the company is authorised to carry on or possessed of property Suitable for the purposes of this Company.

(17) To pay all costs, charges and expenses incurred or sustained in or about the promotion and establishment of the Company, or which the Company shall consider to be in the nature or preliminary expenses, including therein the cost of advertising, commissions for underwriting, brokerage, printing and stationery and expenses attendant upon the formation of agencies.

(18) To construct, maintain, and alter any building or works, necessary or convenient for the purpose of the Company.

(19) To apply for and take out purchase or otherwise acquire any trade mark, patents, patent-rights, inventions, copyright, designs or secret processes, which may be useful for the Company's object and to grant licences to use the same, and to work, develop, carry out, exercise and turn to account the same and adopt such means of making known the business and products of the Company or of any company in which this Company is interested as may seem expedient and in particular by advertising in newspapers, magazines; periodicals, by circulars, by purchase and exhibitions, by publication and distribution of books and periodicals, calendars, almanacs and diaries, by distributing samples and by granting prizes, rewards and donations.

(20) To make, draw, accept, endorse, discount, execute, issue and negotiate, cheques, bills of exchange, promissory notes, debentures and other negotiable or transferable instruments.

(21) To borrow or raise or secure the payment of money in such other manner as the Company shall think fit and in particular by the issue of debentures, debenture bonds or debenture stock perpetual or otherwise. Mortgage or any other securities charged or based upon the undertakings of the company or any part of its property both present and future including its uncalled capital and the rights of the Company's or without any such security, and upon such terms as to priority or otherwise, and generally to borrow money in such manner as the Company shall think fit.

(22) To receive grants, loans, advances or other money on deposit or otherwise, from the Central Government or State Governments, Banks, Companies, Trusts, or individuals with or without allowance of interest there on.

(23) To lend money to such persons or Companies and on such terms as may seem expedient, and in particular to customers and others having dealing with the Company, and to guarantee the performance of contracts by any such persons or companies.

(24) To invest and deal with the money of the Company not immediately required in such manner, other than in the shares of this Company, as may from time to time be determined.

(25) To acquire by subscription purchase or otherwise, and to accept and take, hold and sell, shares or stock in any company, society or undertaking, the object of which shall, either in whole or in part, be similar to those of this Company, or such as may be likely, directly or indirectly, to promote or advance the interests of this Company.

(26) To establish, maintain, subscribe to or subsidise or become member of training institutions, research laboratories, research institutions and experimental workshops for scientific and technical research and experiments.

(27) To provide for the welfare of persons in the employment of the Company, and the wives, widows and families of such persons, by establishing provident or other Funds, by grants of money, pensions, or other payments, and by providing or subscribing to places of instruction and recreation and hospitals, dispensaries, medical and other attendance and other assistance as the Company shall think fit, and to subscribe money to or for and otherwise help any charitable or benevolent object or any exhibition or any public show or useful object.

(28) To establish and regulate branches or agencies of the Company at any place in India or elsewhere and discontinue the same.

(29) Gernally to do all such other matters and things as may appear to be incidental or conducive to the attainment of the above objects or any of them or consequential upon the exercise of its powers or discharge of its duties.

(30) To create any depreciation fund, reserve fund, sinking fund, insurance fund, òr any special or other fund whether for depreciation or for repairing, improving, extending or maintaining any of the property of the Company or for redemption of debentures or redeemable preference shares or for special dividends or for equalising dividends for any other purpose whatsoever, and to transfer any such fund or part thereof to any of the other funds herein mentioned.

(31) To employ or pay experts, foreign consultants, etc. in connection with the planning and development of all or any of the business connected with the Company's operations.

(32) To appropriate, use, or let out land belonging to the Company for streets, parks pleasure grounds, allotments and other conveniences and to present any such land so laid out to the public or to any persons or company conditionally or unconditionally as the Company thinks fit.

(c) The Other Objects

(1) To apply for, tender, purchase or otherwise acquire contracts and concessions for, or in relation to the construction, cxecution, carrying out, equipment, improvement, management, administration or control of works and conveniences and to undertake, execute, carry out, dispose of or otherwise turn to account the same.

(2) To invest the capital of the Company in, or to deal with shares, stocks, bonds. debentures, obligations and other securities of any company or association formed for establishing, executing or working of any industrial undertaking approved by the company.

(3) To issue, or guarantee the issue of, or the payment of interest on the shares, debentures, debenture stock, or other securities or obligations of any company or association, and to pay or provide for brokerage, commission and under-writing in respect of any such issue..

(4) The above mentioned objects of this Company will extend to the Union Territory of Delhi, to every other state in the Indian Union and also to territories beyond the Indian Union.

In is hereby declared that (i) the word "Company" in this Memorandum when applied otherwise than to this Company shall be deemed to include any authority, partnership or other body of persons whether incorporated or not incorporated, whether domiciled in India or elsewhere.

IV. The liability of the members is limited.

V. The share capital of the Company is Rs. 20 lakhs divided into 20,000 equity shares of Rs. 100/- each.

The Share Capital of the Company is Rs. 30,00,00000 (Rupees Thirty Crores) divided into 30,00,000 Equity shares of Rs. 100/- (Rupees one hundred) each.

We, the several persons, whose names and addresses, description and occupations are subscribed are desirous of being formed into a company in pursuance of this Memorandum of Association and we respectively agree to take the number of shares in the capital of the Company set opposite our respective names.

Names, addresses, descriptions and occupations (if any) of subscribers	No. of Shares taken by each subscriber	Names, addresses, description and occupations (if any) of witnesses
1. Lt. Governor of Delhi	4998 (Four thousand nine hundred & ninty eight only)	
Sd/- L. N. Saklani S/o Shri Hirdey Narain Siklani Secretary Industries, Delhi Administration, Delhi For & on behalf of Lt. Governor of Delhi	Sd/- K. P. Chaudhry S/o Shri P. R. Chaudhry Industrial Survey Officer, Office of the Director of Industries	Delhi Administration, Delhi
2. Sd/- Janak Juneja D/o Shri Sarup Singh Under Secretary Industries, Dlehi Administration, Delhi	1 (One)	Sd/- J. L. Kotru, S/o Shri Shiv Ji Kotru, Asst. Director of Industries Delhi, Administration, Delhi
3. Sd/- R. N. Suri S/o Shri J. G. Suri Deputy Director of Industries (Planning & Technical) Office of the Director of Industries, Delhi Administration, Delhi.	(One)	Sd/- B. L. Goel S/o Shri Rameshwar Dass, Office of the Director of Industries, Delhi Administration, Delhi.

Dated this 4th day of February, 1971

The Companies Act, 1956

(Public Company Limited by Shares) Articles of Association of Delhi State Industrial Development Corporation Limited Preliminary

(1) In these articles unless there be something repugnant in the subject-matter or context :

(a) "The Company" means "Delhi State Industrial Development Corporation Ltd.".

(b) "The Act" means the Companies Act of 1956.

(c) "President" means the President of India.

(d) "Directors' means the Directors for the time being of the Company.

(e) "Chairman" means the Chairman of the Board of the Directors for the time being of the Company.

(f) "Office" means the registered office for the time being of the company.

(g) "The Seal" means the common seal of the Company.

(h) "State" means the Union Territory of Delhi.

(i) "Lt. Governor of Delhi" means the Administrator of Union Territory of Delhi.

Unless the context otherwise requires other words or expressions contained in these Articles shall bear the same meaning as in the Act.

(2) Save as otherwise expressly provided for in these Articles the regulations contained table A in schedule I to the Act shall apply.

(3) The regulations for the management of the Company and for the observance of the members thereof and their representatives shall subject to any exercise of the statutory powers of the Company in reference to the repeal or alteration of or addition of its regulations by special resolution as prescribed or permitted by the Act be such as are contained in these Articles.

(4) The Company is a Private Company and accordingly:

(a) the number of members for the time being of the Company (exclusive of persons who are for the time being in the employment of the Company and persons who having been formerly in the employment of the Company were members of the Company while in that employment and have continued to be members after the employment ceased) is not to exceed fifty, but where two or more persons hold one or more shares in the company jointly, they shall, for the purpose of this Article. be treated as a single member.

(b) Any invitation to the public to subscribe for any shares in or debentures stock of the Company is hereby prohibited, and

(c) The right of transfer of shares is restricted as hereinafter provided.

Shares

(5) The share capital of the Company is Rs. 20,00,000 (Twenty Lakhs) divided into 20,000 equity shares of Rs. 100/- each with power to increase the share capital.

"Resolved that in accordance with Articles 5 and 30 of Articles of Association the share capital of the Corporation be raised from Rs. 20 lakhs to Rs. 100 lakhs divided into 1,00,000 shares of Rs. 100/- each. Further resolved that Clause (V) and Article 5 of the Memorandum and Articles of Association of the Delhi State Industrial Development Corporation be amended accordingly".

The Share Capital of the Company is Rs. 30, 00, 00, 000 (Rupees thirty Crores) divided into 30, 00, 000 Equity

Shares of Rs. 100/- (Rupees one hundred) each.

(6) The shares shall be under the control of the Board of Directors who may allot or otherwise dispose of them on such terms and conditions as it consider fit subject to such directions as the President may issue from time to time.

(7) (1) Every person whose name is entered as a member in the register of members shall be entitled to receive within three months after allotment or within two months of reciepts of application for registration of transfer (or within such other period as the conditions of issue shall provide):

(a) One certificate for all his shares without payment; or

(b) Several certificates, each for one or more of his shares, upon payment of one rupee for every certificate after the first.

(2) Every certificate shall be under the seal and shall specify the shares to which it relates and the amount paid up thereon.

(3) In respect of any share or shares held jointly by several persons, the Company shall not be bound to issue more than one certificate, and delivery of a certificate for a share to one of several joint holders shall be sufficient delivery to all such holders.

(8) If a share certificate is defaced, lost or destroyed, it may be renewed or a duplicate of a certificate may be issued if such certificate is proved to have been lost or destroyed, or having been defaced or mutilated or torn and is surrendered to the Company, on payment of a fee of fifty paise and on such terms if any, as to evidence and indemnity and the payment of out of pocket expenses incurred by the Company in investigating evidence, as the directors think fit.

(9) (1) The Company shall have a first and paramount lien :

(a) On every share (not being a fully paid shares), for all moneys (whether presently payable or not) called, or payable at a fixed time, in respect of that share, and

(b) On all shares (not being fully paid shares) standing registered in the name of a single person, for all moneys presently payable by him or his estate to the Company.

Provided that the Board of Directors may at any time declare any shares to be wholly or in part exempt from the provisions of this clause.

(2) The Company's lien, if any, on a share shall extend to all dividends payable thereon.

(10) The Company may sell, in such manner as the Board thinks fit, any shares on which the company has a lien

Provided that no sale shall be made:

(a) unless a sum in respect of which the lien exists is presently payable; or

(b) until the expiration of fourteen days after a notice in writing stating and demanding payment of such part of the amount in respect of which the lien exists as is presently payable, has been given to the registered holder for the time being of the share or the person entitled thereto. by reason of his death or insolvency.

(11) (1) To give effect to any such sale, the Board may authorise some person to transfer the shares sold to the purchaser thereof.

(2) The purchaser shall be registered as the holder of the shares comprised in any such transfer.

(3) The purchaser shall not be bound to see to the application of the purchase money, nor shall his title to the shares be affected by any irregularity or invalidity in the proceedings in reference to the sale.

(12) (1) The proceeds of the sale shall be received by company and applied in payment of such part of the amount in respect of which the lien exists as is presently payable.

(2) The residue, if any, shall, subject to a like lien for sums not presently payable as existed upon the shares before the sale be paid to the person entitled to the shares at the date of sale.

Call On Shares

(13) (1) The Board may, from time to time, make calls upon the members in respect of any moneys unpaid on their shares (whether on account of the nominal value of the shares or by way of premium) and not by the conditions of allotment thereof made payable at fixed times:

Provided that no call shall exceed one-fourth of the nominal value of the shares or be payable at less than one month from the date fixed for the payment of the last preceding call.

(2) Each member shall, subject to receiving at least fourteen days notice, specifying the time or times and place of payment pay to the company, at the time or times and place so specified, the amount called on his shares.

(3) A call may be revoked or postponed at the discretion of the Board.

(14) A call shall be deemed to have been made at the time when the resolution of the Board of Directors authorising the call was passed and may be required to be paid by instalments.

(15) (1) If a sum called in respect of a share is not paid before or/ on the day appointed for payment thereof, the person from whom the sum is due shall pay interest thereon from the day appointed for payment thereof to the time of actual payment at five per cent per annum or at such lower rate, if any, as the Board may determine.

(2) The Board shall be at liberty to waive payment of any such interest wholly or in part.

(16) (1) Any sum which by the terms of issue of any share becomes payable on allotment or at any fixed date, whether on account of the nominal value of the share or by way of premium, shall, for the purposes of these regulations, be deemed to be a call duly made and payable on the date on which by the terms of issue such sum become payable.

(2) In case of non-payment of such sum all the relevant provisions of these regulations as to payment of interest and expenses, forfeiture or otherwise shall apply as if such sum had become payable by virtue of a call duly made and notified.

(17) The Board :

(a) may, if it thinks fit, receive from any member willing to advance the same, all or any part of the moneys uncalled and unpaid upon any shares held by him; and

(b) upon all or any of the moneys so advanced, may (until the same would but for such advance, become presently payable) pay interest at such rate not exceeding, unless the company in general meeting shall otherwise direct, six per cent per annum as may be agreed upon between the Board and the member paying the sum in advance.

Transfer And Transmission of Shares

(18) The instrument of transfer of any share in the company shall be executed both by the transferor and transferee, and the transferor shall be deemed to remain holder of the share until the name of the transferee is entered in the Register of members in respect thereof.

(19) Shares of the Company shall be transferred in the form as prescribed under the Act from time to time.

(20) The right of members to transfer their shares shall be restricted as follows :

(a) A share may be transferred by a member or other person entitled to transfer only to a person or persons approved by the Board and to no other person.

(b) The Board of directors may decline to register any proposed transfer of shares, without assigning any reason therefor.

(21) (A) The Board of Directors may suspend the registration of transfer during the fourteen days immediately preceding the annual general meeting in each year.

(B) The Board of -Directors may decline to recognise

any instrument of transfer unless:

(a) a fee not exceeding Rs. 2 is paid to the Company in respect thereof; and

(b) the instrument of transfer is accompanied by the Certificate of the shares to which it relates, and such other evidence as the Board of Directors may reasonably require to show the right of the transferor to make the transfer. If the Board refuses to register a transfer of any shares, it shall within two months after the date on which the transfer was lodged with the Company send to the transferee and the transferor notice of the refusal.

(22) So far it concerns any share held by any person as a nominee of any body Corporate, on the latter's requiring him to transfer any such share to it or on to any other person or persons nominated by it, or any such person becoming of unsound mind or becoming or being adjudicated an insolvent, or dying or on such person, being a company, being wound up voluntarily or by the Court or subject to the supervision of the Court, the following provisions shall take effect, namely :

(a) The body Corporate may at any time serve the Company with a requisition to enforce the transfer of any such share.

(b) The Company shall thereupon forthwith give to the holder of such share, or where the holder has become of unsound mind, so his committee or other guardian or where the holder has become or been adjudicated an insolvent to the assignee of his estate and effects, or where the holder is dead, to his heirs or legal representatives, or where the holder, being a Company, has been wound up as aforesaid to its liquidator, notice in writing of the requisition and unless within 14 days after wards, the holder, or as the case may be, the Committee or guardian or assignee or heirs or legal representatives of such holder; shall execute in favour of the body Corporate or any person or persons nominated by it, a proper transfer form in respect of such share and hand-over the same alongwith the relative certificate in respect of such share to it or any other person or persons nominated by it and the Body Corporate or such other person as may be nominated by it in that behalf may at any time thereafter execute a transfer in respect of such share for and on behalf of such holder or of his estate and the same shall be deemed to have duly and properly executed for and on behalf of such holder or of his estate and thereupon the holder of his estate shall cease to have any interest whatsoever in such share and the certificate of such share, if not handed over as aforesaid, shall thereupon stand cancelled and be and become void and of no effect, and the Company shall be entitled thereafter to issue a new certificate in lieu thereof in favour of the Body Corporate or such person or persons as it may nominate.

(23) Any person becoming entitled to a share in consequence of the death or insolvency of a member shall, upon such evidence being produced as may from time to time be required by the Board of Directors, have the right either to be registered as a member in respect of the share, or, instead of being registered himself, to make such transfer of the share as the deceased or insolvent person could have made, but the Board shall, in either case, have the same right to decline or suspend registration as they would have had in the case of a transfer of the share by the deceased or insolvent person before the death or insolvency.

(24) A person becoming entitled to a share by reason of the death or insolvency of the holder shall be entitled to the same dividends and other advantages to which he would be entitled if he were the registered holder of the share, except that he shall not, before being registered as a member in respect of the share be entitled in respect of it to exercise any right conferred by membership in relation to meetings of the Company.

Forfeiture of Shares

(25) If a member fails to pay any call, or instalment of a call, on the day appointed for payment thereof, the Board of Directors may at any time thereafter during such time as any part of the call or instalment remains unpaid serve a notice on him requiring payment of so much of the call or instalment as is unpaid, together with any interest which may have accrued.

(26) The notice aforesaid shall :

(a) name a further day (not being earlier than the expire of fourteen days from the date of service of the notice) on or before which the payment required by the notice is to be made;

(b) state that, in the event of non-payment on or before the day so named, the shares in respect of which the call was made will be liable to be forfeited.

(27) If the requirements of any such notice as aforesaid are not complied with, any share in respect of which the notice has been given may, at any time thereafter, before the payment required by the notice has been made, be forfeited be a resolution of the Board to that effect.

(28) (1) A person whose shares have been forfeited shall cease to be a member in respect of the forfeited shares, but shall not withstanding the forfeiture, remain liable to pay to the Company all moneys which, at the date of forfeiture, were presently payable by him to the Company in respect of the shares.

(2) The liability of such person shall cease if and when the Company shall have received payment in full or all such moneys in respect of the shares.

(29) (1) A duly verified declaration in writing that the declarant is a director or the Manager of the Company, and that a share in a Company has been duly forfeited on a date stated in the declaration shall be conclusive evidence of the facts therein stated as against all persons claiming to be entitled to the share.

(2) The company may receive the consideration, if any, given for the share in any sale or disposal

thereof and may execute a transfer of the share in favour of the person to whom the share is sold or disposed of.

(3) The transferee shall thereupon be registered as the holder of the share.

(4) The transferee shall not be bound to see the application of the purchase money, if any, nor shall his title to the share be affected by any irregularity or invalidity in the proceeding in reference to the forfeiture, sale or disposal of the share.

Alteration of Capital

(30) The Company, may from time to time, by ordinary resolution increase the share capital by such sum, to be divided into shares of such amount, as may by specified in the resolution.

(31) Except so far as otherwise provided by the conditions of issue or by these articles, any capital raised by the creation of new shares shall be considered part of the original capital and shall be subject to the provision herein contained with reference to the payment of calls and instalments, transfer and transmission, lien voting surrender and otherwise.

(32) The new shares shall be offered to the members in proportion to the existing shares held by each member and such offer shall be made by notice specifying the number of shares to which the member is entitled and limiting a time within which the offer if not accepted will be deemed to be declined and after the expiration of such notice or on receipt of earlier intimation from the person to whom such notice is given that he declines to accept the shares offered, the Directors may dispose of the same in such manner as they think most beneficial to the Company.

(33) The Company may, by special resolution, reduce in any manner and with and subject to any incident authorised and consent required by law, its share capital.

Borrowing Powers

(34) Subject to the provision of Section 292 of the Act, the Board may from time to time, borrow any sum or sums of money for the purpose of the Company.

(35) The Board may secure the repayment of such moneys in such manner and upon such terms and conditions in all respects as it thinks fit and in particular by creating any mortgage, charge or other security on the undertaking of the whole, or any part of the property of the Company (both present and future) including its uncalled capital for the time being.

General Meetings

(36) The First Annual General Meeting of the Company shall be held by the Company within 18 months of its incorporation and thereafter the annual general meeting of the Company shall be held within 6 months after the expiry of each financial year except in the case when for any special reasons, the time for holding the annual general meeting (not being the first annual general meeting) is extended by the Central Government by a period not exceeding 3 months. Except as provided under the Act, no greater interval than 15 months shall be allowed to lapse between two Annual General Meetings. Every General Meeting shall be held during business hours on a day that is not a public holiday. The notice calling the meeting shall specify it as the Annual General Meeting. The other general meetings, which may be called at such time and place as may be determined by the Directors, shall be called Extraordinary General Meetings.

(37) The Board may, when it thinks fit, call Extraordinary General Meetings.

(38) (1) No business shall be transacted at any general meeting unless a quorum of members is personally present at the time when the meeting proceeds to business.

(2) Save as herein otherwise provided two members present in person shall be a quorum.

(39) (1) The Government as long as they are shareholders of the Company, may from time to time appoint one or more persons (who need not be a member or members of the Company) to represent them at all or any meetings of the Company.

(2) Any one of the persons appointed under Sub-clause (1) of the Article who is personally present at the meeting shall be deemed to be a member entitled to vote and present in person and shall be entitled to represent the Government at all or any such meetings and to vote on their behalf whether on a show of hands or on a poll.

(3) The Government may, from time to time cancel any appointment made under sub-clause (1) of this Article and make fresh appointments.

(4) The production at the meeting of an order of the President evidenced as provided in the Constitution of India shall be accepted by the Company as sufficient evidence of any such appointment or cancellation as aforesaid.

(5) Any person appointed by the Government under this Article may if so authorised by such order, appoint a proxy, whether specially or generally.

(40) The Chairman of the Board shall preside as Chairman at every general meeting of the Company.

(41) If the Chairman is not present within fifteen minutes after the time appointed for holding the meeting the members present shall elect one of their members to be Chairman of the meeting.

(42) (1) The Chairman may, with the consent of any meeting at which a quorum is present, and shall if so directed by meeting, adjourn the meeting from time to time and from place to place.

(2) No business shall be transacted at any adjourned meeting other than the business left unfinished at the meeting from which the adjournment took place.

(3) When a meeting is adjourned for thirty days or more, notice of the adjourned meeting shall be given as in

the case of an original meeting.

(4) Save as aforesaid, it shall not be necessary to give any notice of an adjournment or of the business to be transacted at an adjourned meeting.

(43) In the case of an equality of votes, whether on a show of hands or on a poll, t he Chairman of the meeting at which the show of hands take place or at which the poll is demanded, shall be entitled to a second or casting vote.

(44) Any business other than that upon which a poll has been demanded may be proceeded with, pending the taking of the poll.

(45) The Chairman of any meeting shall be of the sole judge of the validity of every vote tendered at such meeting. The Chairman present at the taking of a poll shall be the sole judge of the validity of every vote tendered at such poll.

Vote of Members

(46) (a) On a show of hands, every member present in person shall have one vote.

(b) On a poll, the voting rights of members shall be as laid down in section 87 of the Act.

(47) A member of unsound mind or in respect of whom an order has been made by any court having jurisdiction in lunacy, may vote whether on a show of hands or on a poll, by his Committee or other legal guardians and any such committee or guardian may on a poll, vote by proxy.

(48) No member shall be entitled to vote at any general meeting unless the calls or other sums presently payable by him in respect of share in the Company have been paid.

(49) (1) No objection shall be raised to the qualifications of any voter except at the meeting or adjourned meeting at which the vote objected to is given or tendered, and every vote not disallowed at such meeting shall be valid for all purposes.

(2) Any such objection made in due time shall be referred to the Chairman of the meeting whose decision shall

be final and conclusive.

(50) The instrument appointing a proxy and the power of attorney or other authority, if any, under which it is signed or executed or a notarially certified copy of that power or authority, shall be deposited at the registered office of the Company not less than 48 hours before the time for holding the meeting or adjourned meeting at which the person named in the instrument purposes to vote or in the case of a poll, not less than 24 hours before the time appointed for the taking of the poll, and in default the instrument of proxy shall not be treated as valid.

(51) An instrument appointing a proxy shall be in either of the forms in Schedule IX to the Act or a form as near thereto as circumstances admit.

(52) A vote given in accordance with the terms of instrument of proxy shall be valid, notwithstanding the previous death or insanity of the principal or the revocation of the proxy or of the authority under which the proxy was executed, or the transfer of the shares in respect of which the proxy is given;

Provided that, no intimation in writing of such death, insanity revocation or transfer shall have been received by the Company at its office before the commencement of the meeting or adjourn meeting at which the proxy is used.

Board of Directors

(53) (1) Unless otherwise determined by the General Meeting, the number of Directors of the Company shall not be more than 9 and less than 2.

(2) All the Directors shall be appointed by the President.

(3) The Directors shall hold office at the pleasure of their appointing authorities or until their office become vacant in terms of the provisions of Section 283 of the Act whichever the earlier and they shall not be liable to retirement by rotation.

(4) The Chairman of the Board shall be appointed by the President.

(5) The Chairman and the Directors appointed by the President shall hold office until removed by the President. As and when the Chairman or Director or appointed by the President vacate office whether on removal or by resignation or otherwise, the President shall fill in the vacancy by nomination.

(53) (A) The Chairman may perform any functions and exercise any authority vested in the Board at in an emergency. Any action so taken by the Chairman will be got ratified in the Next Meeting of the Board.

(54) The remuneration of the Directors shall, in so far as it consists of a monthly payment, be deemed to accrue from day to day.

(55) The Directors shall be paid sitting fees not exceeding Rs. 250/- per meeting as may be fixed from time to time by the Board of Directors, for attending the meetings, of the Board of Directors or any Committee or Sub-Committee thereof.

(56) The Directors shall not be required to hold any qualification shares.

(57) The Board may pay all expenses incurred in getting up and registering the Company.

(58) The Company may exercise the powers conferred by section 50 of the Act with regard to having an official seal for use abroad and such powers shall be vested in the Board.

(59) All cheques, promissory notes, drafts, hundies, bill of exchange and other negotiable instruments and receipts for moneys paid to the Company shall be signed, drawn, accepted endorsed, or otherwise executed as the case may be, by such person and in such manner as the Board shall, from time to time by resolution determine.

(60) Every Director present at any meeting of the Board or of a Committee thereof shall sign his name in a book to be kept for that purpose.

Alternative Directors

(61) The Board, with the prior approval of the President, may

appoint an alternate Director to act for a Director hereinafter in this Article called 'the Original Director' during the latter's absence for a period of not less than three months from this State. Such Director shall not hold office as such for a period longer than that permissible to the original Director. Such appointment shall have effect and such appointee, whilst he holds office as an alternate Director, shall be entitled to notice of meetings of the Board and to attend and vote thereat accordingly, but he shall not require any qualifications and shall *ipso facto* vacate office if and when the absent Director returns to the State in which meetings of the Board are ordinarily held or the absent Director vacates office as a Director.

Proceedings of Boards

(62) (1) The Board of Directors may meet for the despatch of business, adjourn and otherwise regulate its meetings, as it think fit.

(2) A Director may, and the Secretary on the requisition of a director shall at any time, summon a meeting of the Board.

(63) The Board of Directors shall be bound by the directives from the President from time to time.

(64) (1) Save as otherwise expressly provided in the Act, questions arising at any meeting of the Board shall be decided by a majority of votes.

(2) In case of an equality of votes, the Chairman of the Board, if any, shall have a second or casting vote.

(65) If at any time the Chairman is not present within five minutes after the time appointed for holding the meeting, the Directors present may choose one of their members to be Chairman of meeting.

(66) (1) The Board may, subject to the provisions of the Act, delegate any of its powers to committees consisting of such number of members of its body as it thinks fit.

(2) Any committee so formed shall, in the Exercise of the powers so delegated, conform to any regulations

that may be imposed on it by the Board.

(67) (1) A committee may elect a Chairman of its meetings.

(2) If no such Chairman is elected or if at any meeting the Chairman is not present within five minutes after the time appointed for holding the meeting, the members present may choose one of their members to be Chairman of the meeting.

(68) (1) A committee may meet and adjourn as it thinks proper.

(2) Question arising at any meeting of a committee shall be determined by a majority of votes of the members present, and in case of an equality of votes, the Chairman shall have a second or casting vote.

(69) All acts done by any meeting of the Board or of a Committee thereof or by any person acting as a Director, shall notwithstanding that it may be afterwards discovered that there was some defect in the appointment of any one or more of such directors or of any person acting as aforesaid, or that they or any of them were disqualified be as valid as is every such Director or such person had been duly appointed and was qualified to be a Director.

(70) Save as otherwise expressly provided in the Act, a resolution in writing signed by all the members of the Board or of a committee thereof for the time being entitled to receive notice of a meeting of the Board or committee, shall be valid and effectual as if it had been passed at a meeting of the Board or committee, duly convened and held.

(71) The President may appoint one of the Directors as Managing Director of the Company at such terms as may be fixed by him and in accordance with the Act. Any vacancy in the office of the Managing Director may be filled by the President.

(72) (1) A Secretary may be appointed by the Board for such time, at such remuneration and upon such conditions as it may think fit, and any Secretary so appointed may be removed by the Board.

(2) A Director may be appointed as Secretary.

(73) A provision of the Act or these articles requiring or authorising a thing to be done by or to a Director and the Secretary shall not be satisfied by its being done by or to the same person acting both as Director and as or in place of, the Secretary.

The Seal

(74) (1) The Board shall provide for the safe custody of the seal.

(2) The seal of the Company shall not be affixed to any instrument except by the authority of a resolution of the Board or of a Committee of the Board authorised by it in that behalf, and except in the presence of at least two Directors and of the Secretary or such other person as the Board may appoint for the purpose; and those two Directors and the secretary or other person aforesaid shall sign every instrument to which the seal of the Company is affixed in their presence.

Dividends And Reserve

(75) The Company in general meeting may declare dividends, but no dividend shall exceed the amount recommended by the Board.

(76) The Board may, from time to time, pay to the members such interim dividends as appear to it to be justified by the profits of the Company.

(77) (1) The Board may, before recommending any dividend, set aside out of the profits of the Company such sums as it thinks proper as a reserve or reserves which shall at the discretion of the Board, be applicable for any purpose to which the profits of the company may be properly applied, including provision for meeting contingencies or for equalising dividends, and pending such application, may, at the like discretion, either be employed in the business of the Company or be invested in such investments

(other than share the Company) as the Board may, from time to time, think fit.

(2) The Board may also carry forward any profit which it may think prudent not to divide, without setting them aside as a reserve.

(78) (1) All dividends shall be declared and paid according to the amounts paid or credit as paid on the shares in respect whereof the dividend is paid but if and so long as nothing is paid upon any of the shares in the Company dividends may be declared and paid according to the amounts of the shares.

(2) No amount paid or credit as paid on a share in advance of calls shall be treated for the purpose of this regulation as paid on the share.

(3) All dividends shall be apportioned and paid proportionately to the amounts paid or credited as paid on the shares during any portion or portions of the period in respect of which the dividend is paid, but if any share is issued on terms providing that it shall rank for dividend as from a particular date such share shall rank for dividend accordingly.

(79) The Board may deduct from any dividend payable to any member all sums of money, if any, presently payable by him to the company on account of calls or otherwise in relation to the shares of the Company.

(80) (1) Any dividend, interest or other moneys payable in cash in respect of shares may be paid by cheque or warrant sent through the post direct to the registered address of the holder or, in the case of joint holders, to the registered address of that one of the joint holders who is first name on the register of members or to such person and to such address as the holder or joint holders may in writing direct.

(2) Every such cheque or warrant shall be made payable to the order of the person to whom it is sent.

(81) Any one of two or more joint holders of a share may give effectual receipts for any dividends, bonuses or other moneys payable in respect of such share.

(82) Notice of any dividend that may have been declared shall be given to the persons entitled to share therein in the manner mentioned in the Act.

(83) No dividend shall bear interest against the Company.

Account

(84) (1) The Board shall from time to time determine whether and to what extent and at what time and places and under what conditions or regulations, the accounts and books of the Company or any of them shall be open to the inspection of member not being directors.

(2) No member (not being a director) shall have any right of inspecting any account or book or document of the company except as conferred by law or authorised by the Board or by the Company in general meeting.

(3) The financial year of the company shall end on 31st March of each year.

(85) At every Annual General Meeting, the Board shall lay before the Company a Balance Sheet and Profit and Loss Account made up in accordance with the provisions of Section 210 of the Act and such Balance Sheet and Profit and Loss Account shall comply with the requirements of Section 210, 211, 212, 215, 216 and 219 and of Schedule VI to the Act, so far as they are applicable to the Company.

(86) The Board of Directors shall cause an annual report to be made out and attached to every balance sheet a report with respect to the state of the Company's affairs, the amount, if any, which they recommend should be paid by way of dividend and the amount if any which they propose to carry to the Reserve Fund, General Reserve or Reserve Account shown specifically on the Balance Sheet or to be a Reserve, Reserve Account to be shown specifically on the balance sheet or to a Reserve in subsequent balance sheet. The Report shall be signed by the Chairman of the Board of Directors on behalf of the

Directors if so authorised in that behalf by the Directors and when he is not so authorised shall be signed by such number of Directors as are required to sign the balance sheet and the profit and loss account by virtue of sub-sections (1) and (2) of section 215 of the Act.

Capitalization of Profits

(87) (1) The Company in general meeting may, upon the recommendation of the Board, resolve:

(a) that it is desirable to capitalise any part of the amount for the time being standing to the credit of any of the Company's reserve accounts, or to the credit of the profit and loss account; or otherwise available for distribution; and

(b) that such sum be accordingly set free for distribution in the manner specified in clause (2) amongst the members who would have been entitled thereto, if distributed by way of dividend and in the same proportions.

(2) The sum aforesaid shall not be paid in cash but shall be applied, subject to the provision contained in clause (3) either in or towards :-

(a) paying up any amounts for the time being unpaid on any shares held by such members respectively.

(b) paying up in full, unissued shares or debentures of the Company to be allotted and distributed, credited as fully paid up, to and amongst such members in the proportions aforesaid, or

(c) partly in the way specified in sub-clause (a) and partly in that specified in sub-clause (b).

(3) A share premium account and a capital redemption reserve fund may, for the purpose of this regulation, only be applied in the paying up of unissued shares to be issued to members of the Company as fully paid bonus shares.

(4) The Board shall give effect to the resolution passed by the Company in pursuance of this regulation.

(88) (1) Whenever such a resolution as aforesaid shall have been passed, the Board shall:

(a) make all appropriations and applicants of the undivided profits resolved to be capitalised thereby, and all allotments and issues of fully paid shares or debentures if any; and

(b) generally do all acts and things required to give effect thereto.

(2) The Board shall have full power :-

(a) to make such provision, by the issue of fractional certificates or by payment in cash or otherwise as it thinks fit, for the case of shares or debentures becoming distributable in fractions, and also.

(b) to authorise any person to enter, on behalf of all the members entitled thereto, into an agreement with the Company providing for the allotment to them respectively credited as fully paid up, of any further shares or debentures to which they may be entitled upon such capitalization, or (as the case may require) for the payment by the Company on their behalf, by the application thereto of their respective proportions of the profits resolved to be capitalized of the amount or any part of the amounts remaining unpaid on their existing shares.

(3) Any agreement made under such authority shall be effective and binding on all such members.

Winding Up

(89) (1) If the Company shall be wound up, the liquidator may with sanction of a special resolution of the Company and any other sanction required by the Act, divide amongst the members, in specie or kind the whole or any part of the assets of the Company whether they shall consist of property of the same kind or not.

(2) For the purpose aforesaid, the liquidator may set such value as he deems fair upon any property to be divided as aforesaid and may determine how such

division shall be carried out as between the members or different classes of members.

(3) The liquidator may, with the like sanction, vest the whole or any part of such assets in trustees upon such trust for the benefit of contributories as the liquidator, with the like sanction, shall think fit, but so that no member shall be compelled to accept any shares or other securities whereon there is any liability.

Audit

(90) Auditors shall be appointed and their duties regulated in accordance with the provisions of the Act or any statutory modifications thereof for the time being in force.

(91) In addition to the audit to be carried out in accordance with the Act, the Comptroller and Auditor General of India shall have the right to arrange for internal audit by an authority appointed by him. The authority so appointed by the Comptroller and Auditor General of India and all the members of the staff working under that authority shall, at all reasonable times, have access to all accounts, account books, vouchers, documents and other papers of the Company and all reports of the Auditors appointed under the Act. The authority will submit its report to the Comptroller and Auditor General of India, for such action as he may deem fit.

"Resolved that Article 91 of the Articles of Association of Delhi State Industrial Development Corporation be amended and will be read as 'In addition to the audit to be carried out in accordance with the Act, the Comptroller and Auditor General of India shall have power to conduct a supplementary or test audit of the Company's accounts in accordance with the provision of the Act."

(Amended vide Extraordinary General Meeting held on 25th September, 1973)

Indemnity

(92) Subject to the provisions of the Act, every director and other officer or servant of the Company shall be

indemnified by the Company against and it shall be the duty of the Directors to pay out of the funds of the Company, all costs, losses, damages and expenses which any such officer or servant may incur or become liable to by reason of any contract entered into or act or thing done by him as such Director or Officer or servant or in any way in the discharge of his duties including travelling expenses, and in particular and so as not to limit the generality of the foregoing provisions against all liabilities incurred by him as such Director, Manager or other officer or servant in defending any proceed-ings whether Civil or Criminal in which judgement is given in his favour or in which he is acquitted or in connection with any application under Section 633 of the Act in which relief is granted to him by the court.

(93) Subject to the provisions of the Act, no Director or other officer of the Company shall be liable for the acts, receipts, neglects or defaults of any other director or officer or for joining in any receipt or other act for conformity or for any loss or expense happening to the Company through the insufficiency or deficiency of title to any property acquired by order of the Directors for and on behalf of the Company or for the insufficiency of any security in or upon which any of the monies of the Company shall be invested or for any loss or damage arising from the bankruptcy, insolvency or tortuous act of any person with whom any money, securities or effects shall be deposited or for any loss occasioned by any error of judgement or over sight on his part or any other loss, damage or misfortune whatever which shall happen in the execution of the duties of his office or in relation there to unless the same happen through his own negligence, defaults, breach of duty or breach of. trust.

Delegation of Power

(94) "Lt. Governor of Delhi will exercise all the administrative powers with regard to the Company on behalf of the President of India as the latter's nominee."

Names, address, descriptions and occupations (if any) of subscribers	*Names, address, descriptions and occupations (if any) of witnesses*
1	2
1. Lt. Governor of Delhi L. N. Saklani S/o Shri Hirday Narain Saklani, Secretary Industries, Delhi Administration, Delhi For & on behalf of Lt. Governer of Delhi,	K. P. Chaudhry, S/o Shri R. P. Chaudhry, Industrial Survey Officer, Office of the Director of Industries, Delhi Administ-ration, Delhi
2. Janak Juneja D/o Shri Sarup Singh Under Secretary industries, Delhi Administration Delhi	J. L. Kotru, S/o Shri Shiv Ji Kotru, Asst. Director of Industries Delhi Administration, Delhi
3. R. N. Suri S/o Shri J. G. Suri, Deputy Director of Industries (Planning and Technical), Office of the Director of Industries, Delhi Administration, Delhi.	B. L. Goel S/o Shri Rameshwar Dass, Office of the Director of Industries, Delhi, Administration Delhi.

Dated this 4th day of February, 1971.

□□□